IMAGES
of America

Bonner Springs

I0806217

On the Cover: The Bonner Springs High School graduating class of 1905 poses on the stage of the opera house. The graduates look determined to adhere to their class motto, "Climb tho the Rocks be Rugged," seen on the banner above the stage. (Courtesy of Bonner Springs Library, Rudell collection.)

IMAGES
of America

BONNER SPRINGS

Roger B. Miller

ARCADIA
PUBLISHING

Copyright © 2013 by Roger B. Miller
ISBN 978-1-4671-1043-3

Published by Arcadia Publishing
Charleston, South Carolina

Printed in the United States of America

Library of Congress Control Number: 2013933224

For all general information, please contact Arcadia Publishing:
Telephone 843-853-2070
Fax 843-853-0044
E-mail sales@arcadiapublishing.com
For customer service and orders:
Toll-Free 1-888-313-2665

Visit us on the Internet at www.arcadiapublishing.com

This book is dedicated to the early historians of Bonner Springs, and especially to Ella Mae Mitchell, whose preservation of her father's photographs and creation of numerous scrapbooks provided an abundance of material for this project.

Contents

Acknowledgments		6
Introduction		7
1.	Early Beginnings	9
2.	John W. McDanield and His Vision	13
3.	Philo Clark and His Vision	19
4.	J.D. Waters and His Vision	53
5.	After the Depression	73
6.	Attractions, Celebrations, and Organizations	93
Bibliography		127

ACKNOWLEDGMENTS

The Bonner Springs Library has carefully preserved the writings and photographic collections of early Bonner Spring historians. My thanks go to the staff; Kim Beets, the director; and Linda Lozier, the keeper of the Kansas Room. Beth Enloe has been creating a reference file of the *Bonner Springs Chieftain* that has proved invaluable in researching historical articles.

Thank-yous also go to the staff at the Wyandotte County Museum: executive director Patricia Schurkamp, archivist Jennifer McLaughlin, staff assistant Jeff Jennings, and volunteer Monte Gross, who provided access to the files and photographs. David Sandy, who provided much technical assistance, and copy editor Lance Rich also deserve my appreciation. My acquisitions editor, Jason Humphrey at Arcadia Publishing, was encouraging to the author as he delved into the unknown realm of authoring a book.

A thank-you is extended to my wife, Sheila, for her support and encouragement during this endeavor.

This book can only provide limited information about the history of Bonner Springs. For those interested in learning more, the Bonner Springs Library archives house countless photographs, articles, books, and newspapers for more thorough research. Other general sources for information used in the book include the Bonner Springs Centennial Calendar, compiled by Rebecca Barber Meditz; Bonner Springs Historic Preservation Society booklets, compiled by Pat Sheley; and the Wyandotte County Museum and Historical Society archives.

Unless otherwise noted, images appear courtesy of the Bonner Springs Library's Rudell collection. Some photographs are from the Wyandotte County Historical Society and Museum (WCHS&M).

INTRODUCTION

The beginnings and growth of Bonner Springs parallel the growth of America. It was a river town because of its location on the banks of the Kansas River, and when the railroad made its way west, it provided a jump start for more people and businesses to make their way to Bonner Springs.

The fabled history relates that the Spanish explorer Francisco Vazquez de Coronado spent the winter of 1541–1542 at what is now Bonner Springs. The diary of Father Juan Padilla records that the expedition reached the 40th degree (the northern Kansas border) and came to a great river (the Missouri). An inscription found on a stone near Atchison has been translated as, "Thus Far Came Francisco de Coronado. General of an Expedition." The explorers traveled downstream to the mouth of another great river, the Kansas, and preceded upstream 16 leagues to camp before returning to Mexico. Because of the mineral springs, this legend gave the area its first recorded name, Coronado Springs.

The Kanza tribe had settled in the area because of the mineral springs and abundant fish and game, when, in 1812, two French fur traders, brothers Francis and Cyprian Chouteau, established a trading post. The brothers built four log houses in a square, anticipating a hostile reception. However, all was peaceful, and the business was very successful. Steamboat traffic on the Kansas River provided transportation for shipping the furs back to St. Louis as well as receiving stock for the store. The post closed in 1829 when the Kanza Indians were forcefully moved westward by the government, and the Chouteaus lost their customers. The area then became known as the Four Houses.

In 1830, the ferry that had been established across the Kaw River by the Chouteaus was turned over to Henry Tiblow, a Delaware Indian. It was well used, and the area became a place for settlement. As the town grew, it became known as Tiblow Landing, and, in 1860, when the government granted land to the Delaware Indians, Henry Tiblow received 320 acres.

The Kansas Pacific Railway was completed in 1866 from Wyandot City (now Kansas City, Kansas) to Topeka. John William McDanield worked on its construction and then served as the engineer on the first passenger train that ran from Kansas City to Topeka, on which Wild Bill Hickock was a bodyguard for one of the officials. McDanield noted the vast amount of timber in the area, which could be used for fuel as well as railroad ties, and soon bought land stretching from Lake Forest to Wolf Creek, naming the town Tiblow. It officially became a town on September 9, 1870, and a post office was established on June 6, 1871, with McDanield as postmaster.

Several of the springs were analyzed for their mineral content, and the results showed benefits that would attract visitors. To promote the springs, now known as Mammoth Springs, a special train brought prospective investors from Kansas City to Bonner Springs on November 25, 1884. A *Wyandott Herald* reporter cited its proximity to Kansas City, the springs themselves, the fine park of native trees, the site of a racetrack, and the beautiful residential sites as advantages that would assure the success of the venture.

In 1885, John McDanield sold 300 acres to Philo Clark and his town company, which had plans to capitalize on the medicinal and healing springs in the area. Clark changed the name to Bonner Springs because Robert Bonner, the publisher of the *New York Ledger*, was a trotting-horse breeder of note, and Clark thought he would help promote the proposed racetrack. There is no record of that happening.

By 1896, the town boasted a broom factory, a soda factory, a gristmill, a livery stable, a hotel, a restaurant, and a bakery. The *Wyandotte Chieftain* newspaper was established, with E.L. Matthews as editor. He advocated that Bonner Springs should become a city, and a petition was submitted to the county commissioners. It was refused because it lacked a sufficient number of petitioners. Subsequent attempts were successful, however, and Bonner Springs became a third-class city on November 10, 1898. Philo Clark was elected mayor.

In 1896, the postmaster general selected Bonner Springs as one of the first testing points for the rural free delivery (RFD) system. Charles Everett took the first RFD route out of the Bonner Springs post office. The test was a success, and the RFD system was born.

In 1900, the population was 1,025 and civic activities were blossoming, with the formation of various literary and musical groups. The Ladies Reading Circle was organized in 1897 and is still active, as is the New Century Club, formed in 1900. A 600-seat opera house also hosted a variety of performances. In October 1908, a fire destroyed 19 business houses on Oak Street. The loss was reported of $70,000—over $350,000 in today's dollars.

An electric interurban railroad was started by John McDanield to run from Bonner Springs to the cement plant and on to Lake Forest. It was eventually enlarged by J.D. Waters to provide twice-daily transportation from Kansas City, Kansas, to Lawrence.

McDanield sold the land that included Lake Ellen to J.D. Waters in 1910 to build an exclusive resort. He renamed it Lake of the Forest, and it has since developed into a community of 166 homes. In 1920, Belle, the widow of Theodore Naish, gave hundreds of acres of land to the Boy Scouts of America, naming it Camp Naish. Thousands of Scouts still come to camp yearly.

Unfortunately, natural disasters are inevitable in the area. In 1952, a tornado destroyed property in the Loring area, and, in 1951, the flooding Kansas River covered much farmland but did not reach the business district.

A new bridge over the Kansas River was constructed in 1960, taking the place of the wagon bridge that had been used for 55 years. In the 1960s, the new post office building was dedicated and a new Methodist church was built, as well as the Commercial State Bank. The building boom was on; in the early 1960s, new businesses included the Rio Theater, L.P. Gas, the Sinclair Station, and the Bonner Springs Credit Union. The new city hall was completed in 1963. In addition to housing the city offices and jail, it was also the headquarters for the volunteer fire department.

In 1969, urban renewal began revitalizing the downtown business district. The master plan was to beautify downtown with islands, trees, and kiosks. Most businesses updated and improved their stores. The kiosks, however, were not the right addition to Oak Street, and were removed a few years later.

In the 1980s, business activity moved north to Kansas Highway 7, with a Wal-Mart and a McDonald's built first. A new junior high school was built adjacent to the high school. The old high school gym and shop areas were renovated to make a new library, senior center, and community center.

In the 2000s, major construction began in all the buildings of School District 204. The district partnered with the YMCA to build an activity center between the high and junior high schools. It houses an Olympic-sized swimming pool as well as a heated pool. There is also exercise and strength equipment in abundance, as well as a basketball court. The project was a great example of two organizations working together in a symbiotic relationship that benefited the whole community. A revitalization program for downtown Bonner Springs was also started, and it resulted in new sidewalks, sewers, curbing with handicap exits, and streetlamps.

Despite the occasional flood, fire, or tornado and the economic downturns and disappointments of failed promotions, the citizens of Bonner Springs continue to have pride in their city. We invite you to view the past in the following pages and share the proud history of a town that is looking forward to the future.

One

Early Beginnings

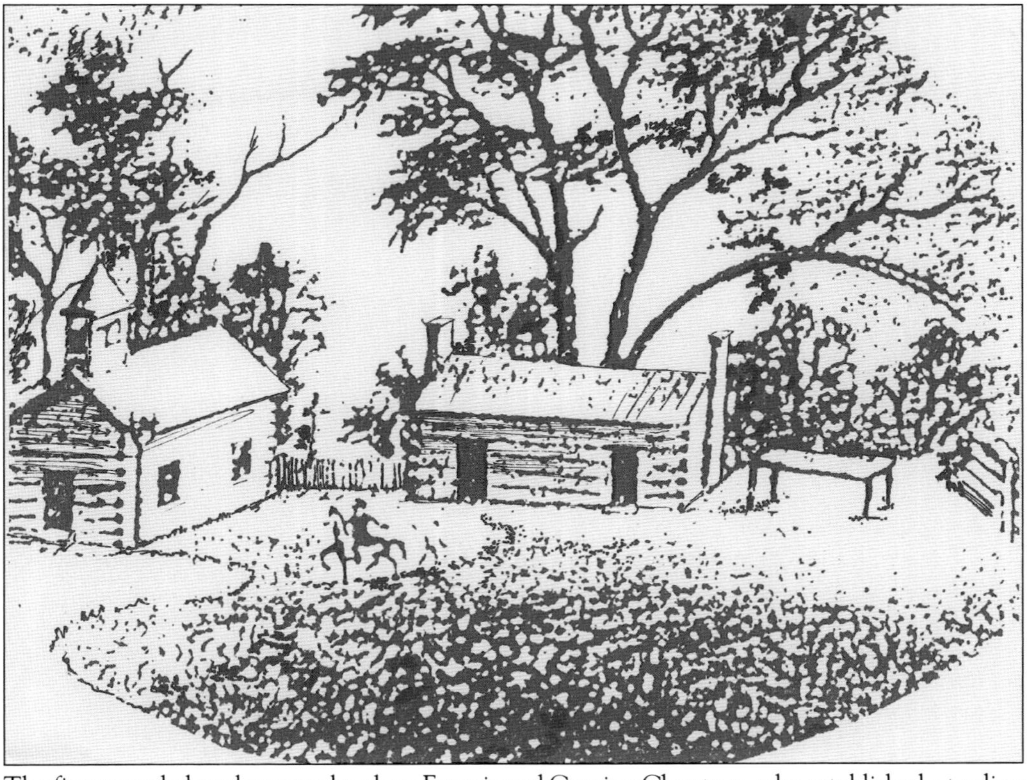

The first recorded settlers were brothers Francis and Cyprian Chouteau, who established a trading post in 1812. This early sketch by an unknown artist was restored by local artist Mary Ann White, and it illustrates two of the four log houses built by the Chouteaus to store their furs while awaiting shipment down the Kansas River to St. Louis. Two were located along Front Street at Elm Street, and two were a block west on Second Street.

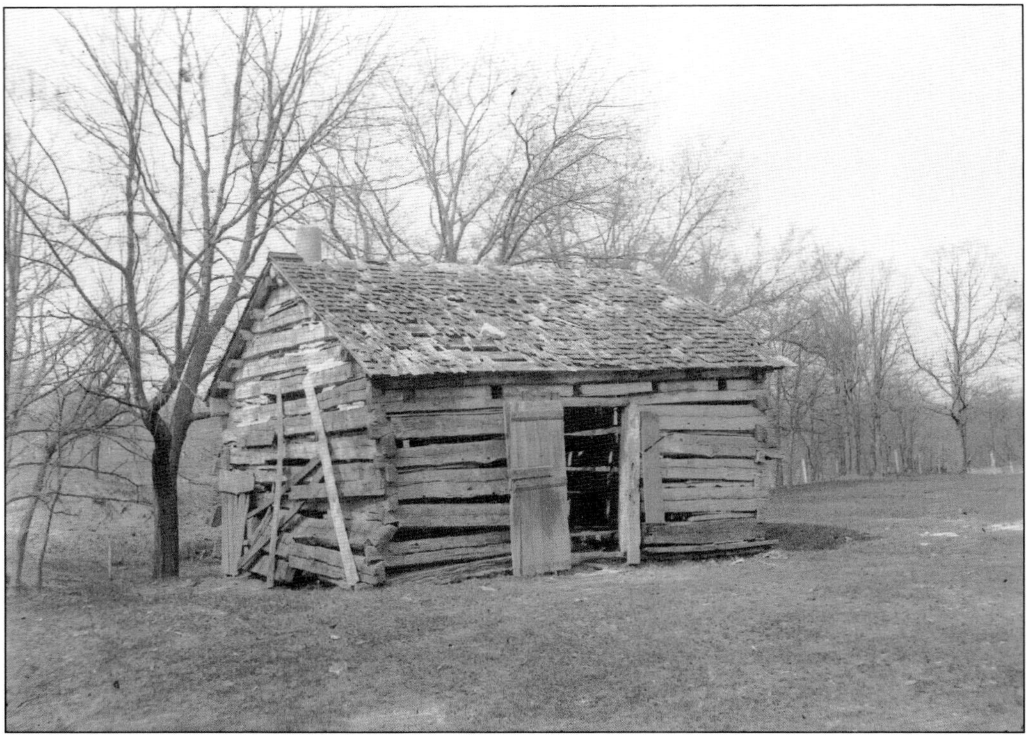

The Chouteaus built this "medicine hut" for their Indian customers, who used the springs to cure many ailments. The hut was located on a hill above Indian Creek in Saratoga Park (now Lions Park). It lasted almost 100 years before finally falling into decay.

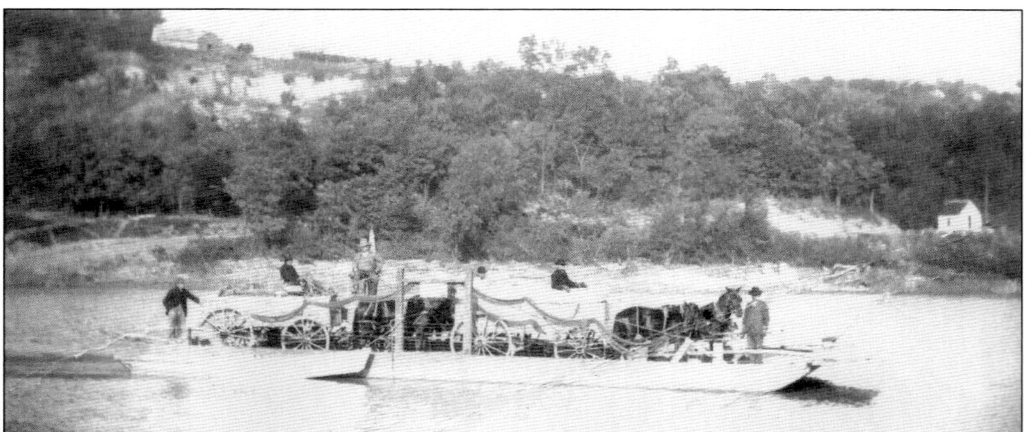

Ferries such as this one were used to cross the Kansas River. When the Chouteaus left in 1830, they gave the ferry to the family of Henry Tiblow, who repaired it and began the business.

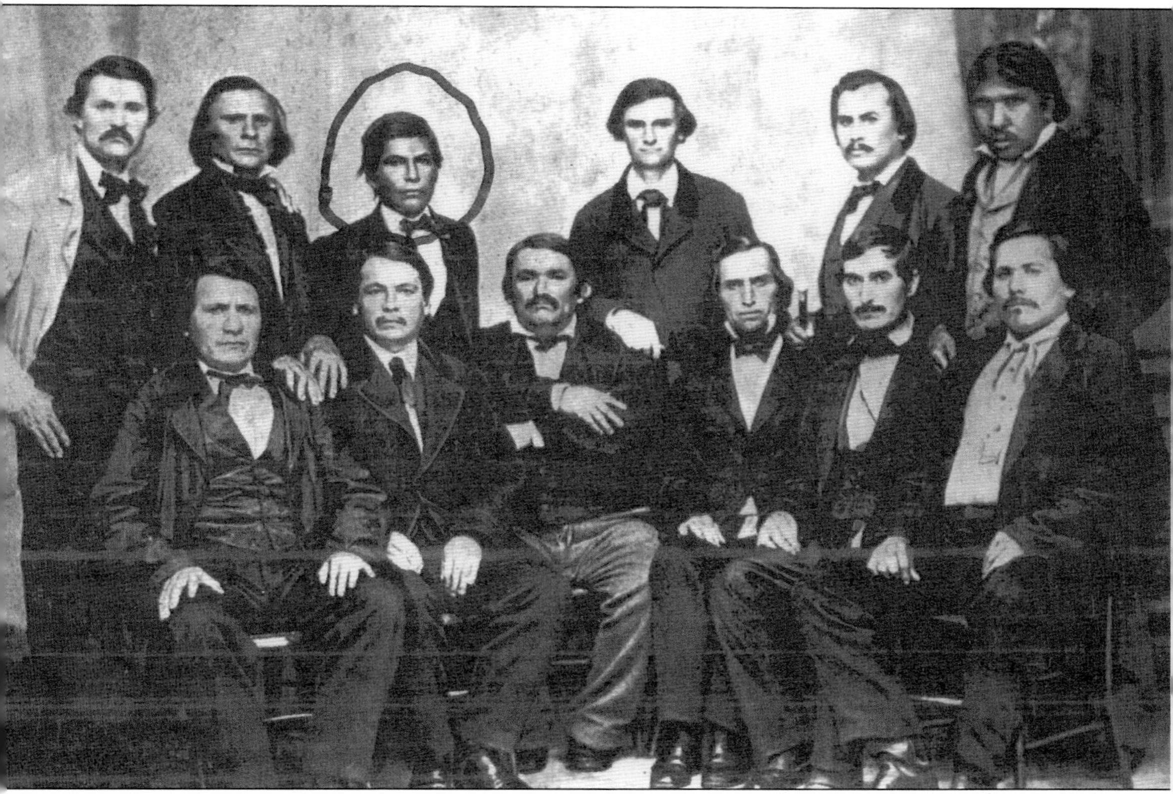

This delegation went to Washington, DC, in 1866 to make a treaty for the Delaware Indians to move with the Cherokees to Indian Territory in what was to become Oklahoma. The delegates are, from left to right, (first row) Jim Ketchem, Jim Conner, John Connor, Charles Journeycake, Isaac Journeycake, and John Sarcoxie; (second row) ? McDaniel (Cherokee), Black Beaver, Henry Tiblow, J.G. Pratt, Charles Armstrong, and Andrew Miller. This is the only known photograph of Tiblow, the Delaware Indian who figured prominently in the history of Bonner Springs. His ferry across the Kansas River was a very successful venture, earning as much as $75 a day. He was an interpreter for the Shawnee and the Delaware, and his witness is on many government documents. He moved to Oklahoma in 1868. Tiblow died on December 6, 1881, and is buried in the Armstrong-Secondine Cemetery, near Nowata, Oklahoma.

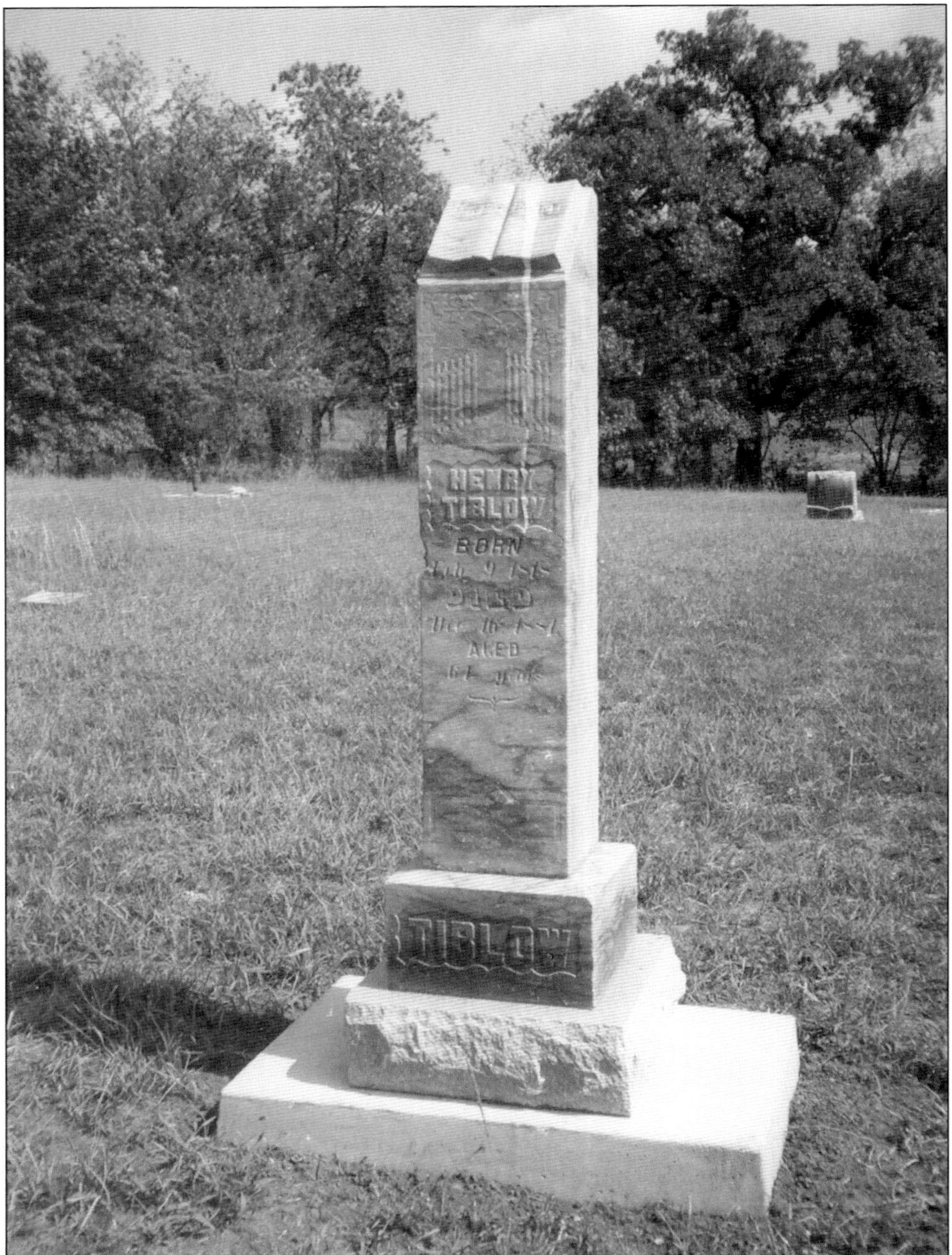

Until the Bonner Springs centennial celebration in 1998, the burial place of Henry Tiblow was unknown. The committee publicized that fact, and received information that resulted in a trip to the cemetery, where the gravestone was found in disrepair. It had toppled over and had broken in several pieces. After it was repaired, a search began for the gravesite of Tiblow's wife, Mary Ann "Polly." Further investigation found that, after her husband's death, she had moved to live with her daughter in Big Cabin, Oklahoma. She died in 1907, and her tombstone resembles her husband's.

Two

John W. McDanield and His Vision

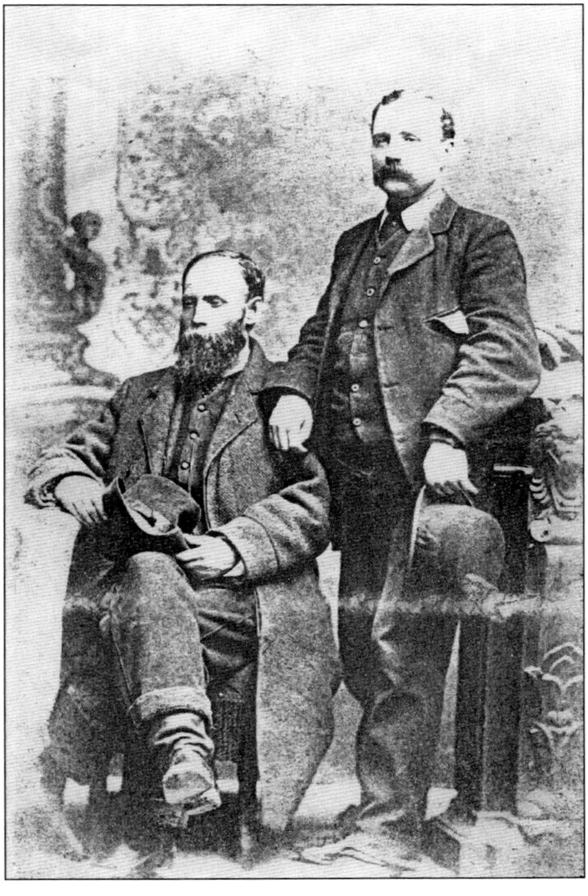

John Wesley McDanield (seated), called "Red John" because of his red hair, is known as the founder of Bonner Springs. He is seen here with his brother and partner Sylvester. They were the first owners of the town they named Tiblow, after their friend Henry Tiblow. When the railroad was completed from Kansas City to Topeka in 1866, John McDanield was the engineer, and he thought the lands around the Tiblow ferry location would be an ideal place to settle, as well as provide timber for railroad ties. The brothers then bought land along the river and settled.

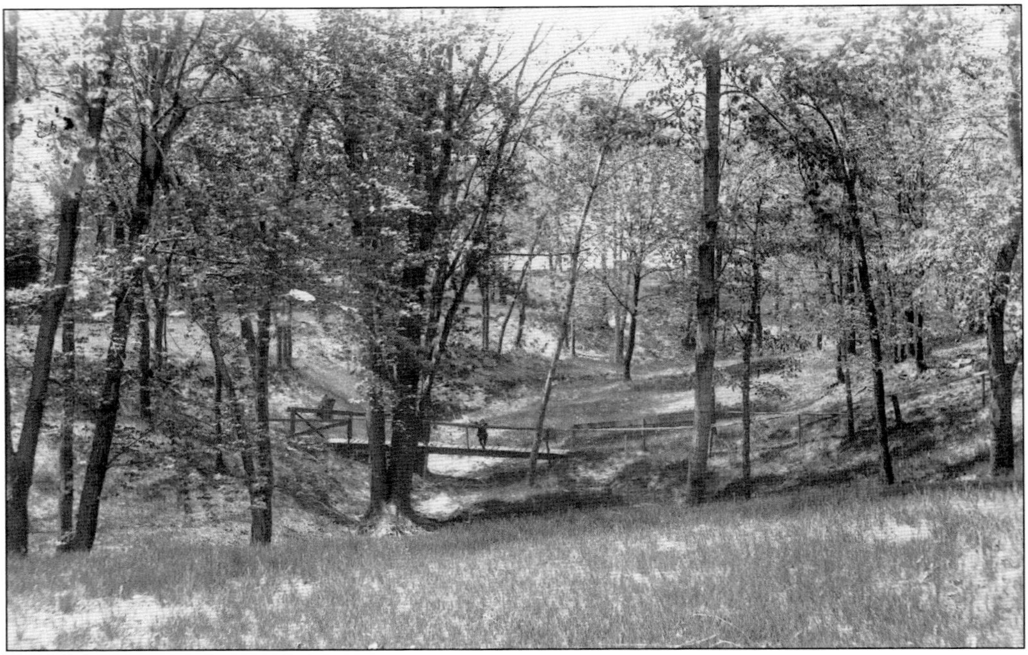

The land John McDanield purchased included the mineral springs as well as a cemetery used by the Delaware Indians. The area seen here, known as McDanield Grove, was west of Forest Street. McDanield created two lakes in the area: Lake Ellen, named for his wife, which became Lake of the Forest, and Lake McDanield, located farther north of the city.

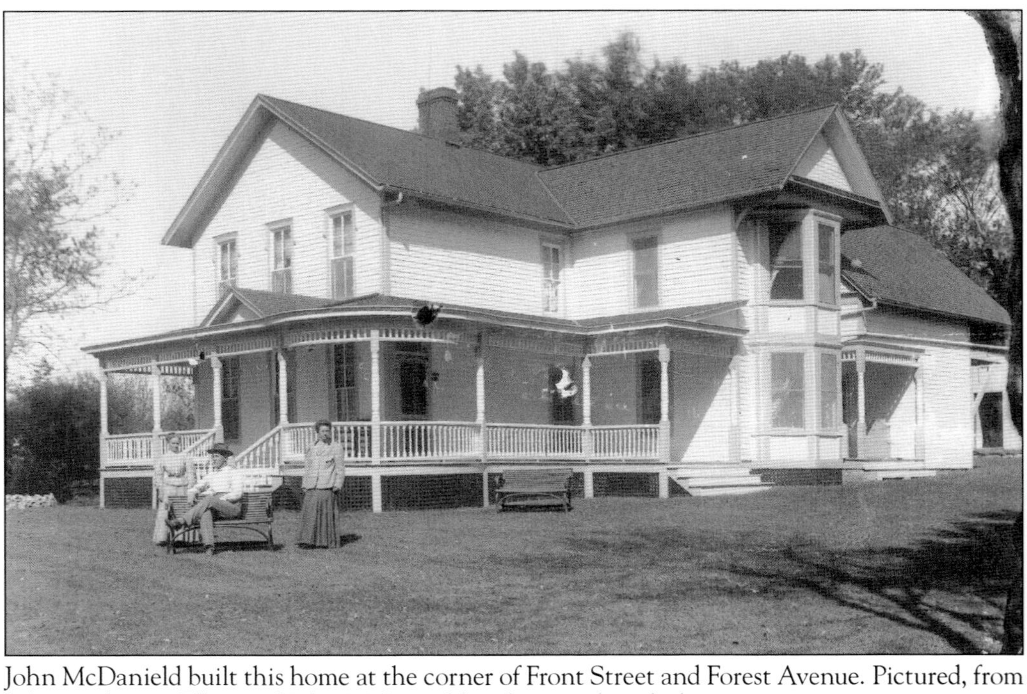

John McDanield built this home at the corner of Front Street and Forest Avenue. Pictured, from left to right, are Ellen and John McDanield and an unidentified woman.

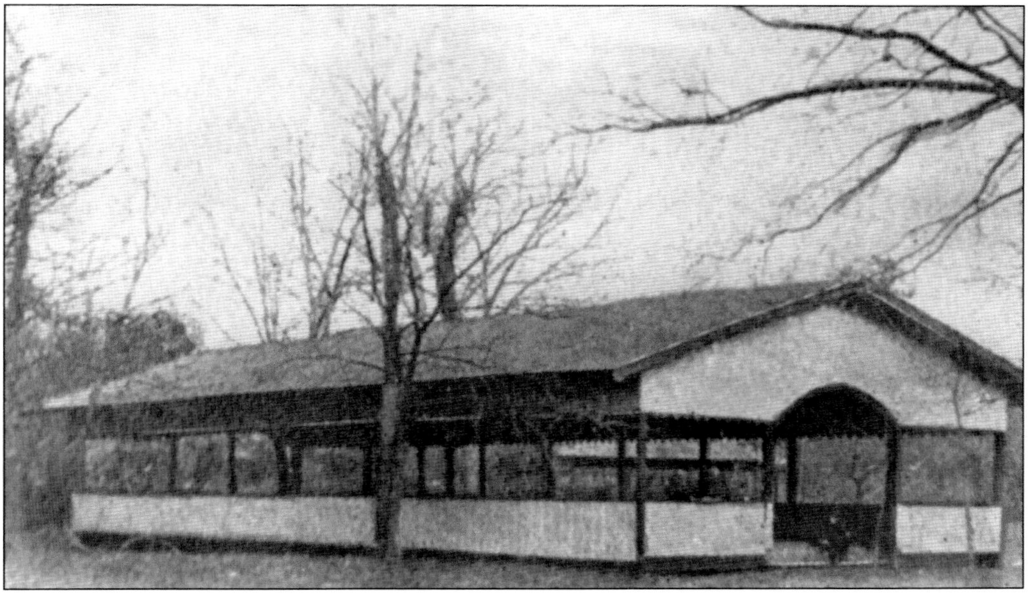

The dance pavilion in McDanield Grove was a popular place for entertainment in the early days of Bonner Springs. It was eventually moved to Saratoga Park (now Lions Park), located south of Morse Avenue between Neconi and Garfield Avenues.

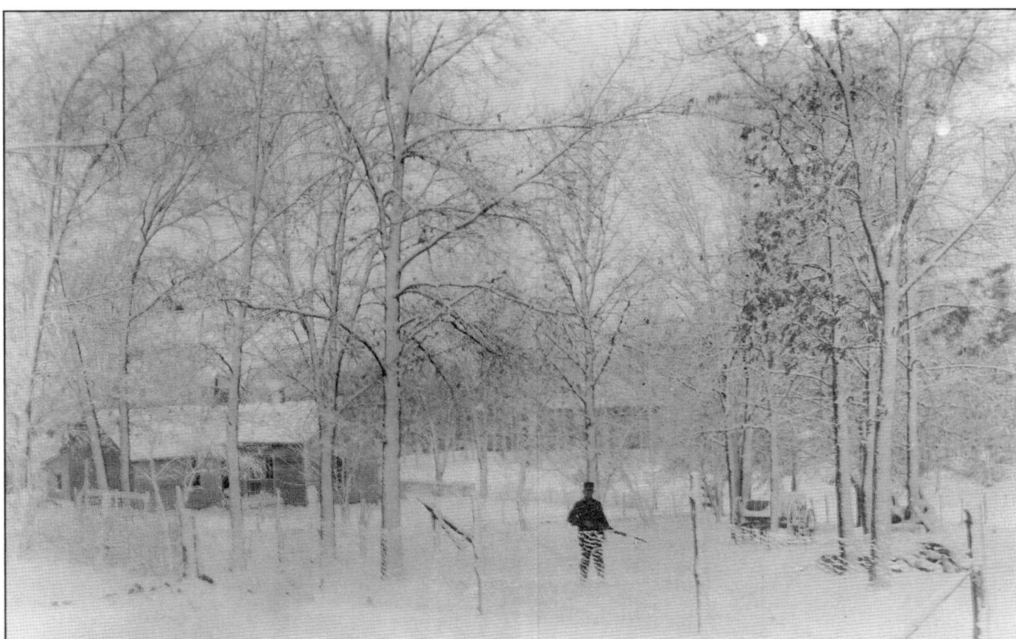

McDanield Grove was also popular for hunting because of the abundance of timber in the area. This photograph was taken from the house at 322 Armour Street. Urbin Rudell is the man in the center with the gun. The house in the background is on Neconi Avenue.

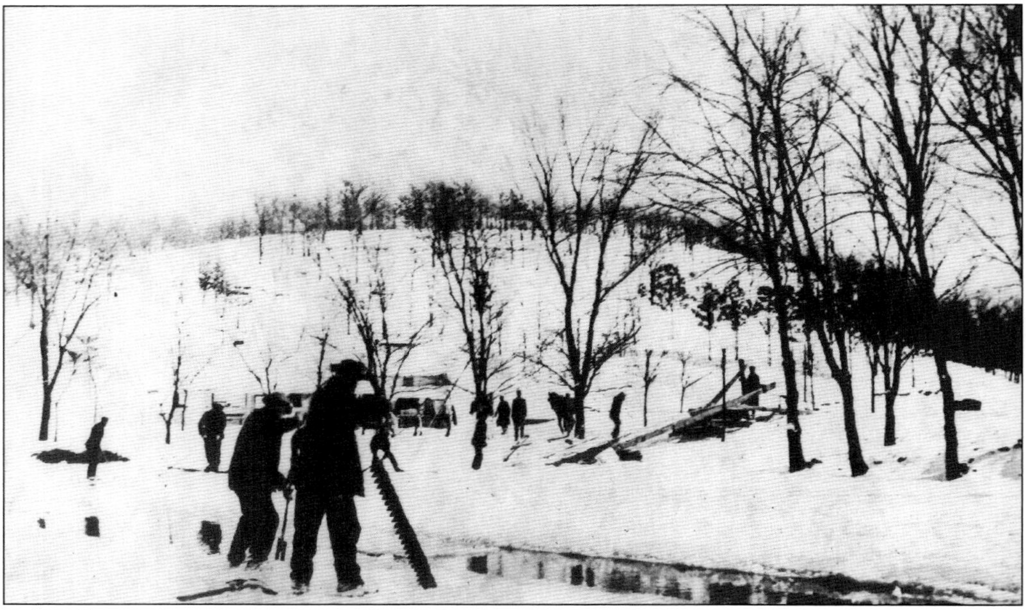

Lake Ellen was used as a source of ice when it froze over during the winter. Blocks of ice were sawed from the lake and stored in an icehouse on the south side of the lake, where the Lake of the Forest clubhouse is now located. The Union Pacific Railroad had the contract and was able to cool its cars in the summer.

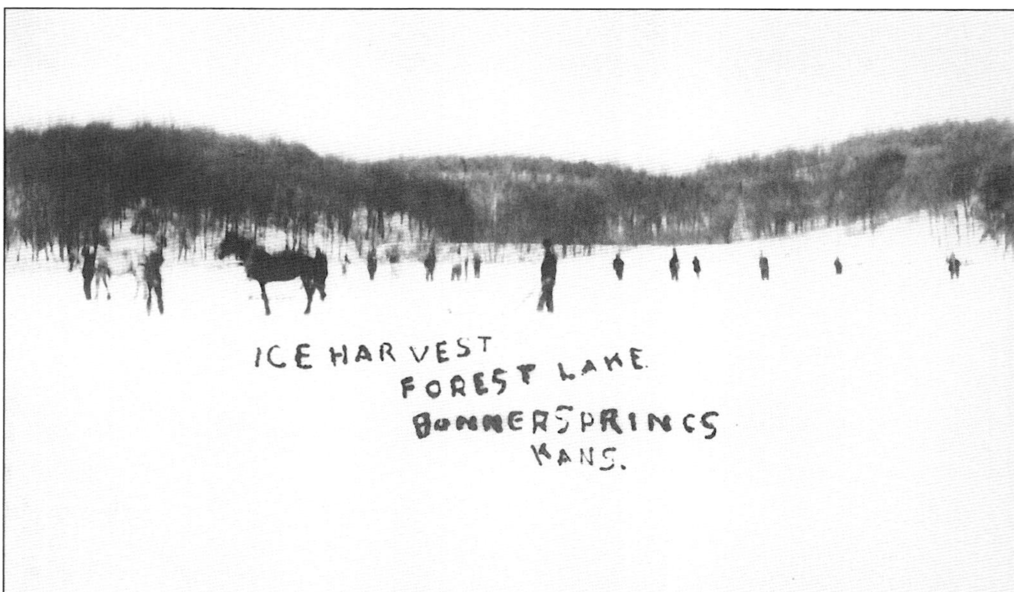

This postcard shows the ice harvest. After being covered with sawdust and burlap in the icehouse, the huge ice cakes could survive for several months.

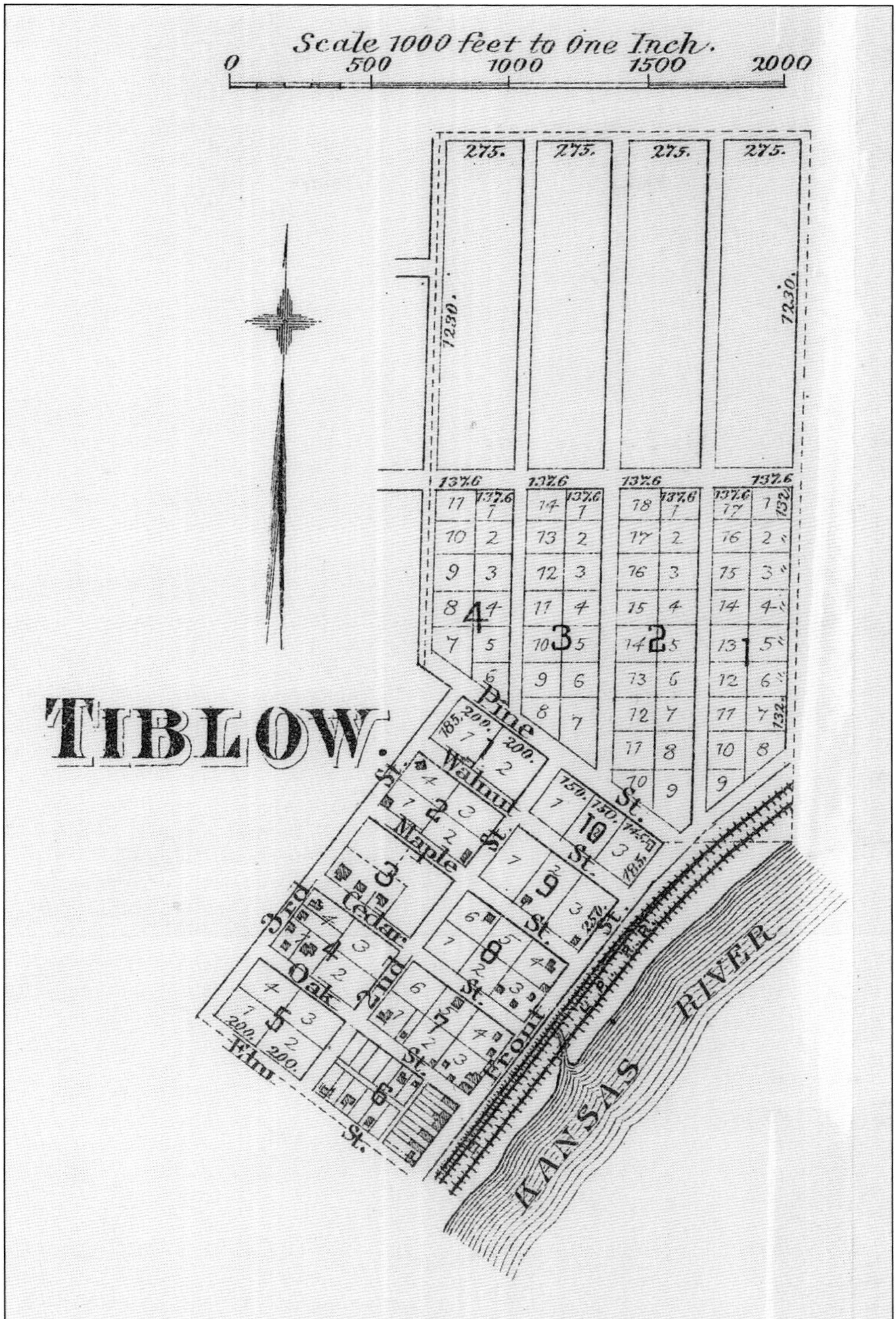

In 1870, the new town was platted and lots were ready to be sold. Henry Warner sold his store in Wyandot City (now Kansas City, Kansas) and built the first store in Bonner Springs.

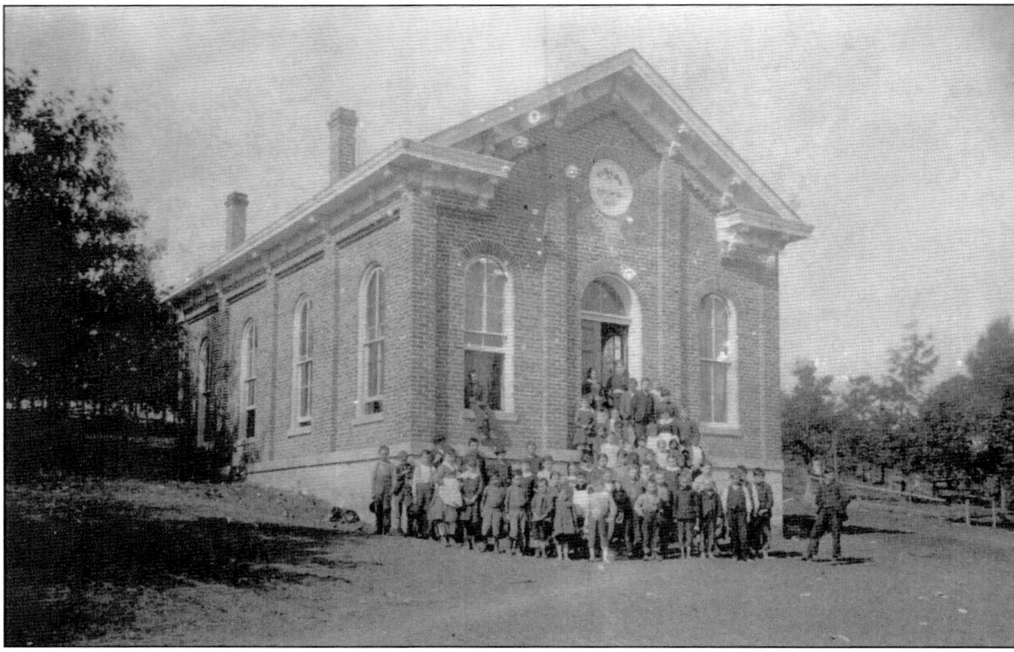

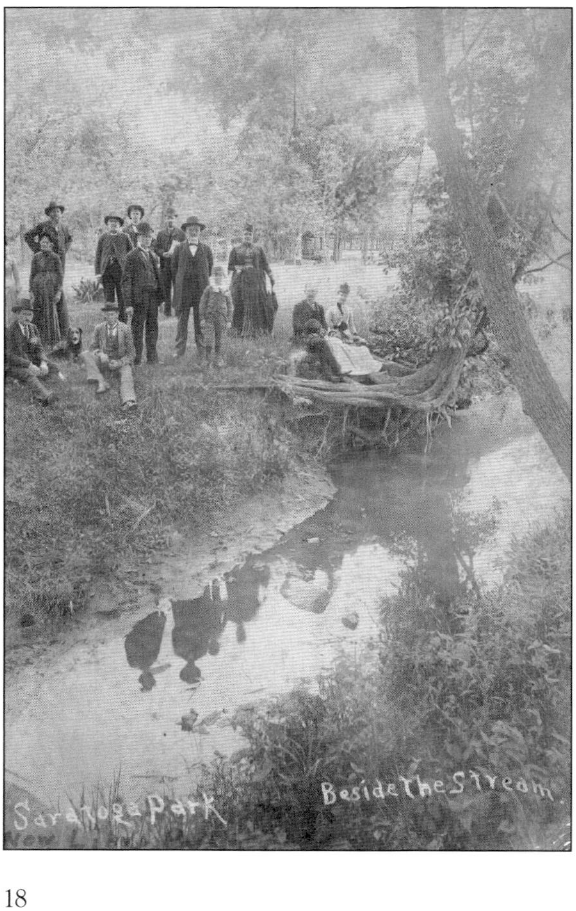

In 1867, the first school was established in one of the original four houses, which was called the Swayback house because of its sagging roof. Teacher Fannie Reed had three students—John Nelson, Charles McGarvin, and Dame Hiatt. In 1873, this brick school building was constructed on land donated by John McDanield. It was named the Tiblow school. The Christian church started meeting there as well. In 1871, the Tiblow post office was established, with John McDanield as the postmaster.

A popular, peaceful scenic gathering place was Saratoga Park beside what is now called Indian Creek. Now named Lions Park, it was located south of Morse Avenue between Neconi and Garfield Avenues.

Three

Philo Clark and His Vision

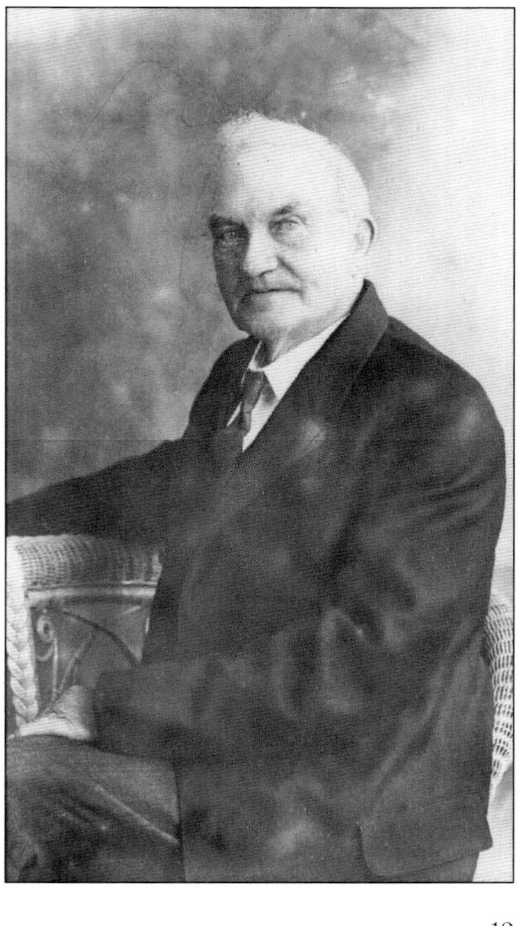

At the Wyandot Convention, held in Wyandot City in 1859, a young telegrapher spoke to an expectant nation that was eager to know whether Kansas would be a free state or a slave state. That man was Philo Clark, a successful real estate developer from Kansas City, Missouri. At the beginning of the Civil War, he and his partner, John Kump, opened a soda pop manufacturing plant in Kentucky near a large Army camp, which became very successful. They decided to establish a factory on a barge and float down to Vicksburg, Mississippi, where a large number of troops were stationed. However, the boat struck a snag and sank, along with the fortunes of the two entrepreneurs. Clark eventually rebuilt his finances, and, in 1885, he purchased 300 acres of land from John McDanield. He then laid out the town, which he named Bonner Springs after the publisher of the *New York Ledger*, Robert Bonner. Because the name Tiblow was not retained, as John McDanield had wanted, he and his brother Sylvester were not buried in Bonner Springs. Instead, they were both laid to rest in Oak Grove Cemetery, in Kansas City, Kansas. McDanield's dream of the area becoming a booming resort community was ahead of its time, but he eventually saw the city grow into a livable and prosperous one.

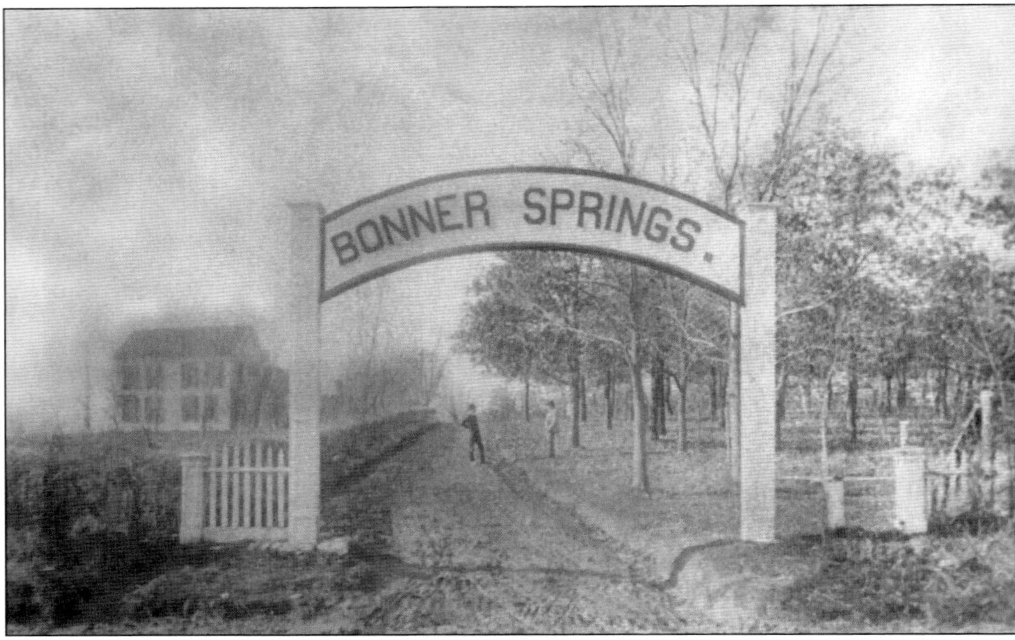

The newly named city of Bonner Springs is ready for development in this photograph, with the arch over Forest Street welcoming prospective buyers. The home at the top of the hill is Homestead Acres, which Sylvester McDanield built for his parents, Bartholomew F. and Sarah McDanield.

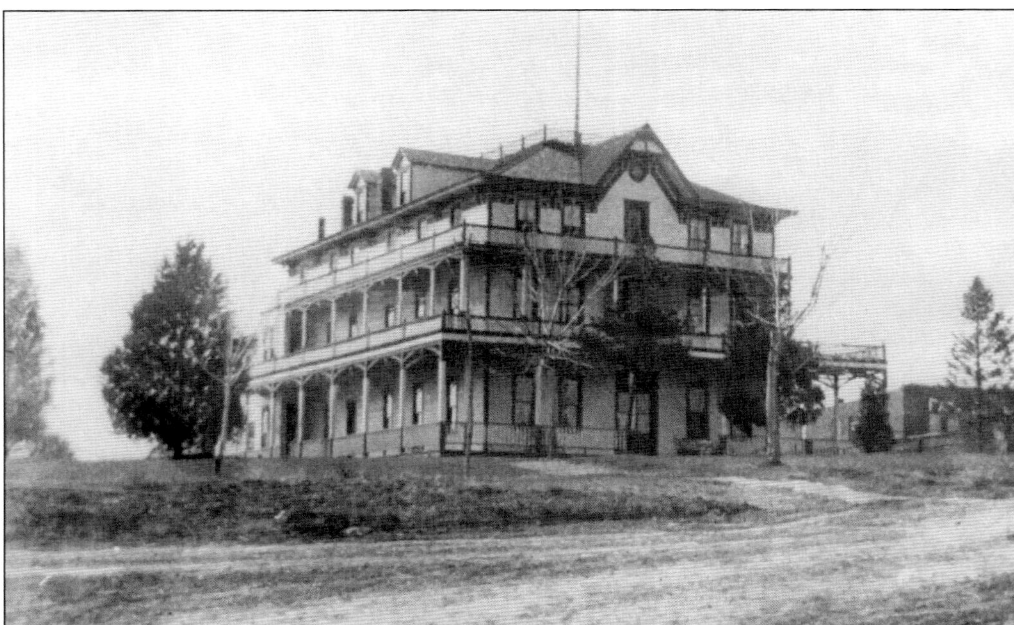

The 60-room Coronado Hotel, located at the top of Oak Street, where McDanield School is now, was built by Philo Clark. Unfortunately, it eventually failed and was then sold to Dr. M.P. Sexton in 1891 for use as a sanitarium. It burned in 1903 and was replaced by a stone structure on North Nettleton Avenue. Three patients and one employee were killed in the fire.

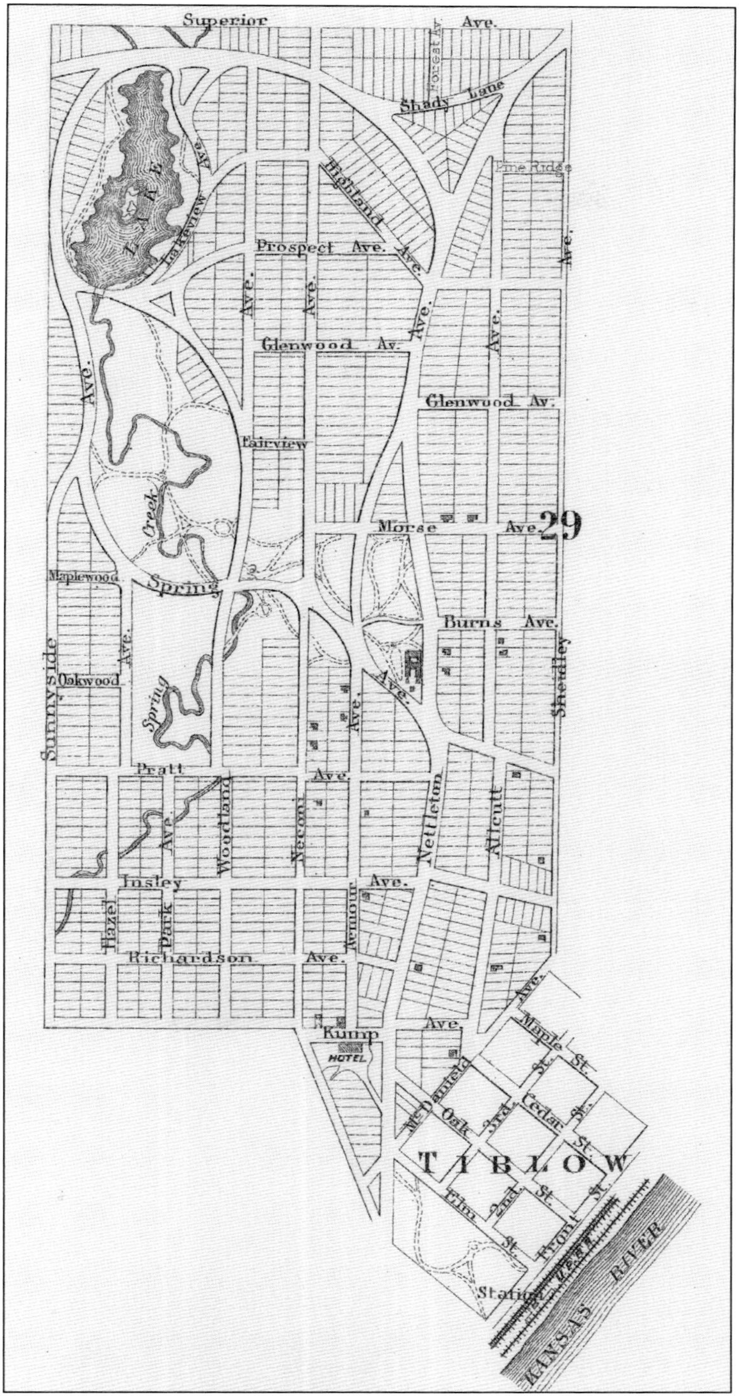

This Bonner Springs plat shows the original 10 square blocks of Tiblow, along with the expansion to the north that goes past the lake. Most of the street names remain today, and are named after trees or prominent citizens. Kump Avenue was named after Philo Clark's brother-in-law and partner in his bottling business, John Kump.

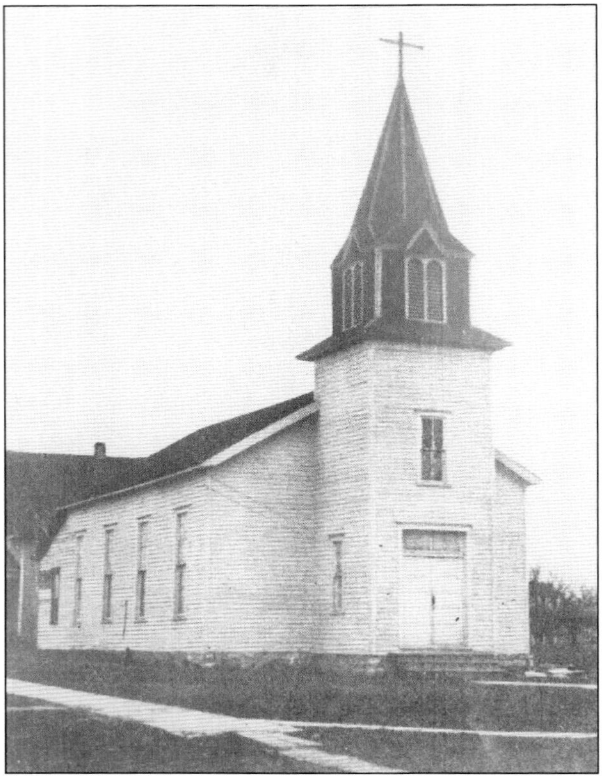

After the city fathers gave a plot of land to the first congregation for a church, the Christian church (left) was built in 1887. It was later sold to the Catholic congregation and renamed Sacred Heart.

Just a few years later, in 1890, the Methodist church (below) was built at the corner of Allcutt and Cedar Streets.

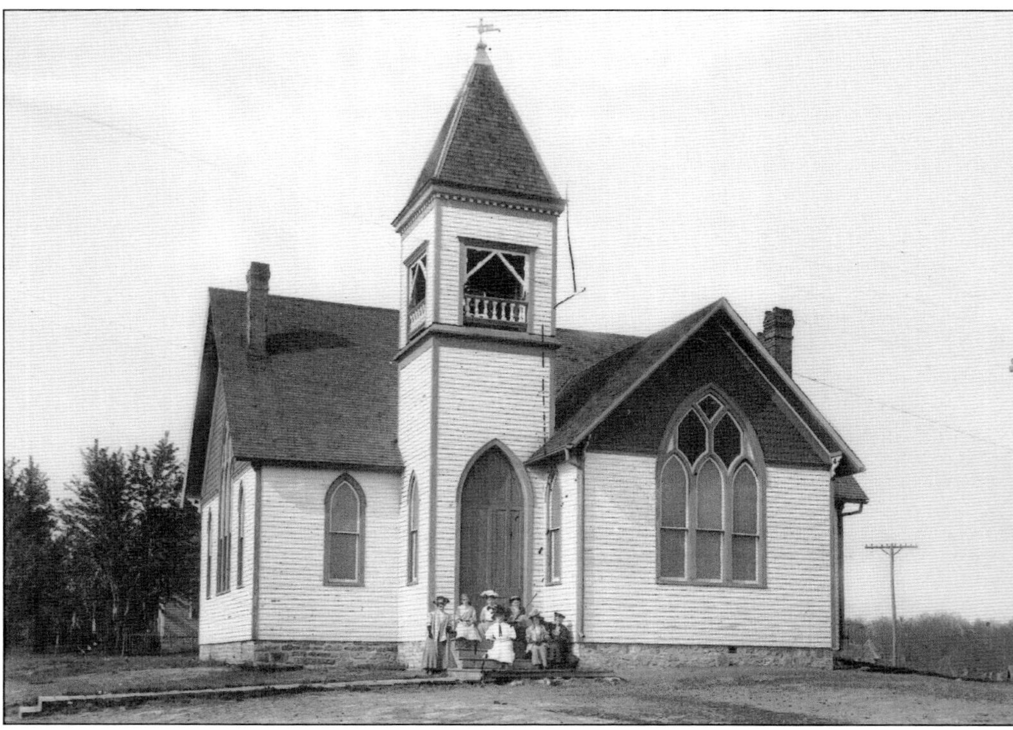

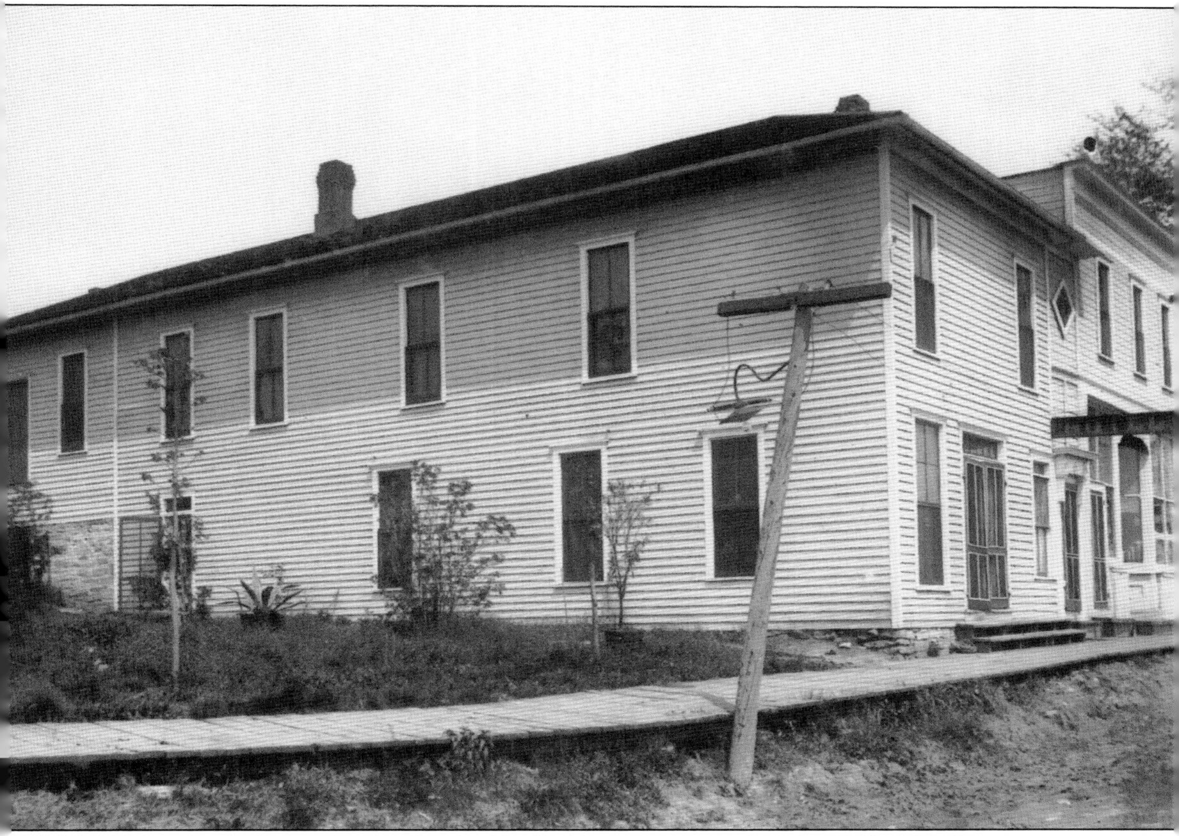

The Riverview Hotel was just one of many new buildings constructed in the 1890s. New businesses included a broom factory, a soda factory, a gristmill, a livery stable, a restaurant, and a bakery. By that point, the post office was called Bonner Springs, and Marcus Bearden was the postmaster.

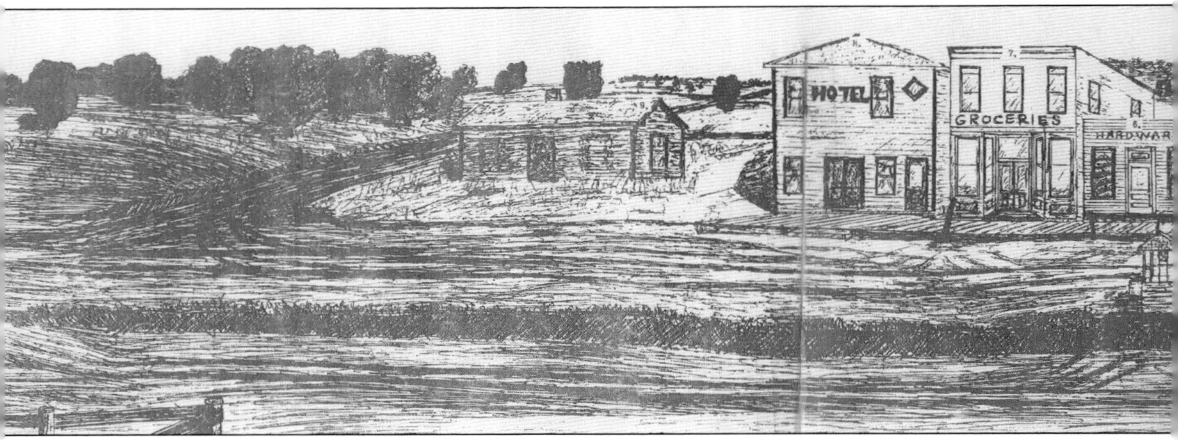

Lifelong Bonner Springs resident Frank Shaw drew this sketch of Front Street as it appeared in the late 1890s, based on the buildings that remained and the memory of those who remembered that time. Elm Street is on the left and Oak Street is on the right. On the right side of Oak Street may be a part of Cole's blacksmith shop and the houses of Oscar Hyroot and Herman Kohlts. In the center foreground are the town well and the wooden watering trough. The buildings are listed here from right to left, starting with the general store of John Stotts and his father-in-law, Si Johnson (1). Frank Warner's store (2) is next. Warner later became an important builder and developer in Bonner Springs. Next to his store is the general store of John "Wes" McDanield (3). There were two John McDanields in Bonner Springs, one was known as "Wes" and the other

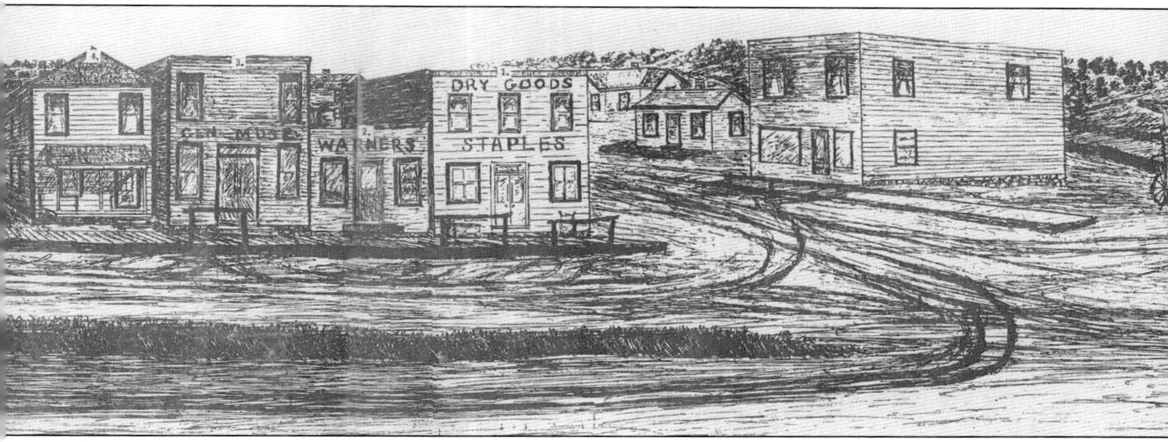

was known as "Red John" for his red hair. The residence of John "Wes" McDanield (4) was later moved to Spring and Clark Streets and became the Caldwell Apartments. The home and office of a Mr. Dillhorn (5), a notary public brought to Bonner Springs by "Red John" McDanield to attest to signatures on documents arising from McDanield's many land title transfers, is next. Then Dick Brauner's hardware store (6), followed by a general store owned by Dr. Downs (7), a practicing physician who lived at Second and Elm Streets. The Riverview Hotel (8) was operated by Maude Michael, and the vacant house on Elm Street (9) was rumored to have been a saloon known as Peggy's Place. On the extreme left, across Elm Street, was McDanield's Grove, where picnics and celebrations were held.

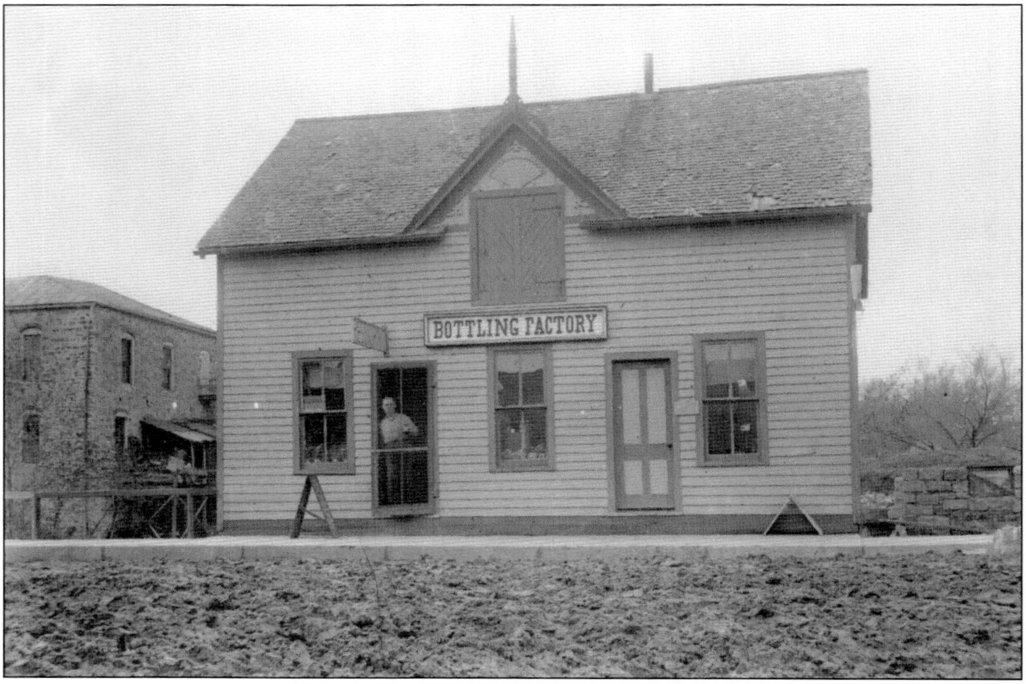

Soda pop was very popular in the early days, and there were many local bottlers and no national brands. Seen here standing in the doorway of his bottling factory is Albin Holmquist.

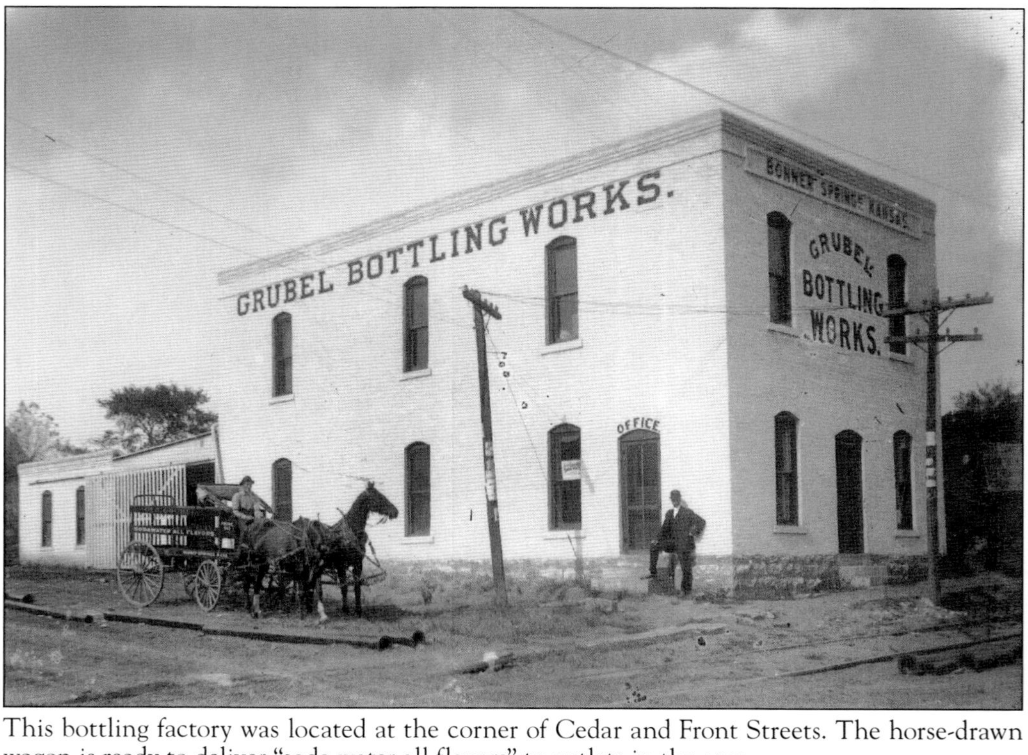

This bottling factory was located at the corner of Cedar and Front Streets. The horse-drawn wagon is ready to deliver "soda water all flavors" to outlets in the area.

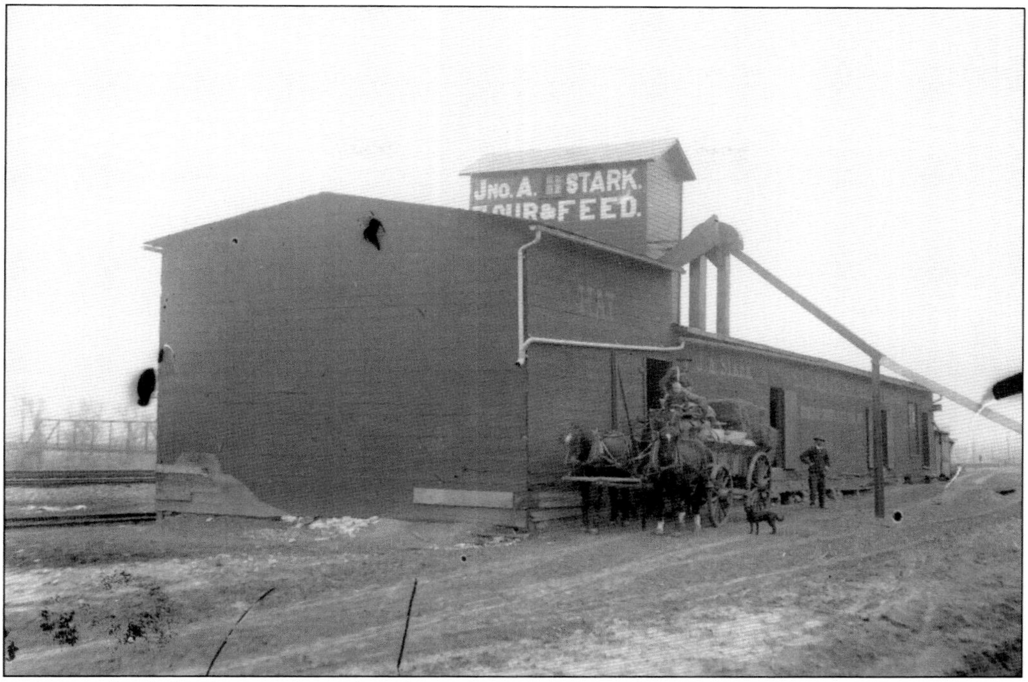

A farmer loads his hay and supplies from the feed store. The area around Bonner Springs was ideal farmland.

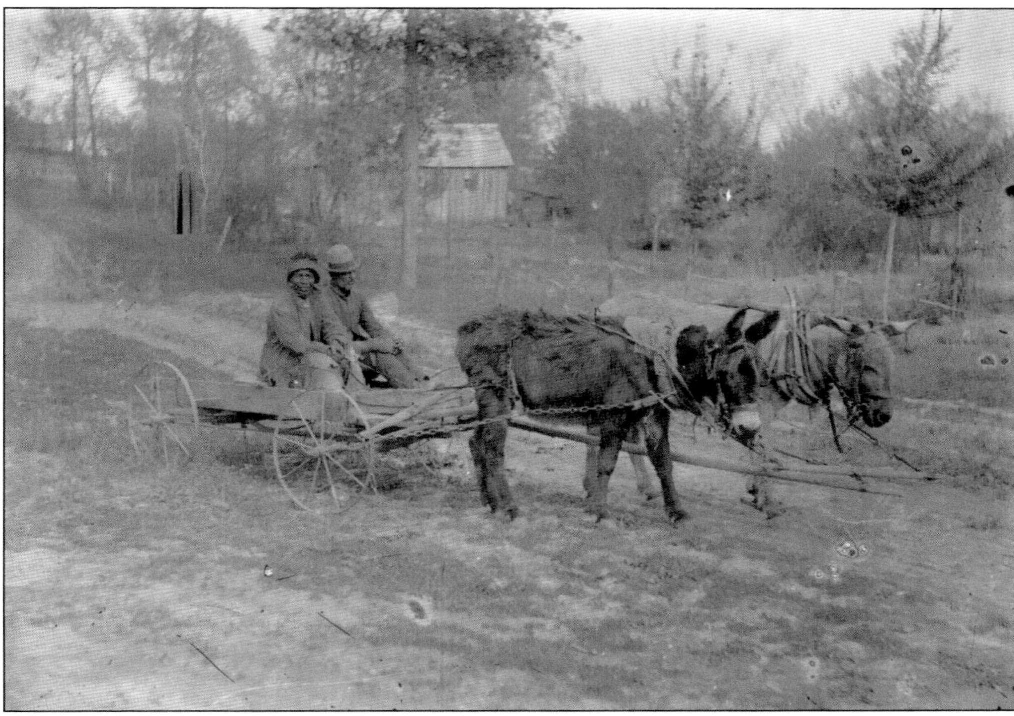
This photograph, captioned "Archie and Friend," was taken in the Grandview area, west of Nettleton, where many African American residents lived.

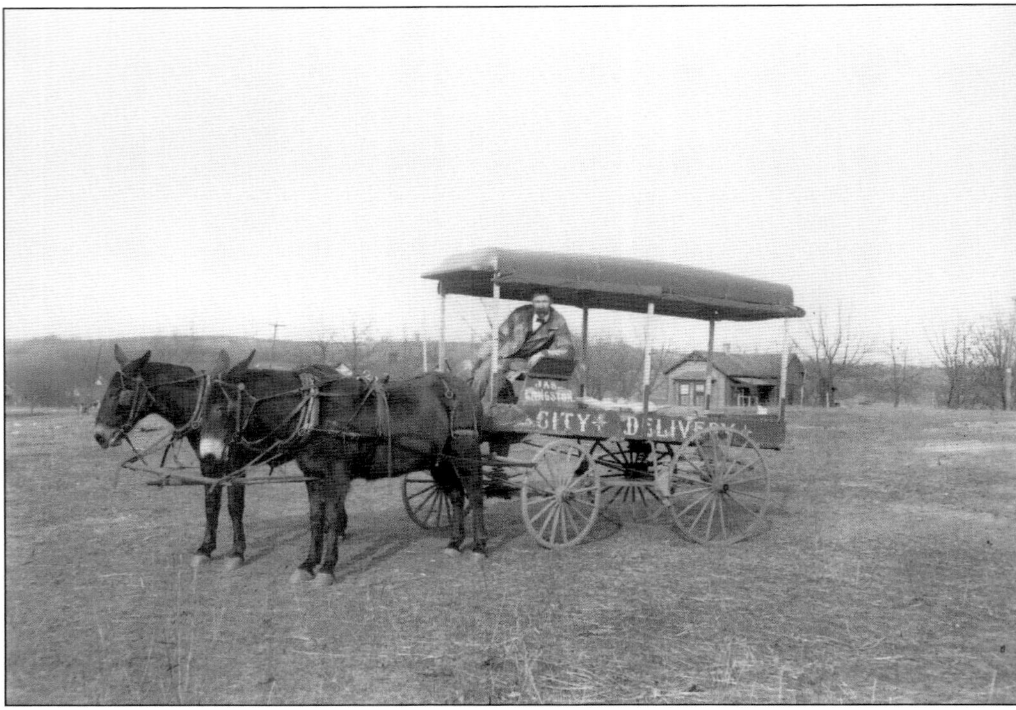

James Langston is seen here in his City Delivery wagon, which transported anything that needed to be moved or delivered.

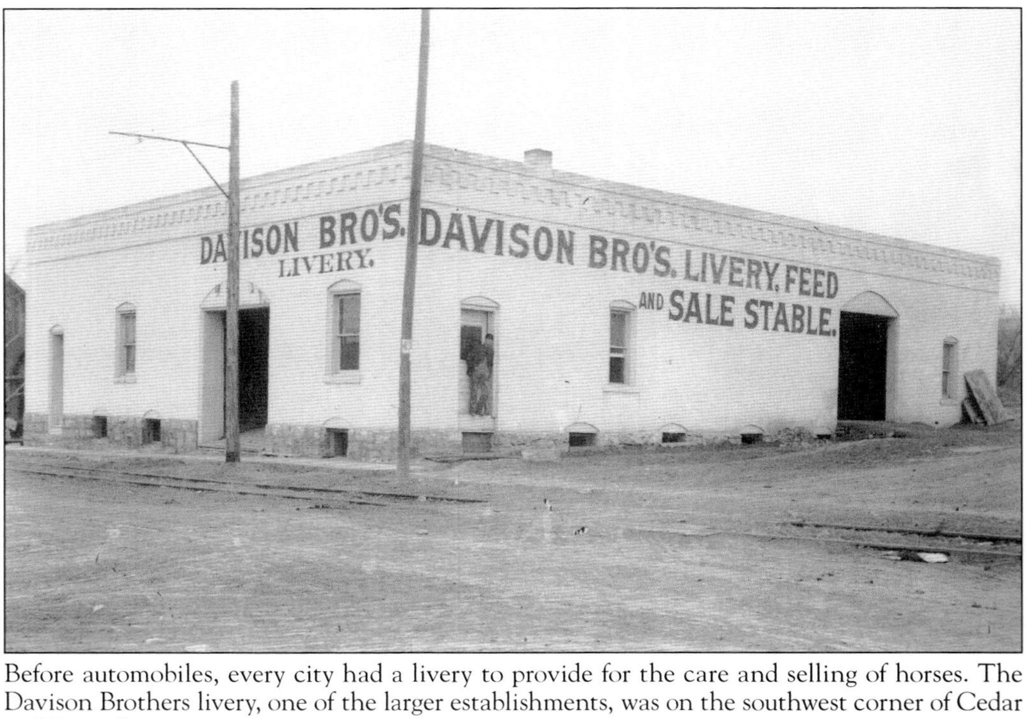

Before automobiles, every city had a livery to provide for the care and selling of horses. The Davison Brothers livery, one of the larger establishments, was on the southwest corner of Cedar and Front Streets.

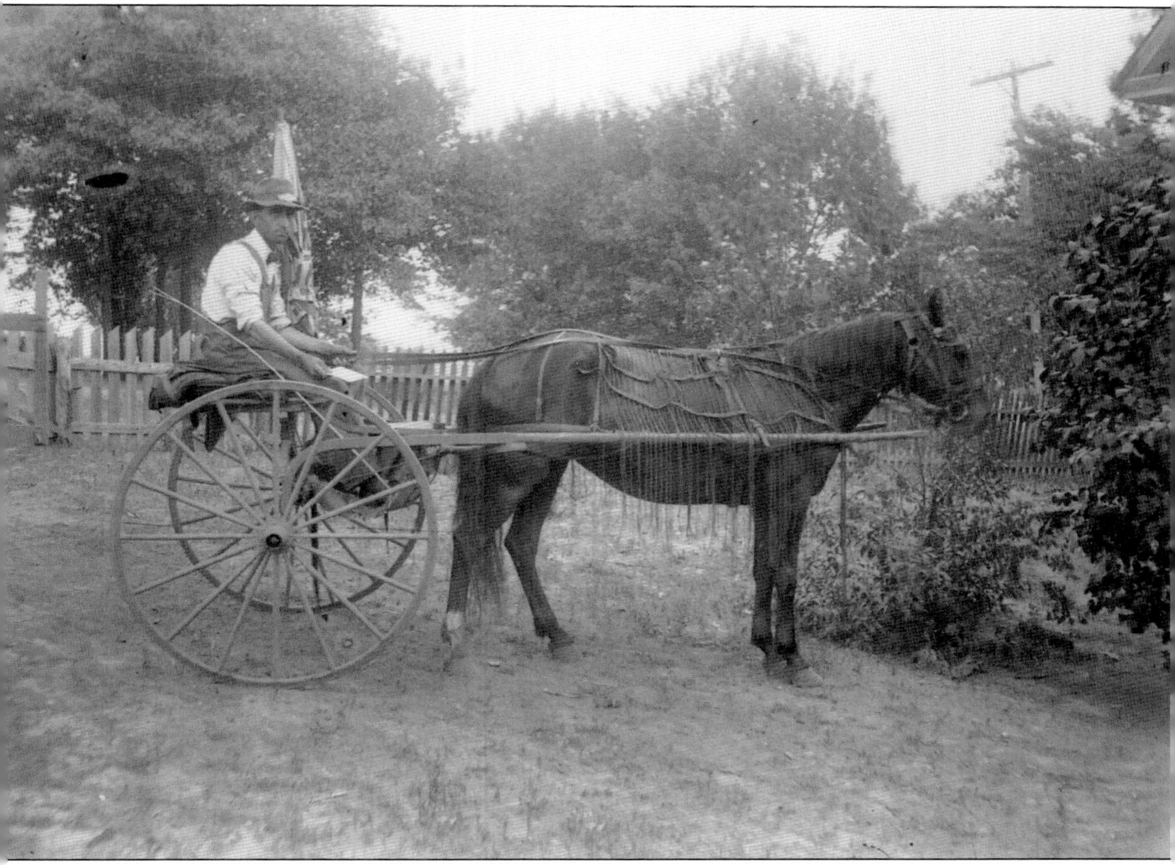

Through his eyes and his lens, Urbin Rudell spent more than half a century capturing significant people, places, and events in Bonner Springs. He became interested in photography at about age 15, when he acquired a German-made camera and became a self-taught photographer. He worked at the David & Son store until the Depression, when he acquired the contract to deliver mail from the post office to the train depot and the mail car. Mail coming in was then hauled to the post office. He held this position from 1933 until his retirement in 1955. His daughters Ella Mae Mitchell and Mildred Bundy preserved his collection of glass negatives, and they are now in the possession of the Kansas State Historical Society in Topeka, Kansas. Copies of the images are archived at the Bonner Springs Library.

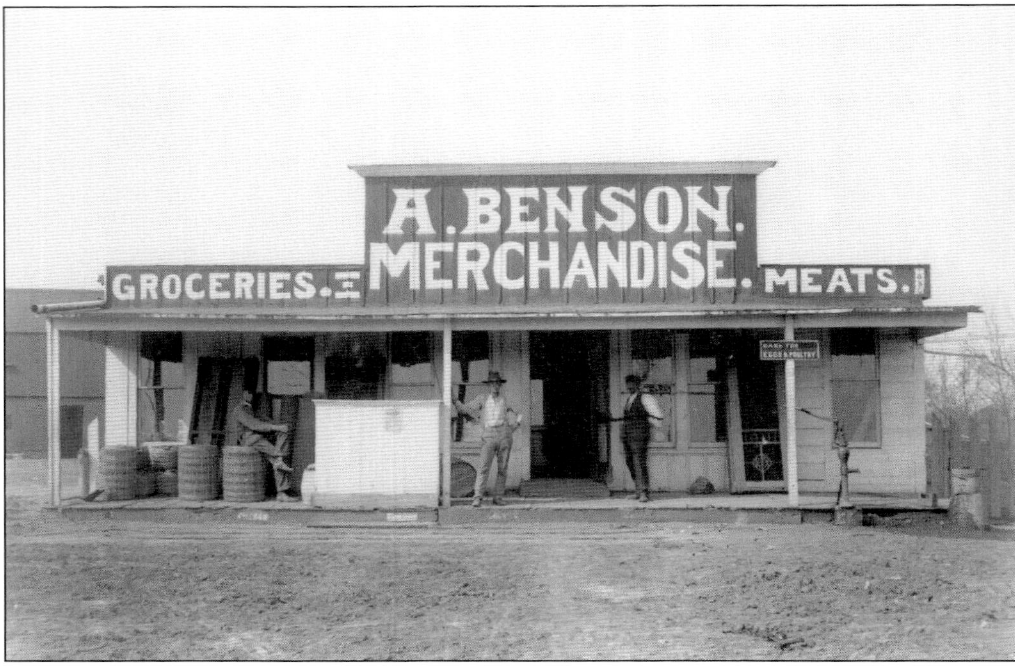

August Benson's general store, on Front Street and Santa Fe Road, advertised "cash for eggs and poultry."

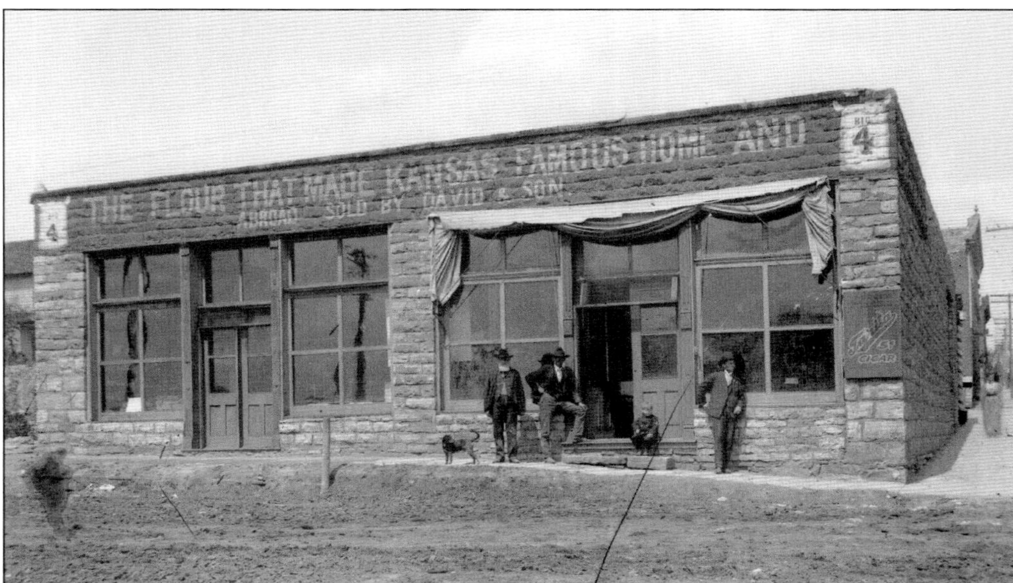

David & Son was on the corner of Oak and Front Streets. Seen here are, from left to right, J.J. Smith, Calvin L. David, young Calvin David, and L.S. David, the son of Calvin L. David. Their product, Big 4 Flour, is touted on the building. Unfortunately, it seems that the painter miscalculated the width of the building. One could also get a good nickel cigar at that time, according to the sign.

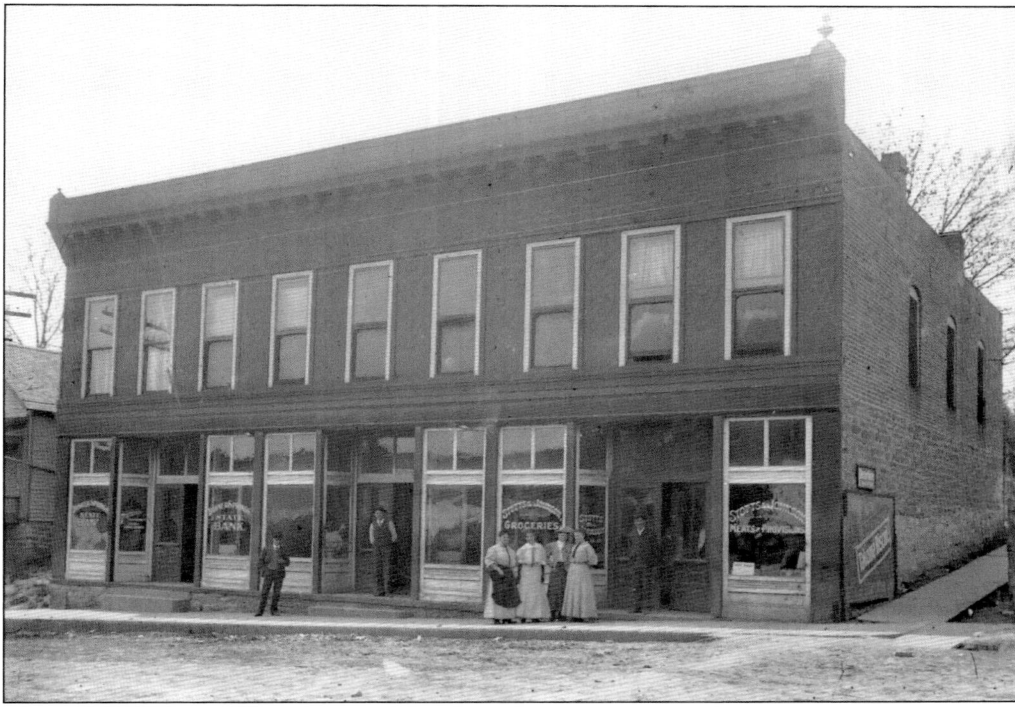

The Ryan Building was on the southeast corner of Oak and Second Streets. It was replaced by Interstate Savings and Loan.

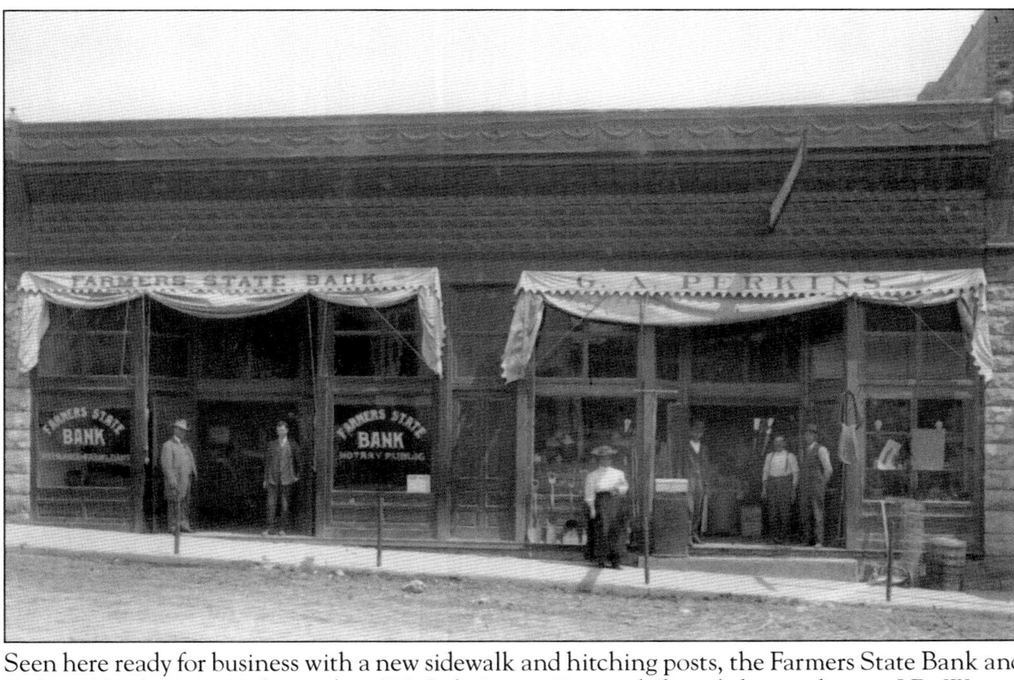

Seen here ready for business with a new sidewalk and hitching posts, the Farmers State Bank and Perkins Hardware were located at 125 Oak Street. Pictured, from left to right, are J.D. Waters, John Jackson, an unidentified woman, Urbin Rudell, and two unidentified men.

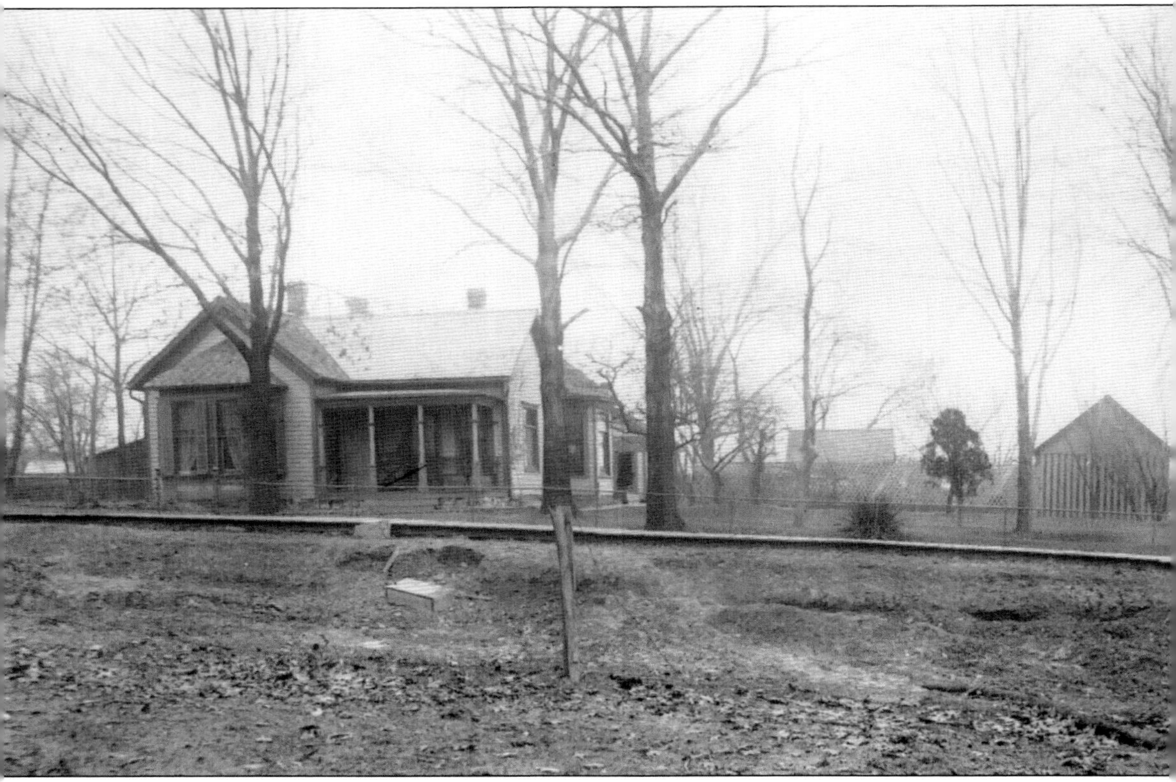

The home of E.L. Matthews is seen here. Matthews was the editor and publisher of the *Wyandotte Chieftain* newspaper, which he started in 1896. He immediately started campaigning to have Bonner Springs incorporated as a city. A meeting was called on July 2 of that year, and, on October 15, a petition was submitted to the county commissioners. After several rejections, Bonner Springs was granted incorporation rights as a third-class city on November 10, 1898. Philo Clark was elected as mayor, and W.S. Twist installed a telephone system. One report in the newspaper notes that Dave Rhodes was fined $12.50 by Judge J.D. Waters for "naughty talk" at the barbershop.

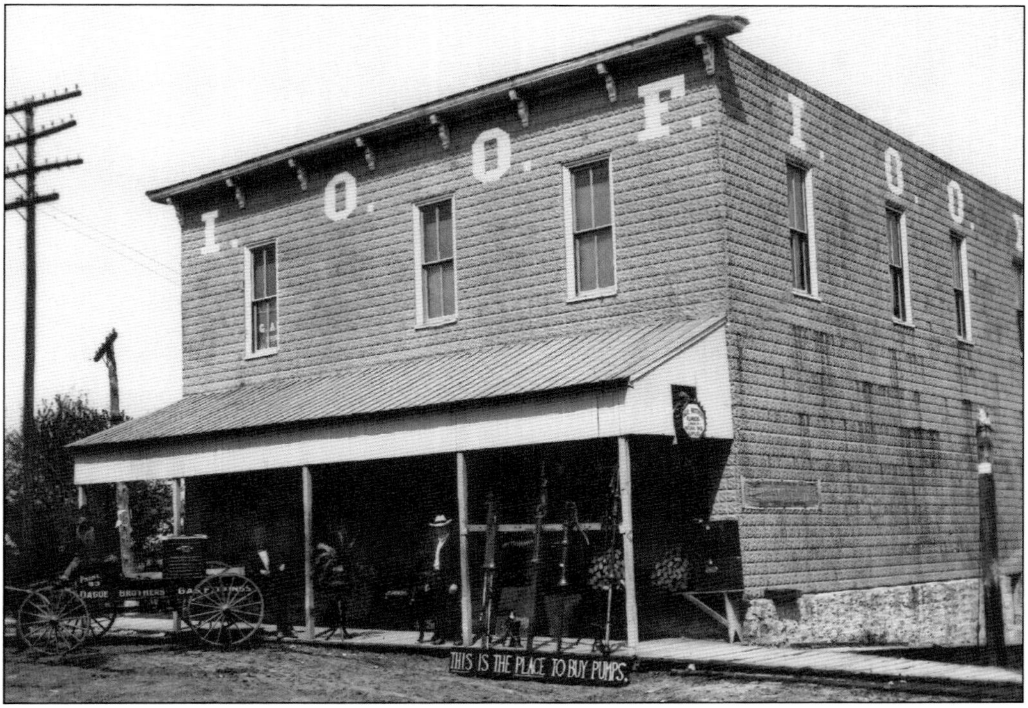

This building, at the southeast corner of Nettleton and Kump Avenues, was home to the A.B.C. Dague Pump Company, on the first floor, and the Independent Order of Odd Fellows hall, on the second.

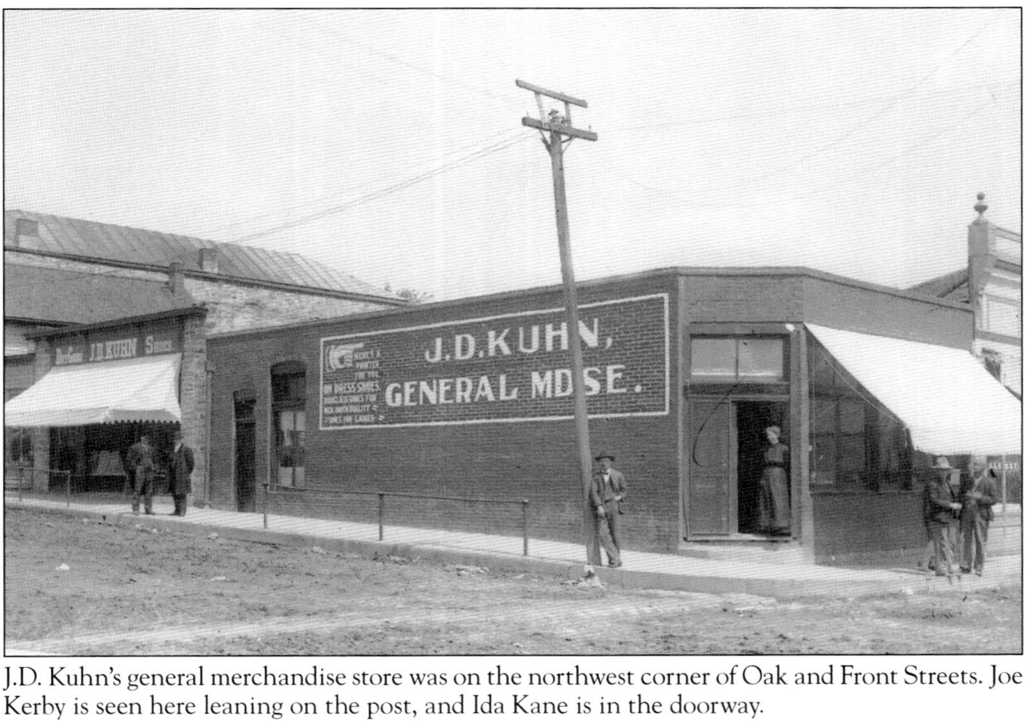

J.D. Kuhn's general merchandise store was on the northwest corner of Oak and Front Streets. Joe Kerby is seen here leaning on the post, and Ida Kane is in the doorway.

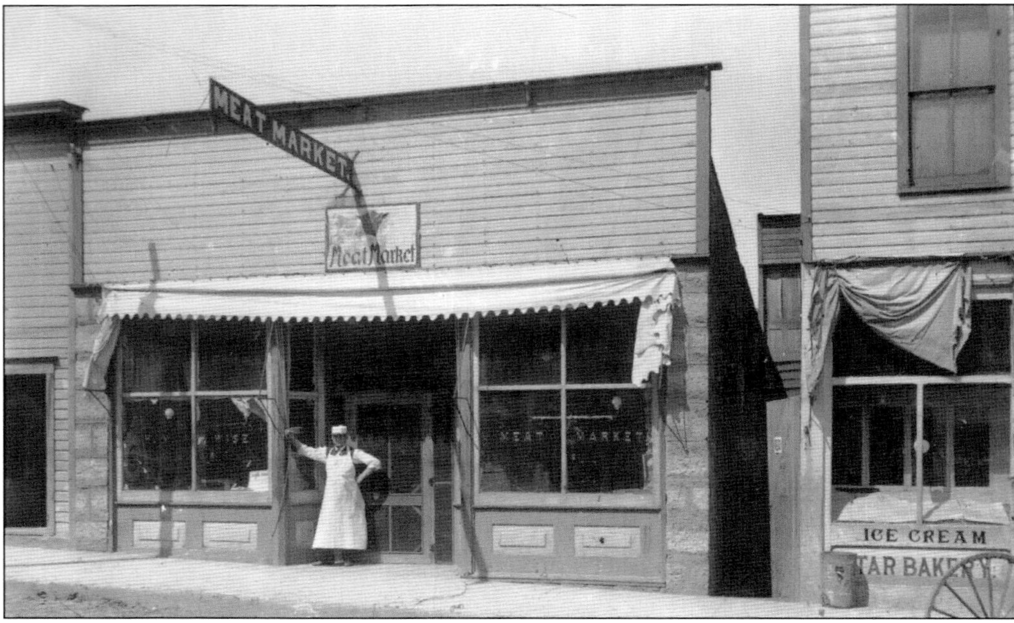

H.V. Wise is ready to greets customers at 121 Oak Street. He advertised himself as "Bonner Springs' butcher," offering a wide variety of fresh and salted meats.

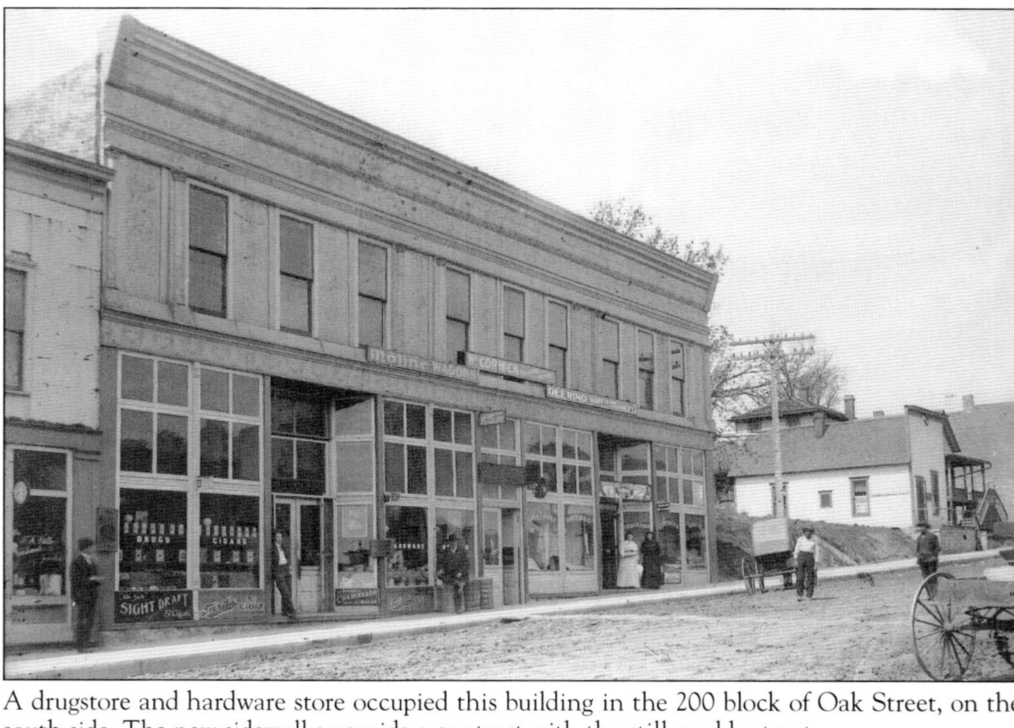

A drugstore and hardware store occupied this building in the 200 block of Oak Street, on the south side. The new sidewalks provide a contrast with the still-muddy street.

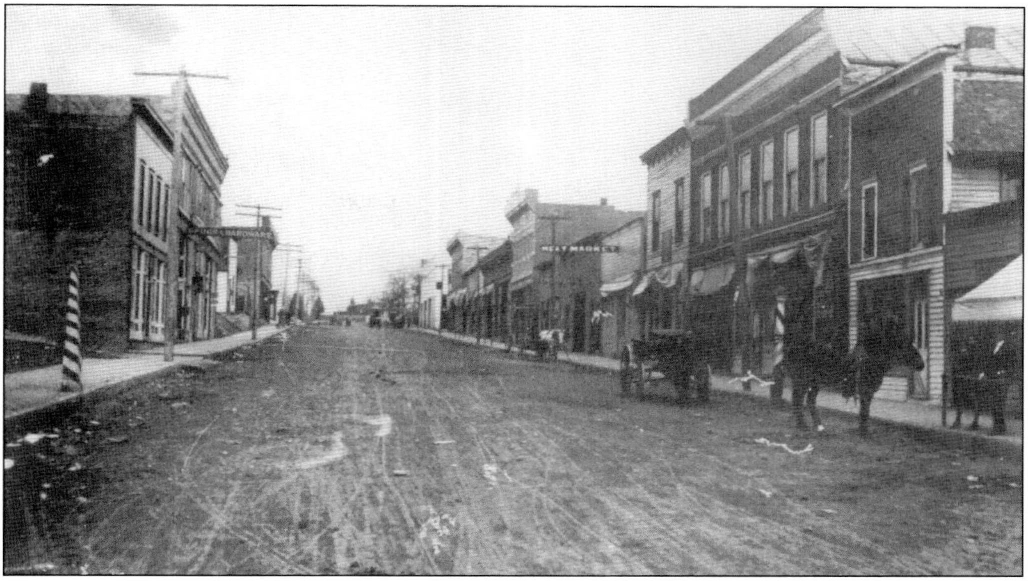

The view in this photograph, looking west on Oak Street, shows that it was almost complete with businesses in 1907. Although there was a new sidewalk, the street was still dirt. It was not paved until 1913.

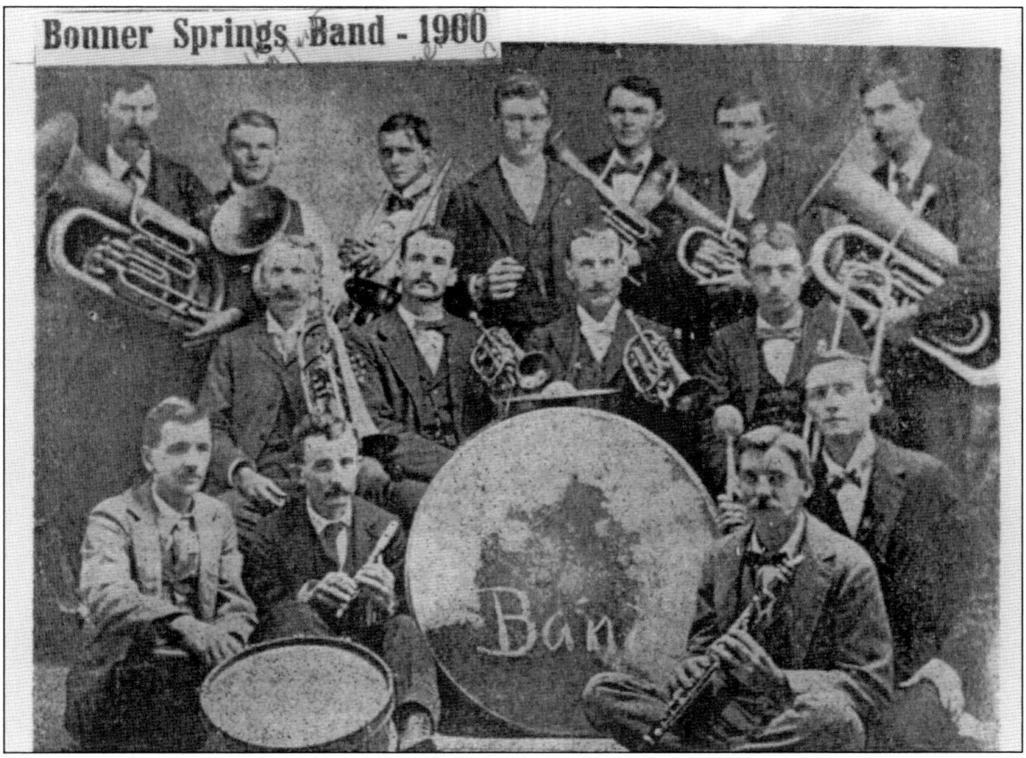

This clipping from the newspaper shows the city band in 1900. Many concerts were given at the wooden bandstand in the park, behind the Masonic lodge. Today, the band plays during the summer at the new band pavilion in Kelly Murphy Park.

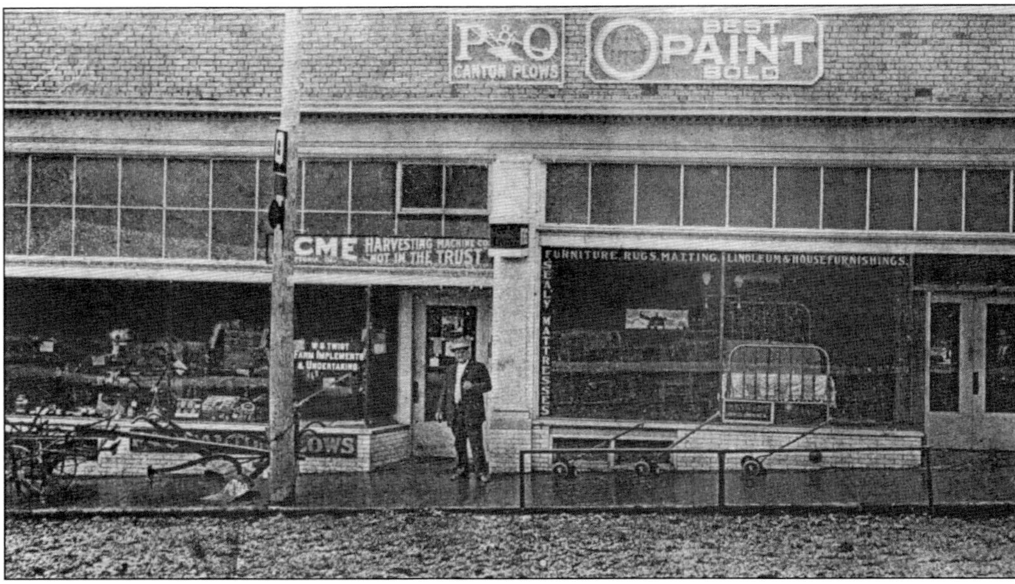

W.S. Twist stands proudly in front of his furniture store. He was also an undertaker, as were many builders of caskets at that time. He sold his undertaking business to his employee Frank Alden in 1904. The Alden-Harrington Funeral Home is still in operation today.

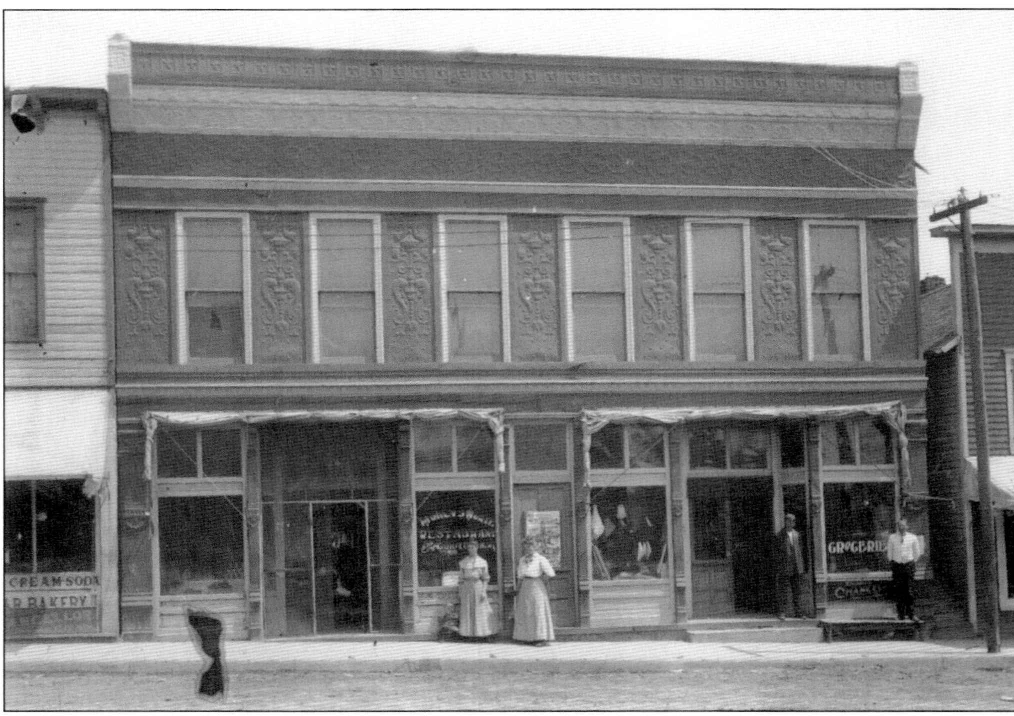

The Moneys Worth Restaurant and Confectionary occupied the first floor of this building, along with a grocery. An opera house was above. Traveling shows and local events kept the opera house busy. It burned in the fire of 1908.

The Bonner Springs Sanitarium

Bonner Springs, Kansas

(Suburban to Kansas City, Mo.)

A private hospital and sanitarium for the care and treatment of mild nervous and mental cases.

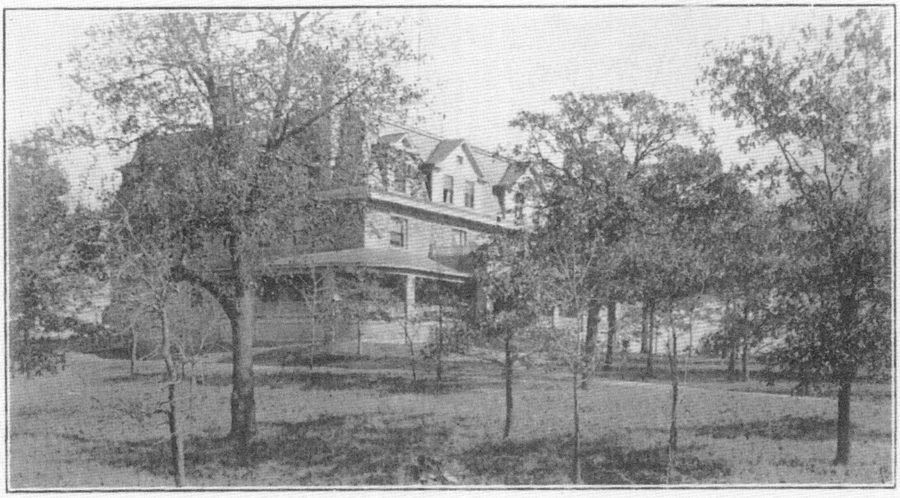

New stone buildings, fully equipped, modern in every respect. Nineteen acres of ground. High and very sightly location. Sunshine, pure air, mineral springs, freedom from noise, dust, heat and distractions of the city. Strictly ethical

DR. HENRY C. HAYS

Resident Superintendent

Kansas City Office, Suite 900 Rialto Bldg.

This brochure touts the Bonner Springs Sanitarium, operated by superintendent Dr. Henry C. Hayes. At the time, Bonner Springs was still being advertised as a place for rest and recovery from the hustle and bustle of the big city.

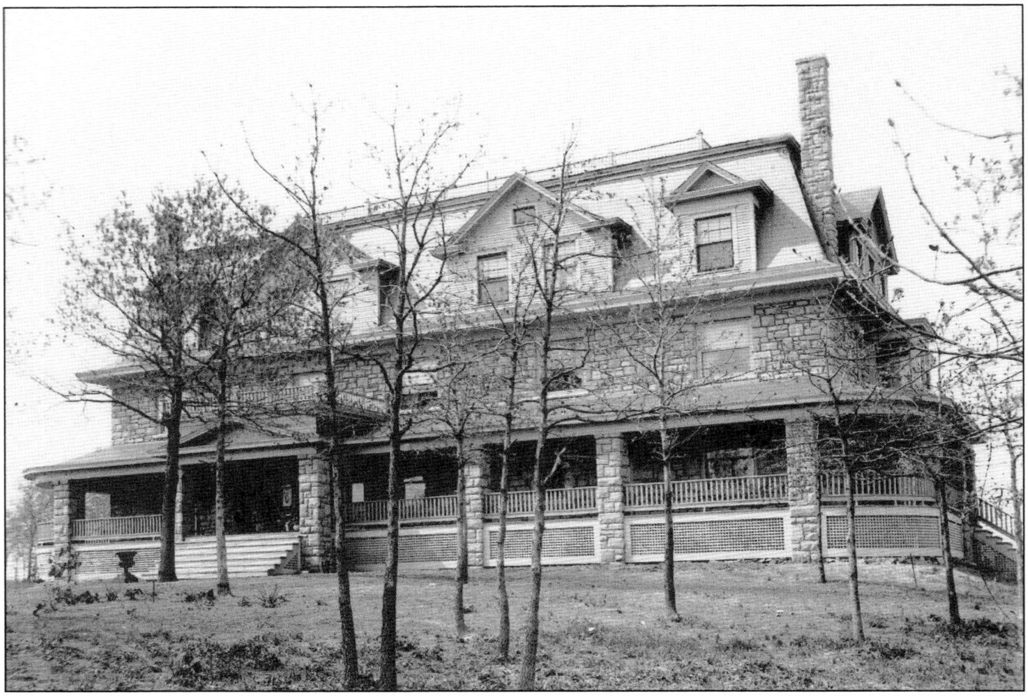

This imposing structure, the Bonner Springs Sanitarium, was built on the 700 block of North Nettleton Avenue by Dr. M.P. Sexton in 1905. It was constructed away from the town so his patients would not be disturbed by noise. He sold it to Dr. Henry C. Hayes in 1907.

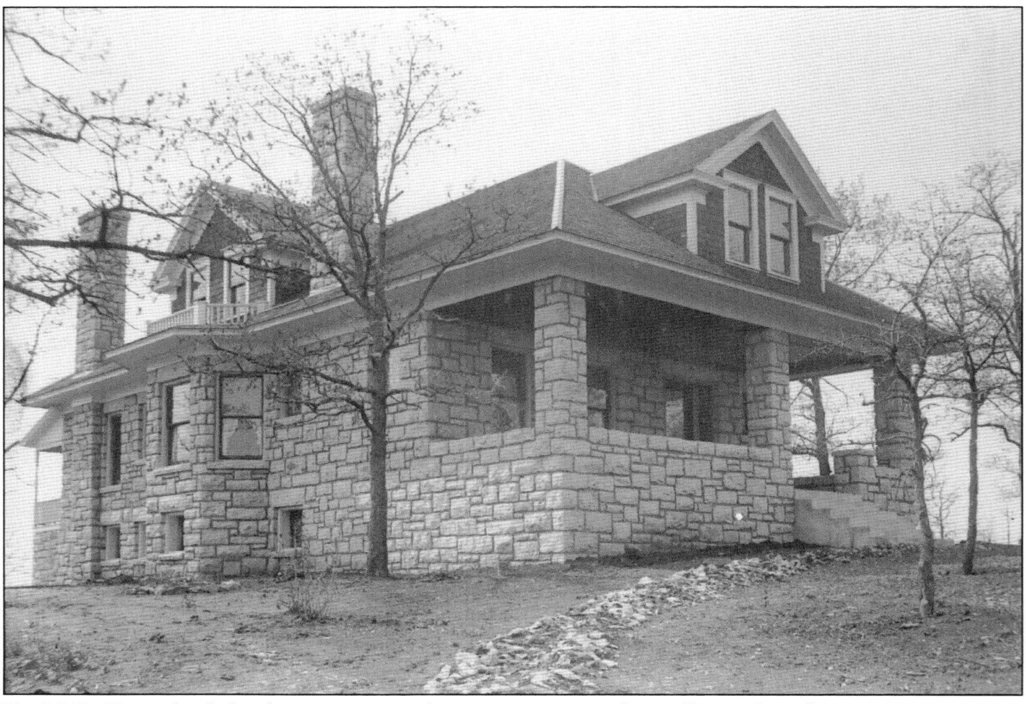

Dr. H.C. Hayes built his home next to the sanitarium, and it still stands today.

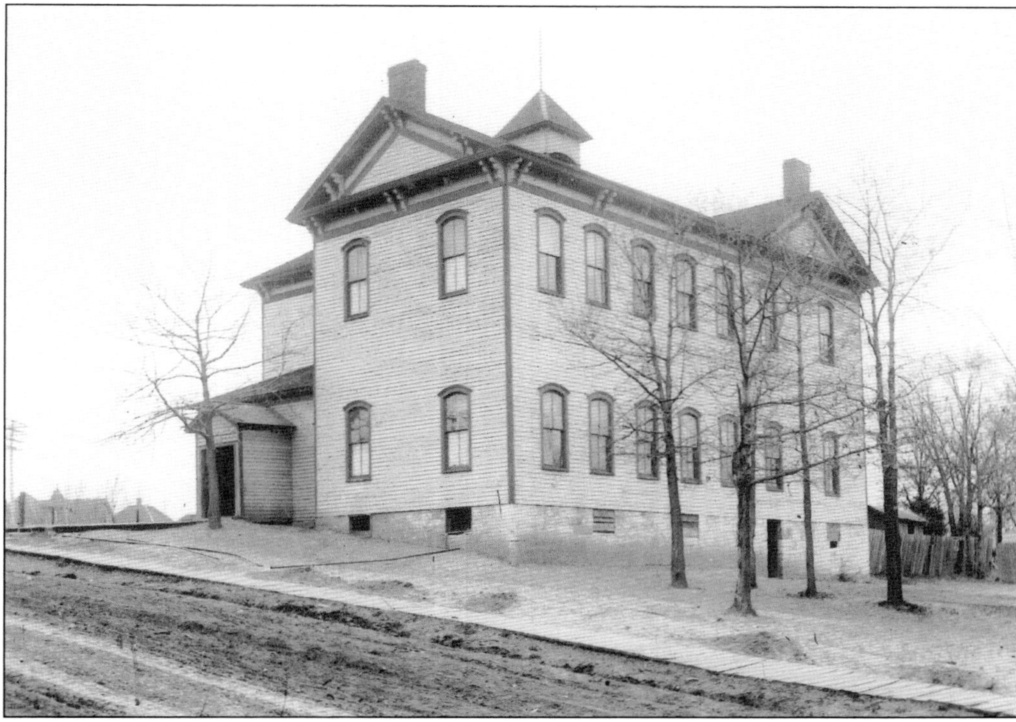

The new Tiblow School replaced the original school on the corner of Third and Cedar Streets. It was replaced with a brick building in 1918. Note the layered-board sidewalk going up the hill.

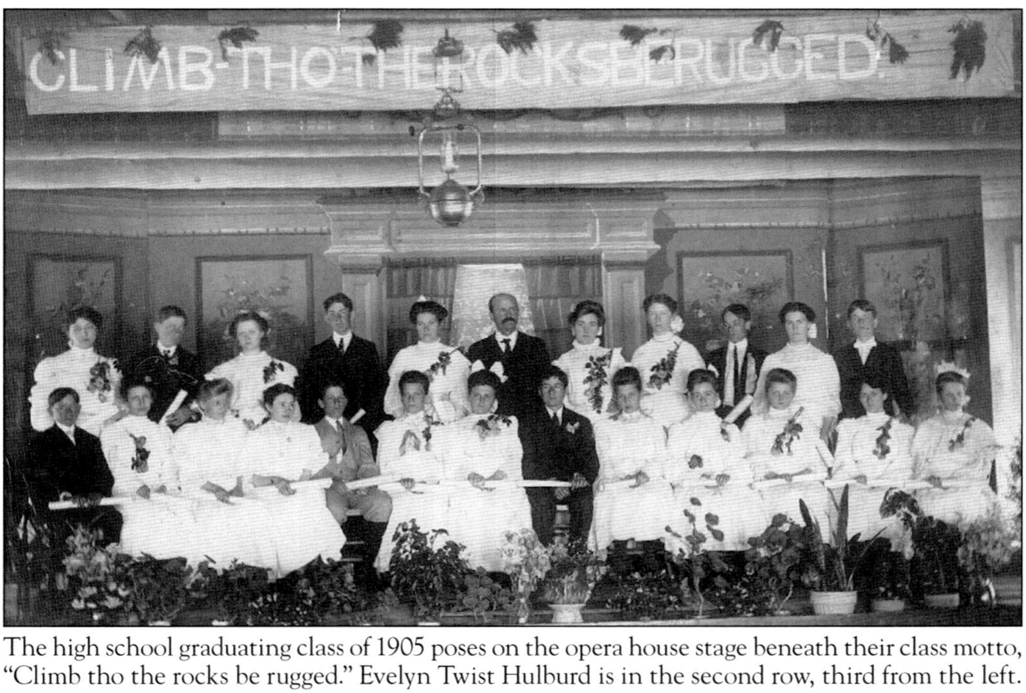

The high school graduating class of 1905 poses on the opera house stage beneath their class motto, "Climb tho the rocks be rugged." Evelyn Twist Hulburd is in the second row, third from the left. She was instrumental in forming the Business and Professional Women's Club in 1945.

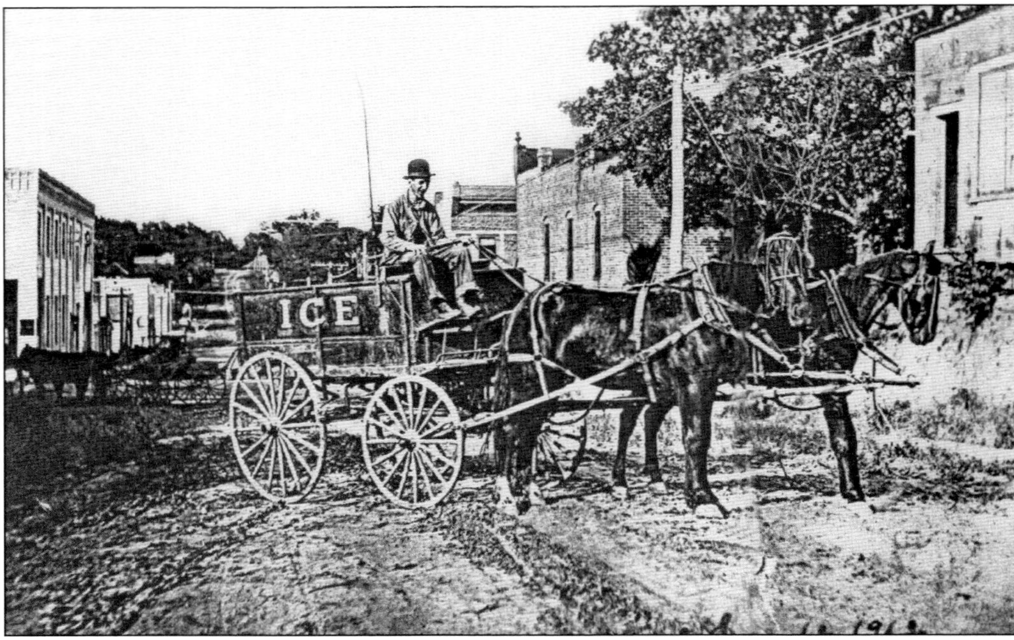

The ice delivery wagon, driven by Earl Thorp, was an important asset for households and businesses.

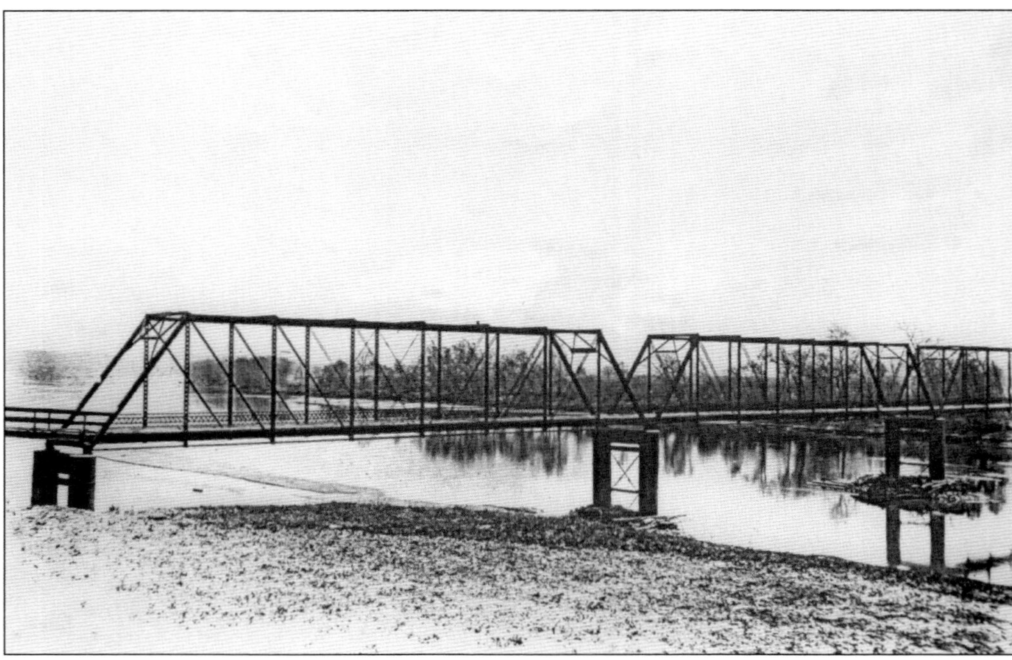

In 1905, the wagon bridge was constructed across the Kansas River, connecting Bonner Springs with Johnson County. It lasted until 1960, when it was replaced with the present bridge on Kansas Highway 7.

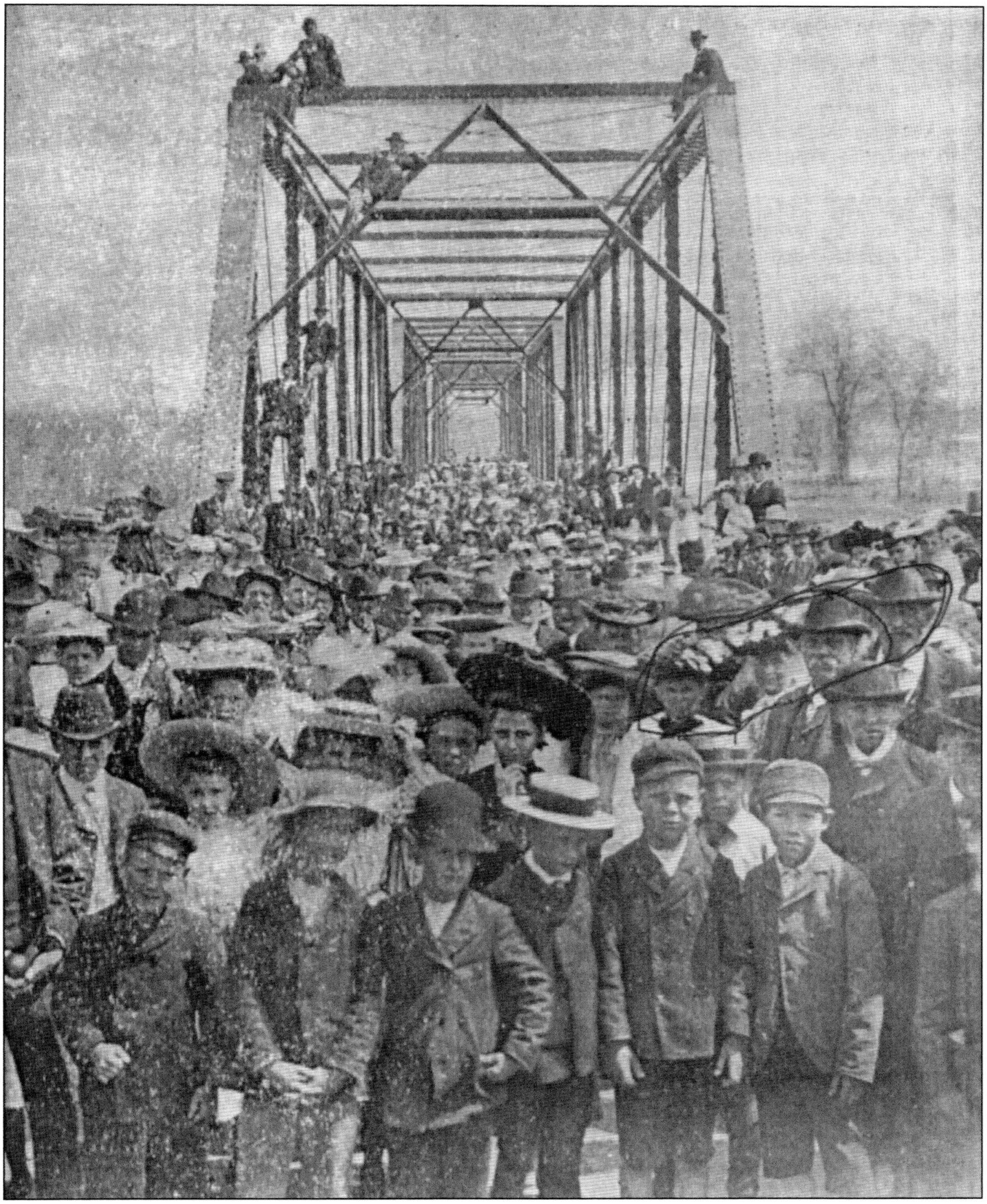

The dedication of the bridge brought a large turnout. As clearly seen, hats were the style of the day.

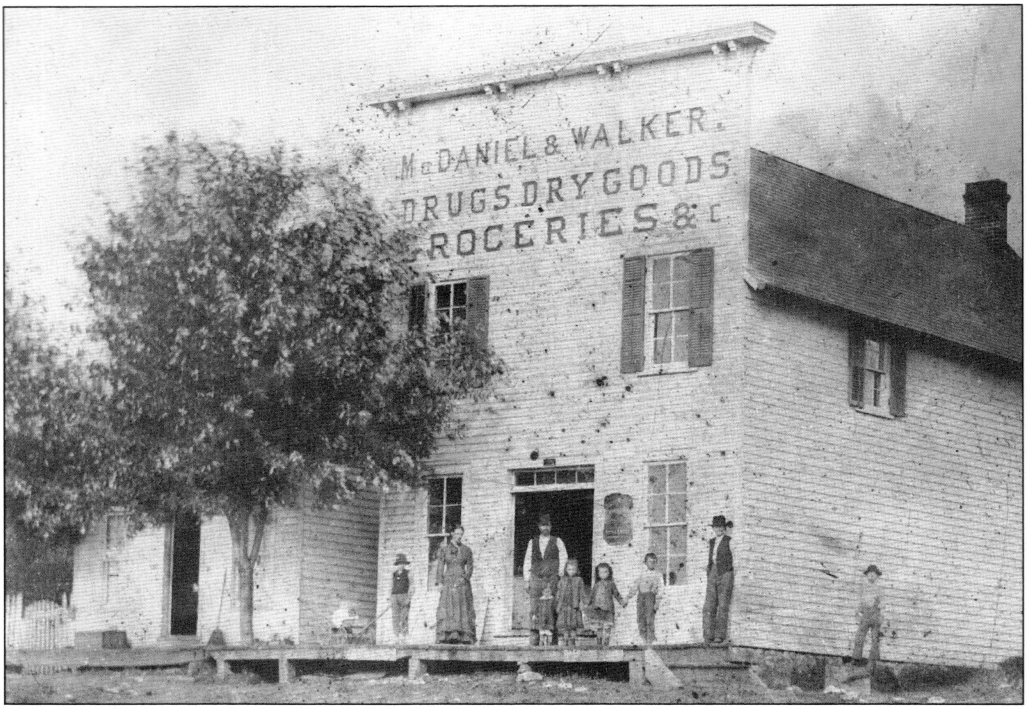

The location of the McDaniel & Walker store is unknown; it was one of several general stores in the early days of Bonner Springs.

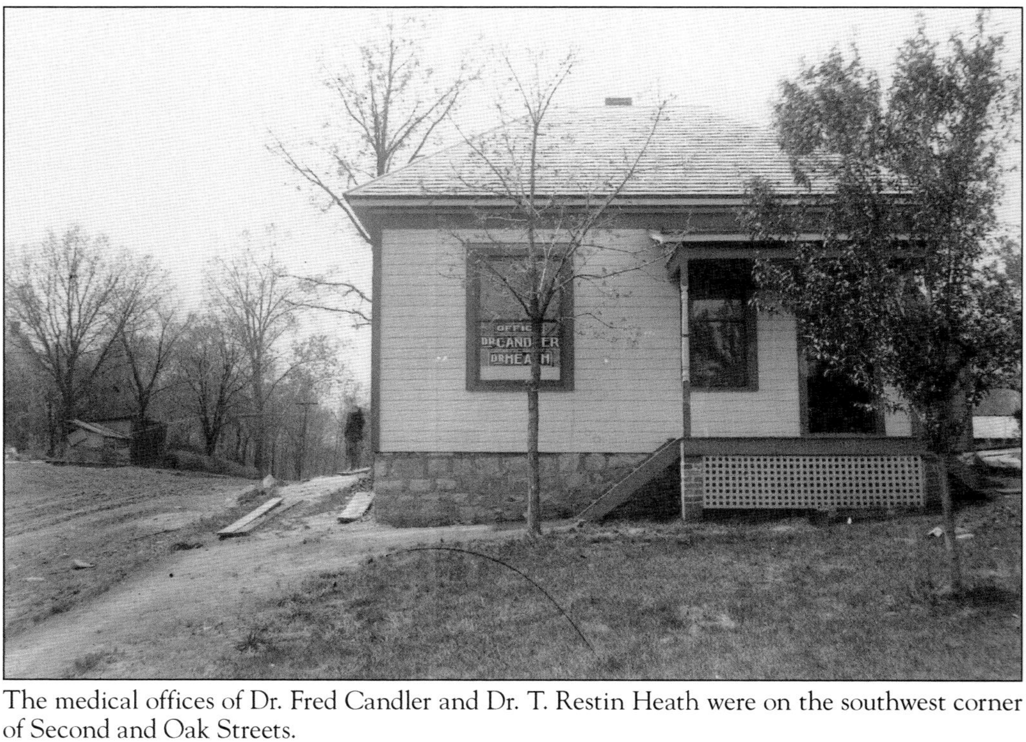

The medical offices of Dr. Fred Candler and Dr. T. Restin Heath were on the southwest corner of Second and Oak Streets.

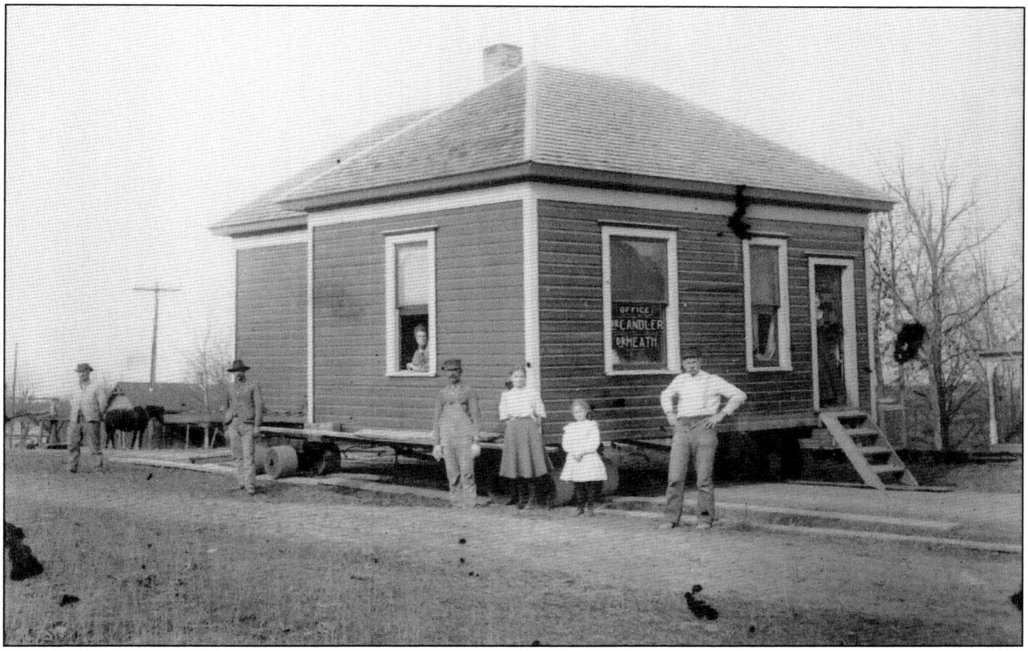

Apparently, the location on the previous site did not suit the doctors, as they moved their office to the 100 block of Allcutt Street. Many buildings were moved to better locations over the years. Without basements or many electrical and water hookups, it was advantageous to relocate a building rather than construct a new one.

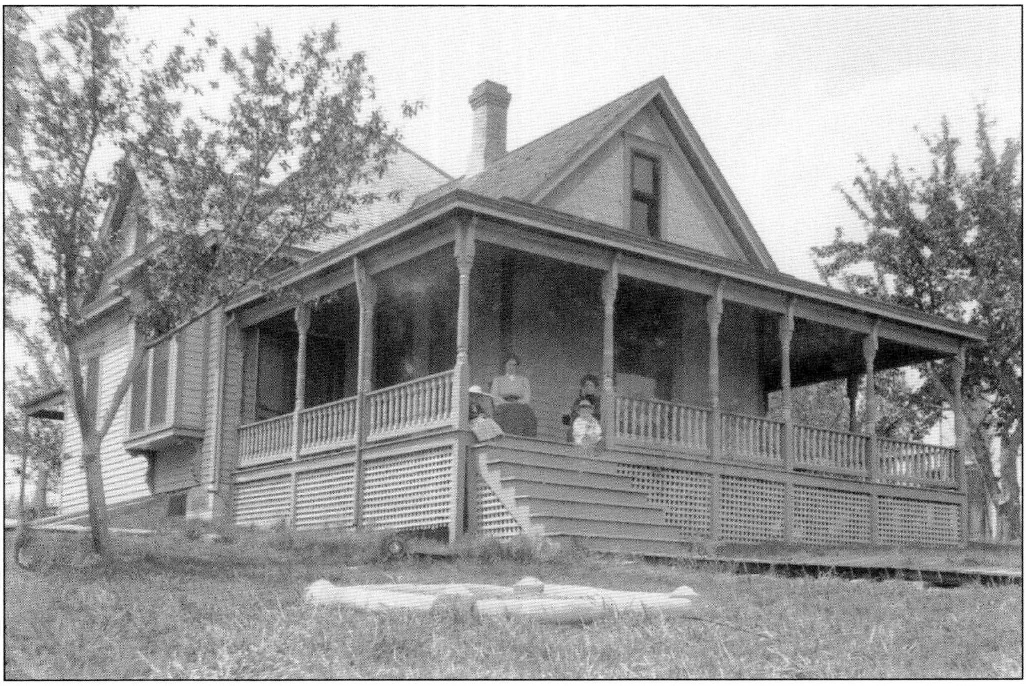

The home of Dr. Fred Candler was originally next to his office, but was later moved to the Forest Park Addition, at the corner of Elm and Second Streets.

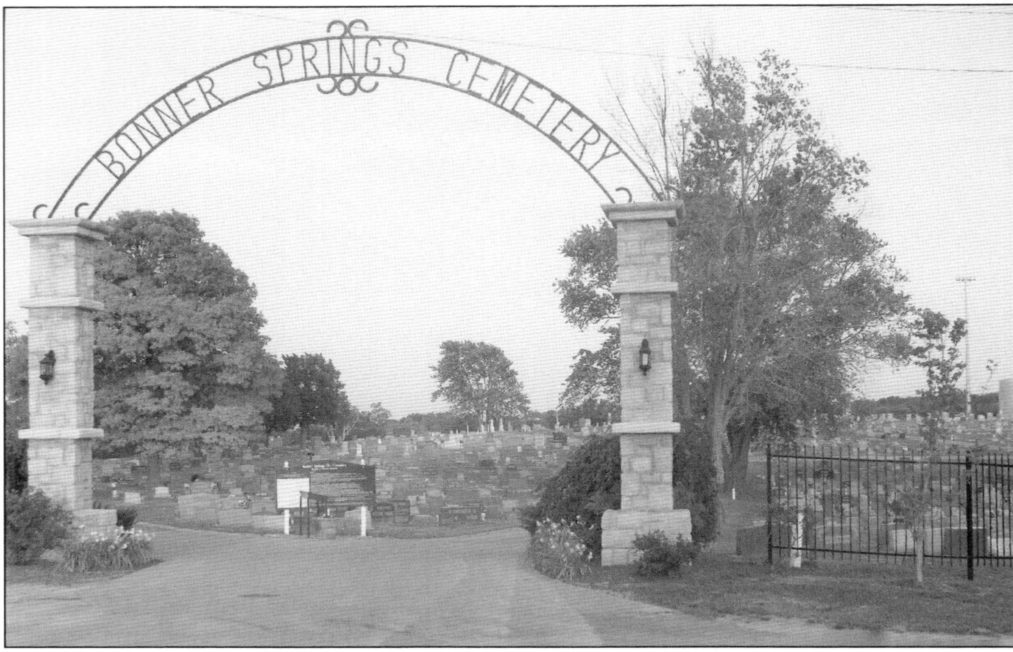

In 1903, Sylvester McDanield gave 10 acres of land in the northern part of the city for use as a cemetery. The bodies in the old cemetery, between Cedar and Second Street, were moved. W.S. Twist reported that, in 1907, about 150 bodies still remained to be moved. The old cemetery was turned over to the city for a park. (Courtesy of City of Bonner Springs.)

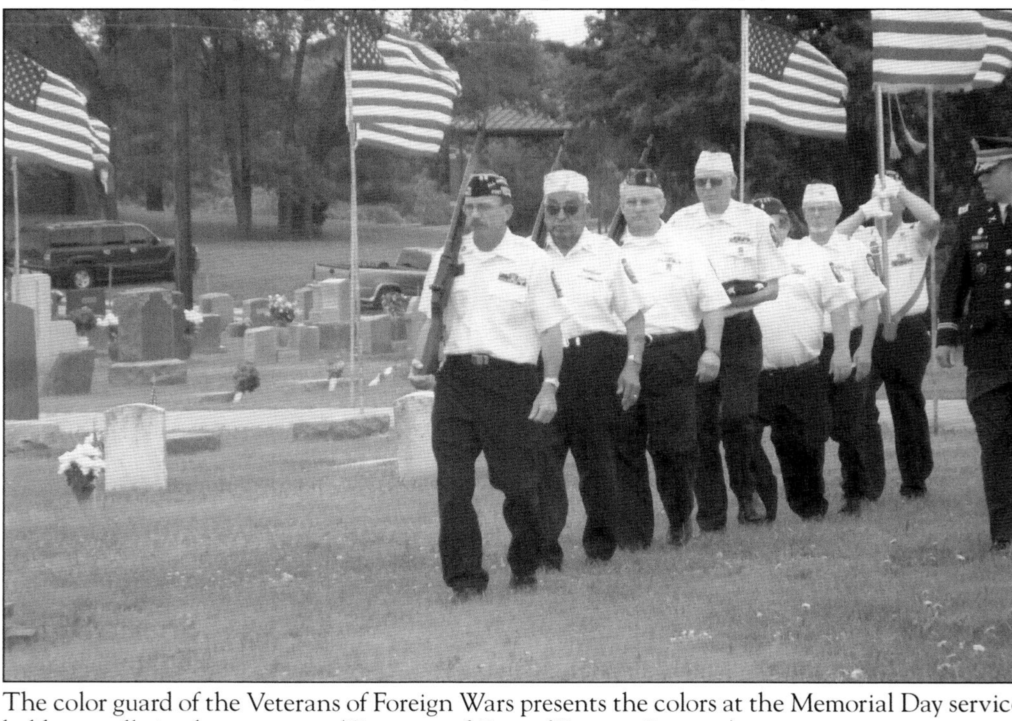

The color guard of the Veterans of Foreign Wars presents the colors at the Memorial Day service held annually in the cemetery. (Courtesy of City of Bonner Springs.)

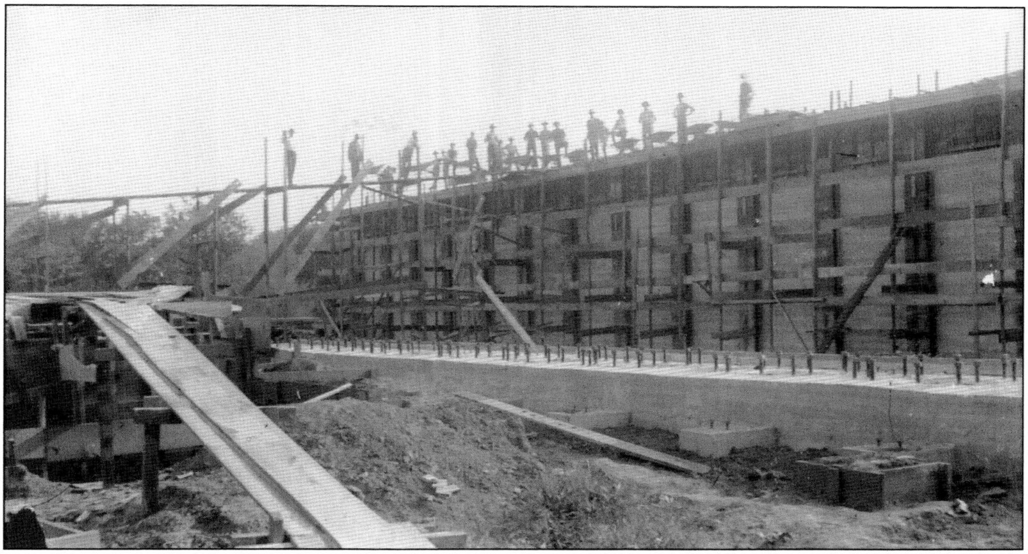

In 1906, "proven, unlimited" shallow natural gas was discovered in the area, and the stage was set to make Bonner Springs a manufacturing community. Tests proved that the stone from the hill east of Bonner Springs was 30-percent better than any being used by cement manufacturers in other parts of the state. A charter was granted to the Bonner Springs Portland Cement Company, and investors were sought.

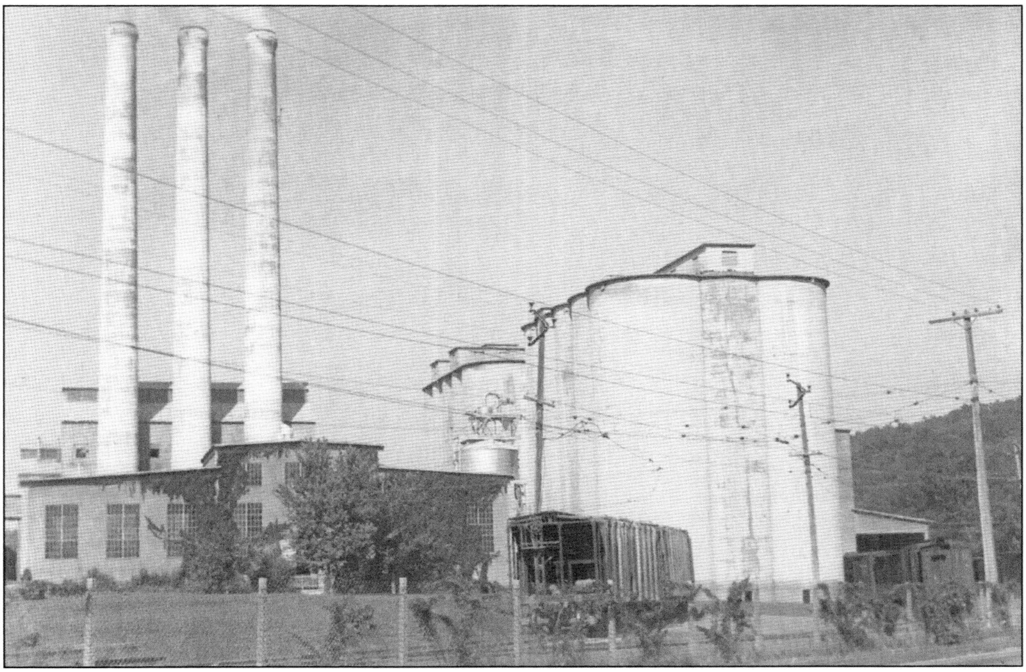

The plant was finished in March 1908, and it began operating on April 15. The first shipment of cement was two carloads made in May. Financial troubles began soon, however, and it operated intermittently through 1909. It was open for eight months in 1910 before running into financial troubles again. At that point, a new corporation was formed by J.D. Kuhn, and operations continued.

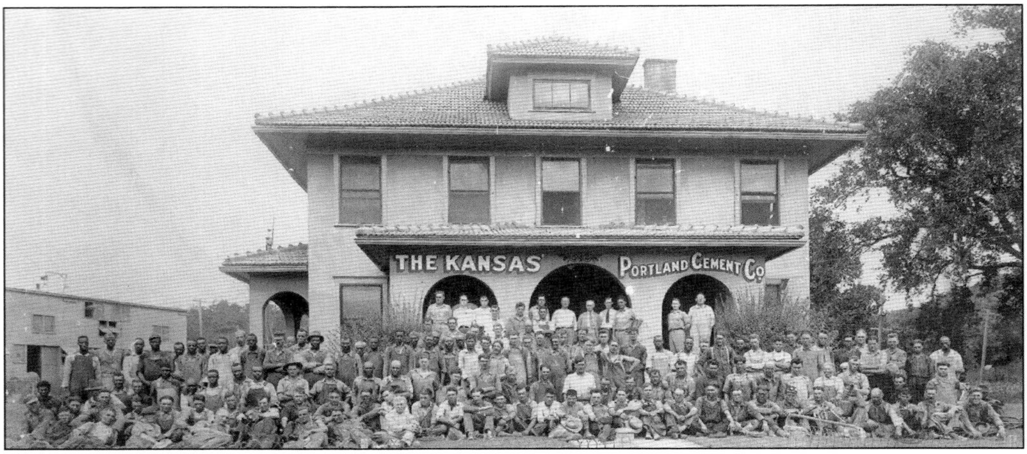

In 1923, the International Cement Corporation purchased the plant, and construction started on a new, modern plant that used the "wet" process rather than the "dry"—grinding the rock in water instead of out of water. The new name was the Kansas Portland Cement Company.

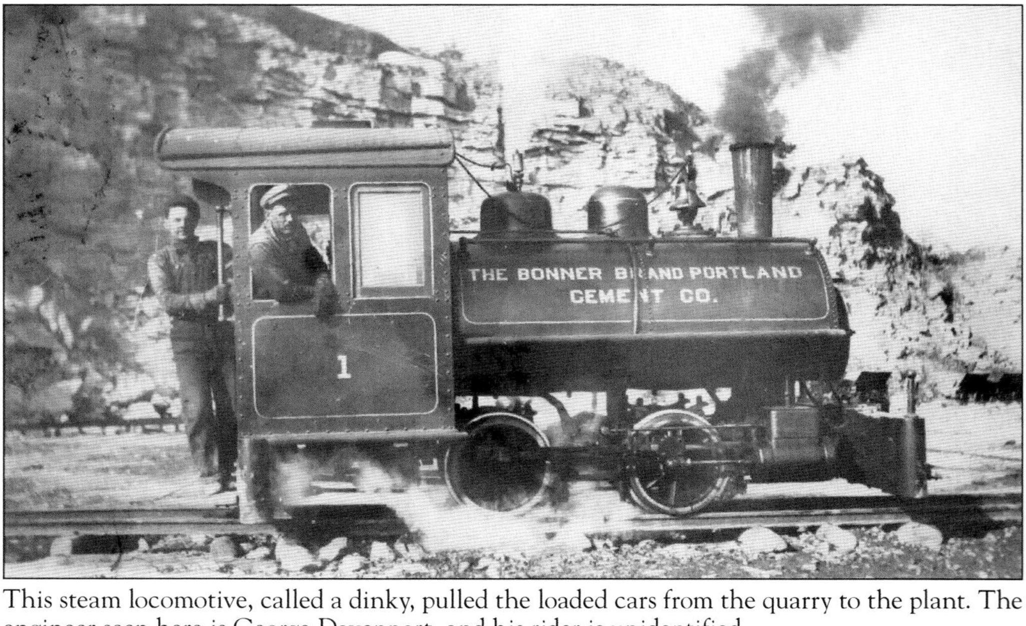

This steam locomotive, called a dinky, pulled the loaded cars from the quarry to the plant. The engineer seen here is George Davenport, and his rider is unidentified.

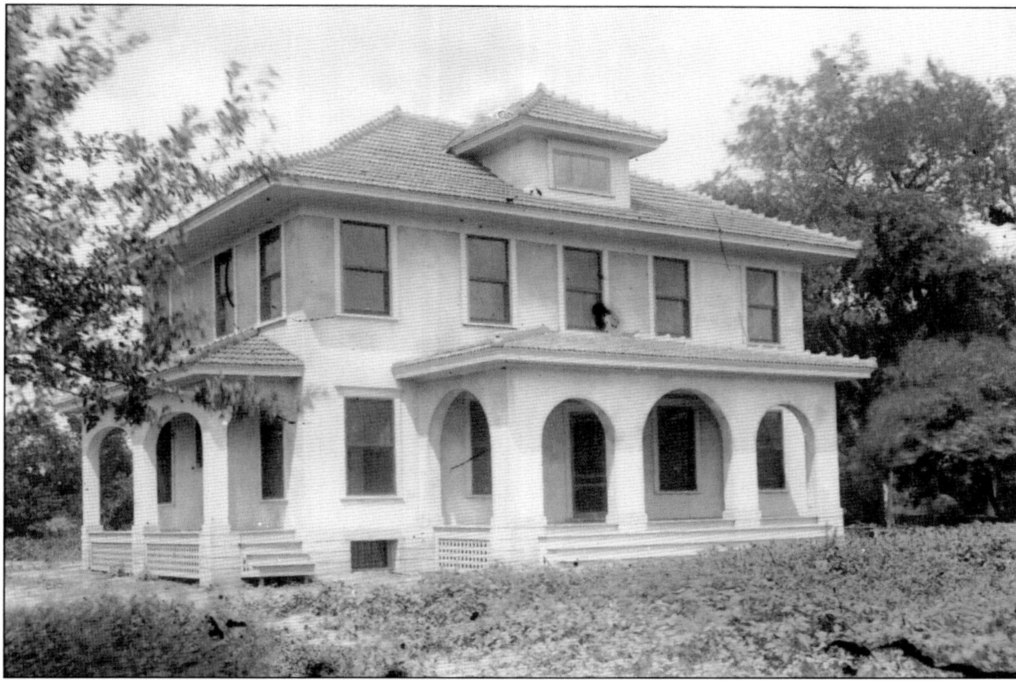

The International Cement Company's headquarters building was constructed on the grounds, as was a laboratory for the analysis of the rock and the finished product.

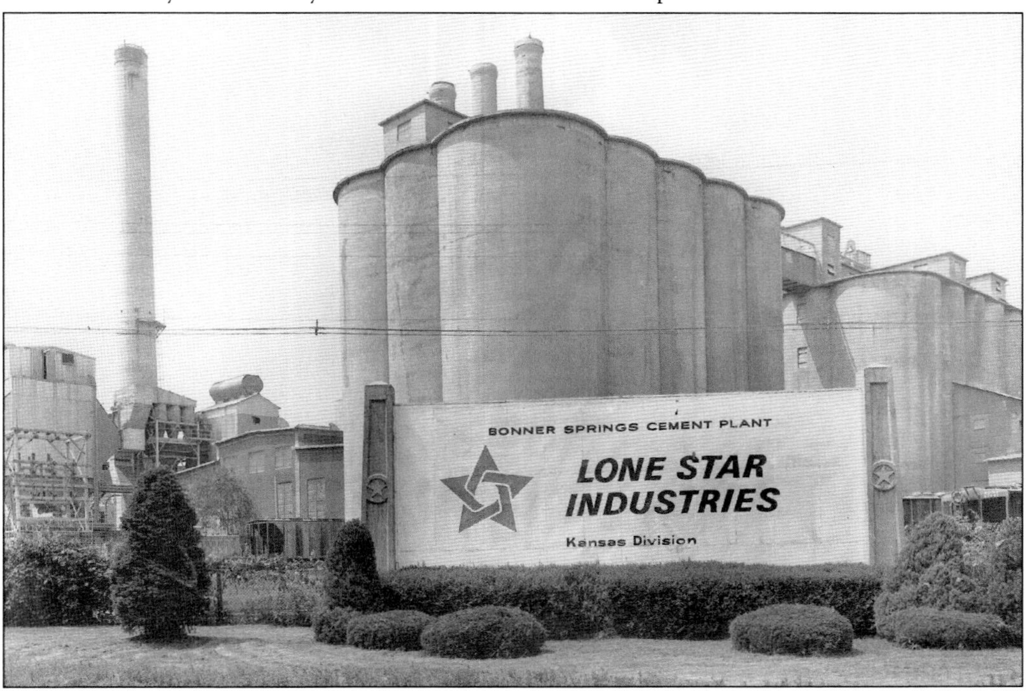

In 1929, the name of the plant was changed to the Lone Star Cement Corporation, in honor of the parent plant in Dallas. The plant closed in 1990, except for the shipping of cement made elsewhere by trucks and the railroad.

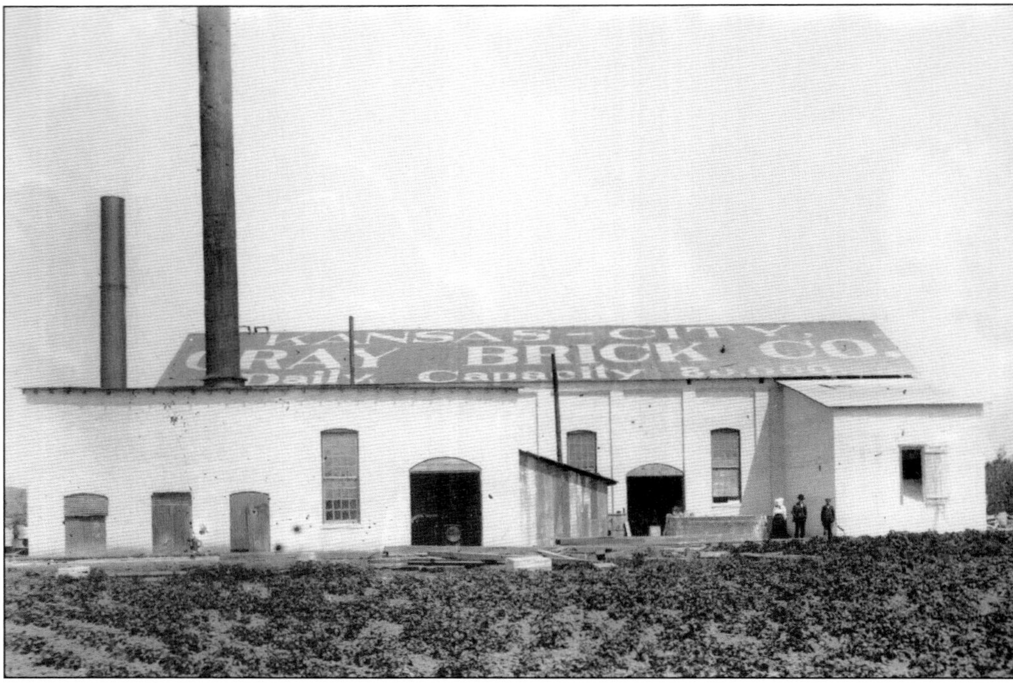

The Gray Brick Company was located across the railroad tracks from the cement plant. It produced concrete bricks that were used in the construction of many buildings in Bonner Springs.

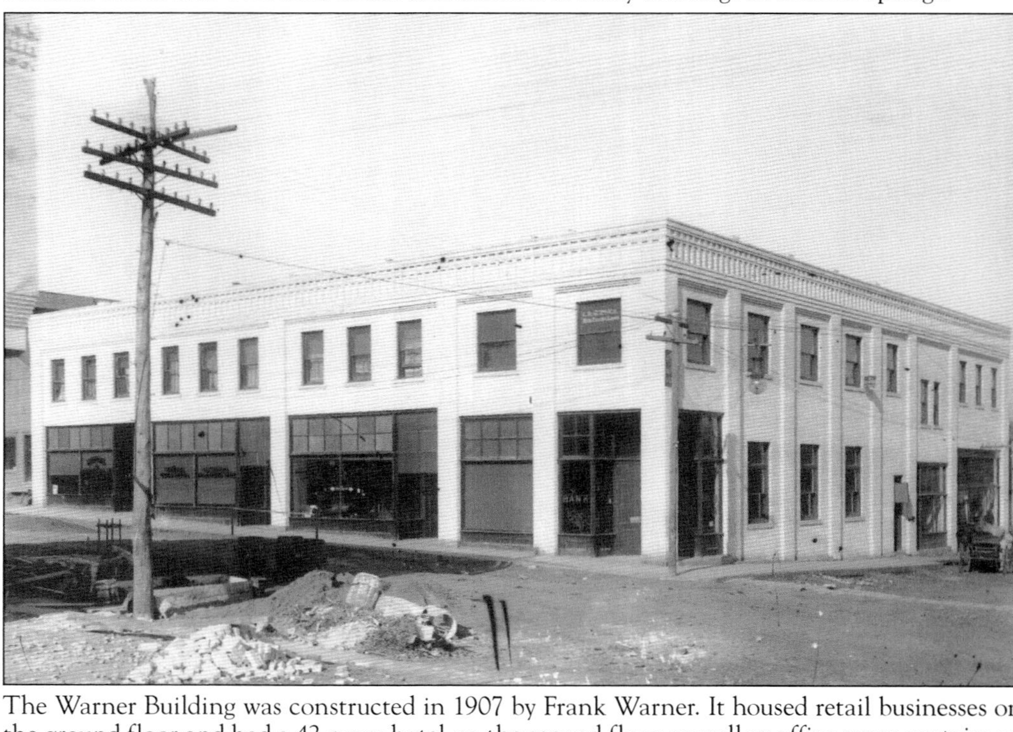

The Warner Building was constructed in 1907 by Frank Warner. It housed retail businesses on the ground floor and had a 42-room hotel on the second floor, as well as office space upstairs on the corner.

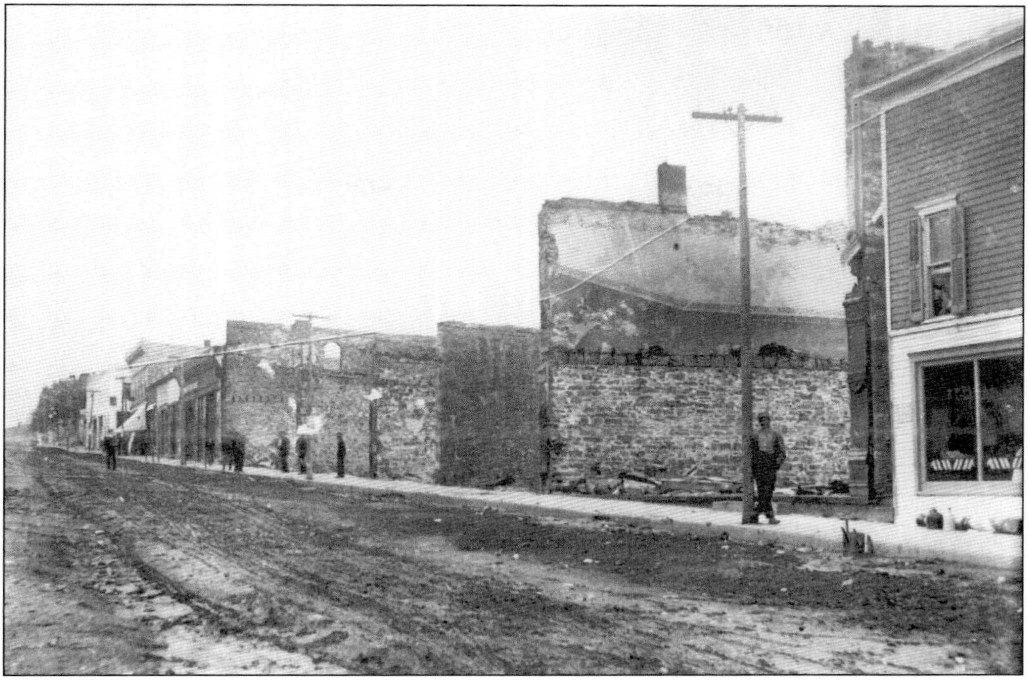

In October 1908, a total of 19 businesses in the 100 block of Oak Street were destroyed by fire. There were no water mains at that time, even though the city council had debated the issue for some time. A bucket brigade from the Kansas River was ineffective in combating the blaze, which caused $70,000 in damage, or about $350,000 in today's dollars.

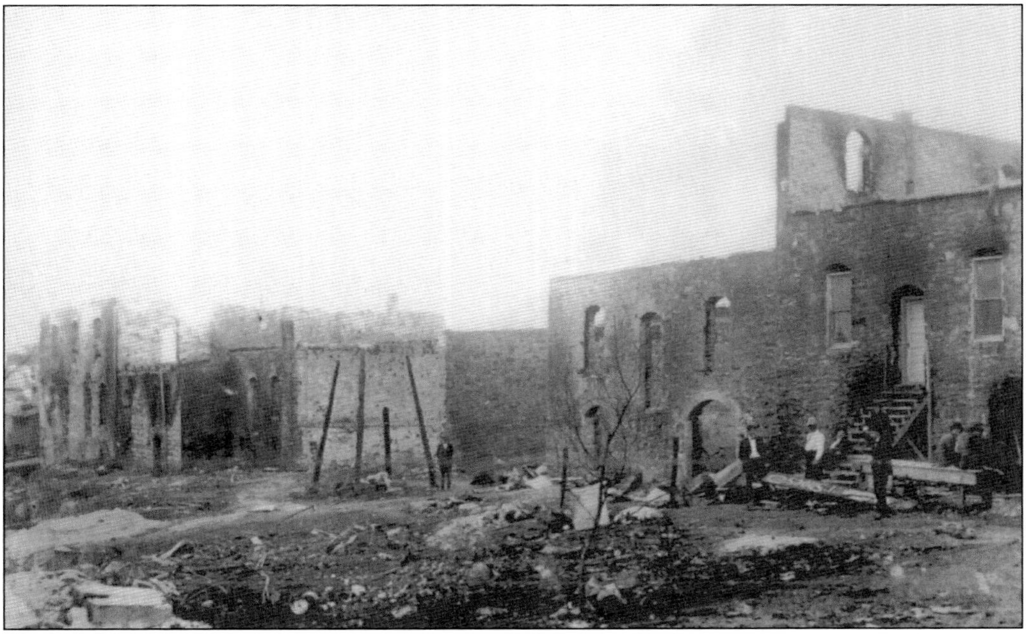

This is a view of the backs of the buildings that were destroyed. Everything was gone except for the fire walls.

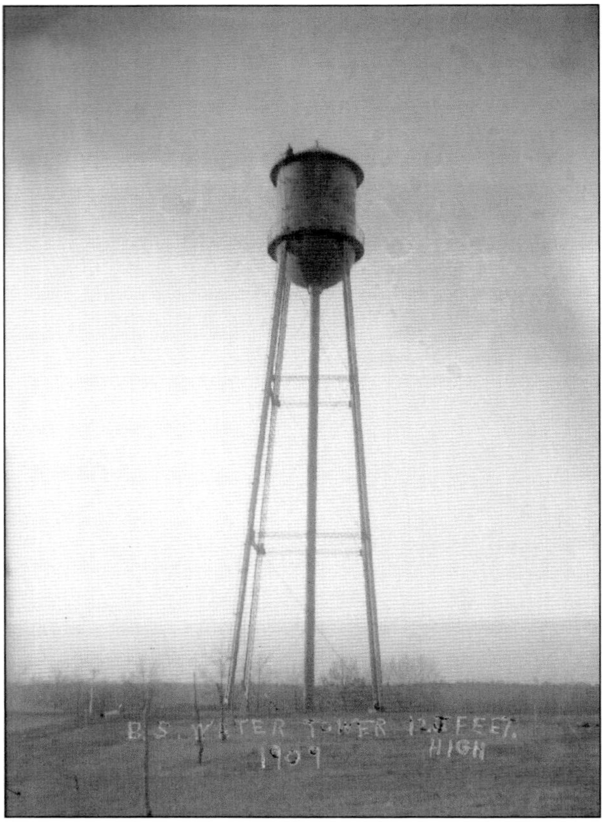

After the disastrous fire, the city installed a water system, and the water tower was erected at a high point in the city, at Oak Avenue west of Spring Street, in 1909. The city also started a volunteer fire department, which has grown to become a standard for other fire departments to follow.

The new water-pumping station for the volunteer fire department was across the Kansas River. The child in the doorway is Ruth Kenton.

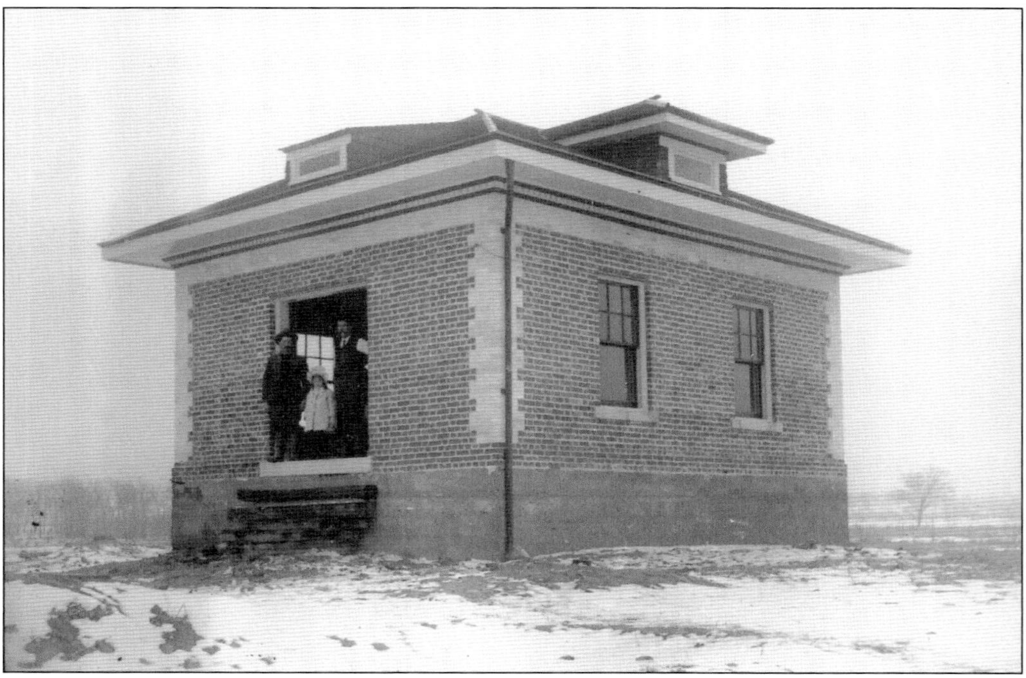

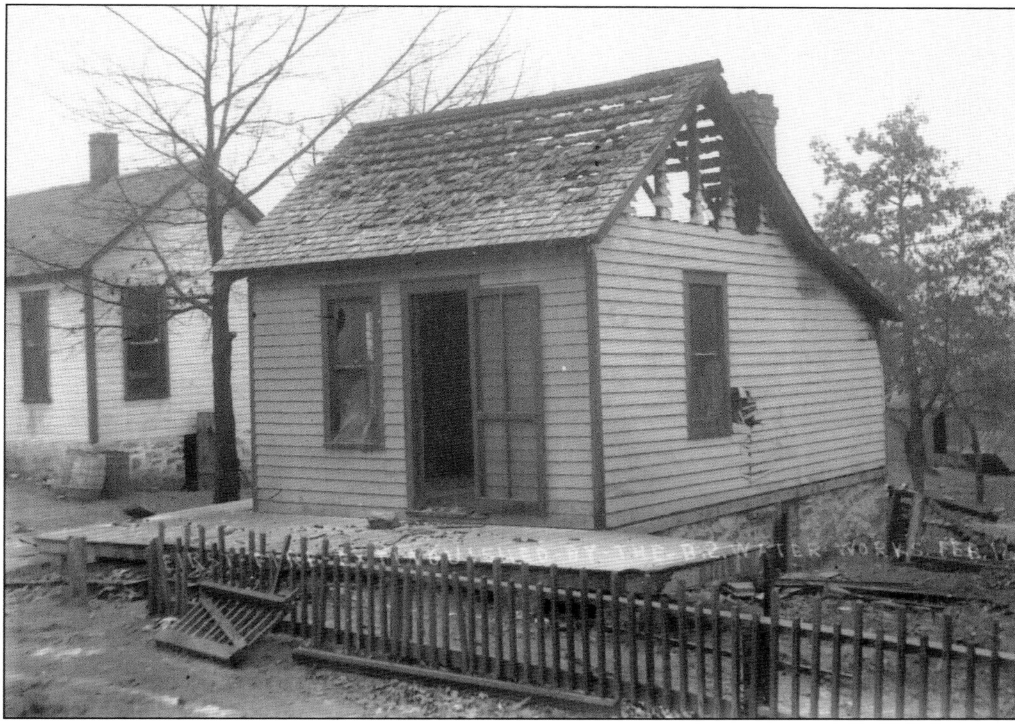

This is what remained after the first fire that occurred after the water system was installed. Unlike the fire of 1908, the structure was at least partially saved.

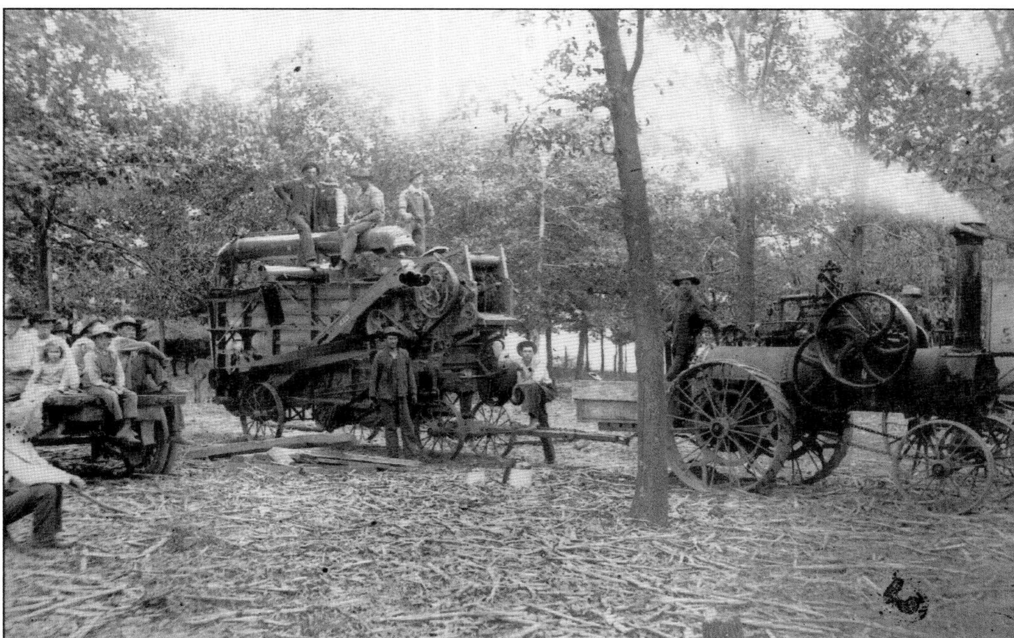

Agriculture was a large part of the economy, and this threshing scene shows the men and machinery it took to reap the fruits of their labors.

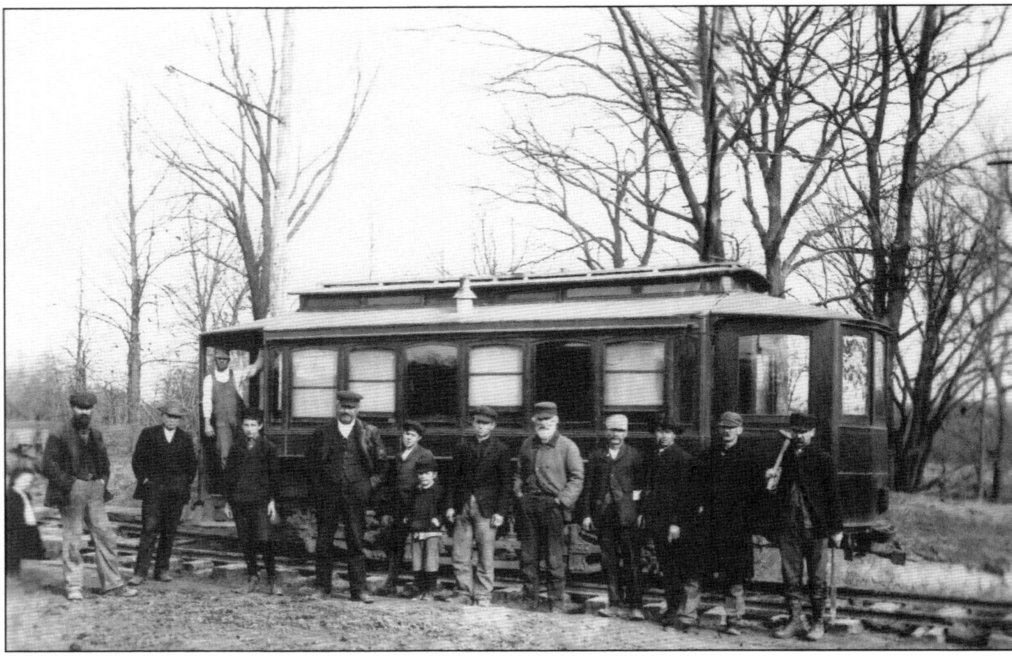

The Kaw Valley electric interurban train was started by John McDanield. It went from Bonner Springs to the cement plant and on to Lake Forest. Pictured, from left to right, are an unidentified young girl, ? Siberts, ? Sconce, an unidentified man on the train, Earl Thorp, August Benson, two boys (one of whom is Claud Benson), J. Douglas, C.C. Carter, unidentified, Arthur Berlin, H.V. Jewett, and William Axe.

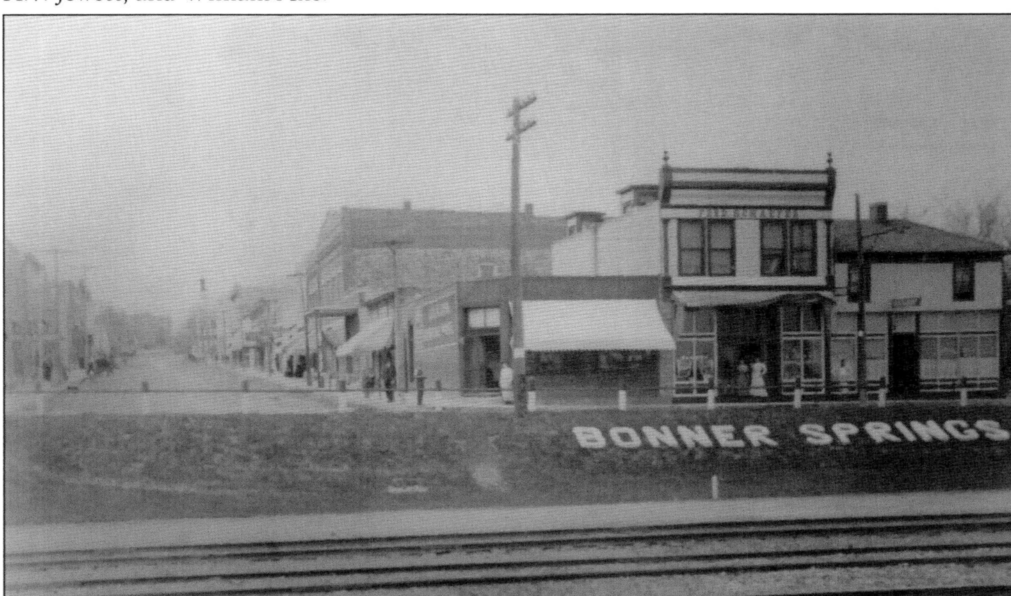

This view west up Oak Street shows the new brick McDanield High School at the top of the hill. The "Bonner Springs" concrete letters in the foreground were in full view of those passing through on the trains.

Four

J.D. Waters and His Vision

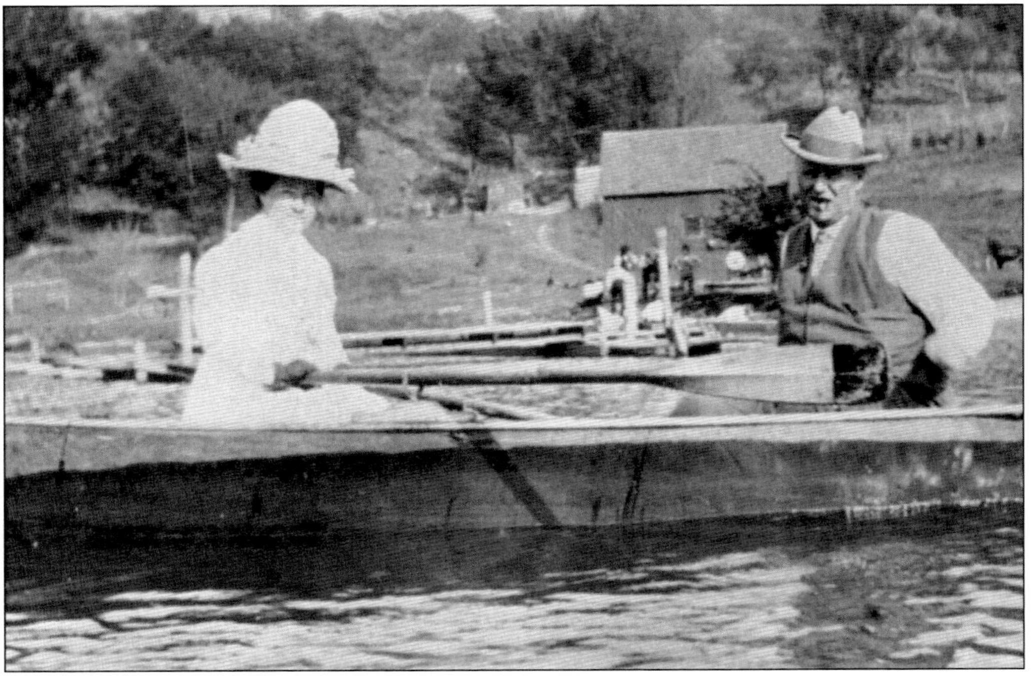

J.D. Waters and his wife, Rose, enjoy a boat ride on the Lake of the Forest. He was an early advocate for the lake and its surrounding area becoming a haven for city dwellers.

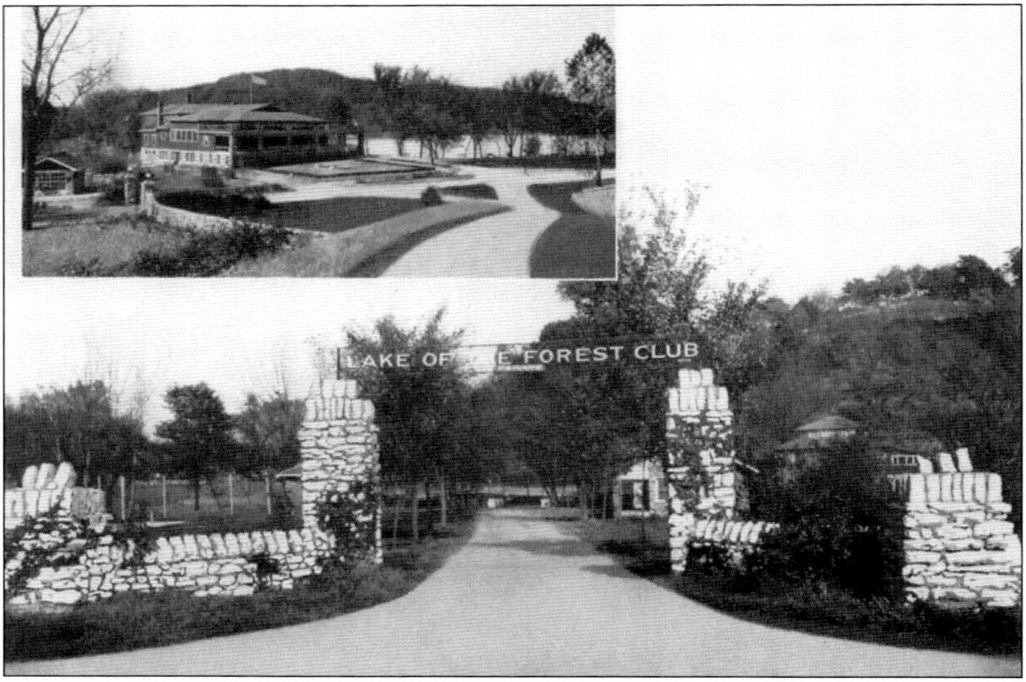

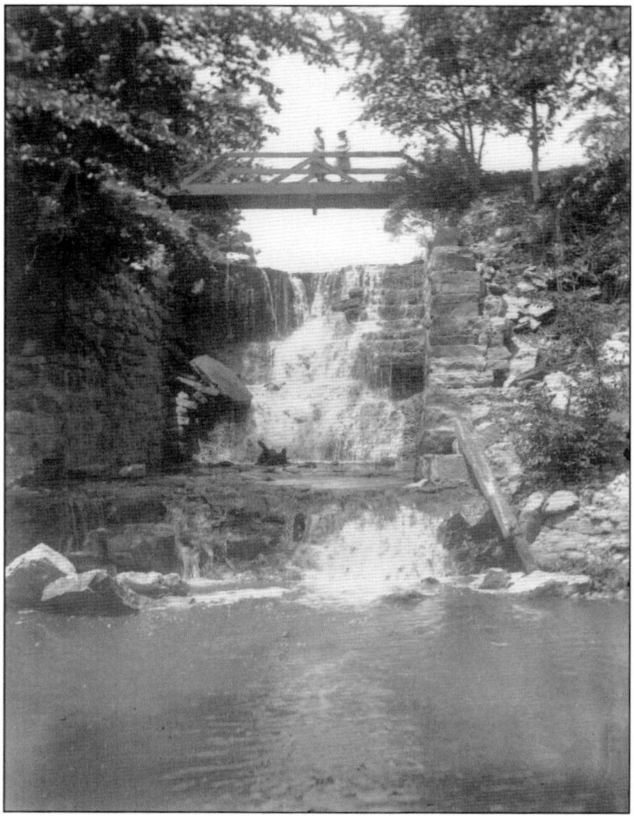

John McDanield sold land, which included Lake Ellen, to J.D. Waters to build an exclusive resort. Waters renamed it Lake of the Forest. It consisted of only summer cottages in the beginning. Today, it has 166 permanent residences, along with the clubhouse, built in 1917 and seen above in the inset.

The lake spillway provided a scenic waterfall for hikers to enjoy.

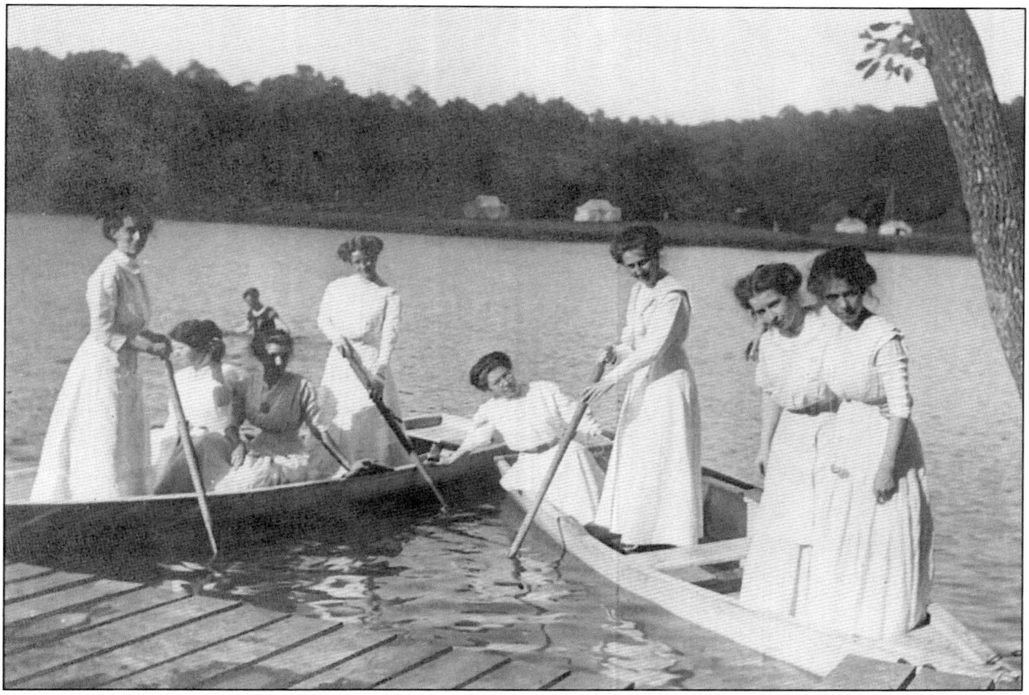

These young ladies are dressed for a canoe ride and ready to man the oars.

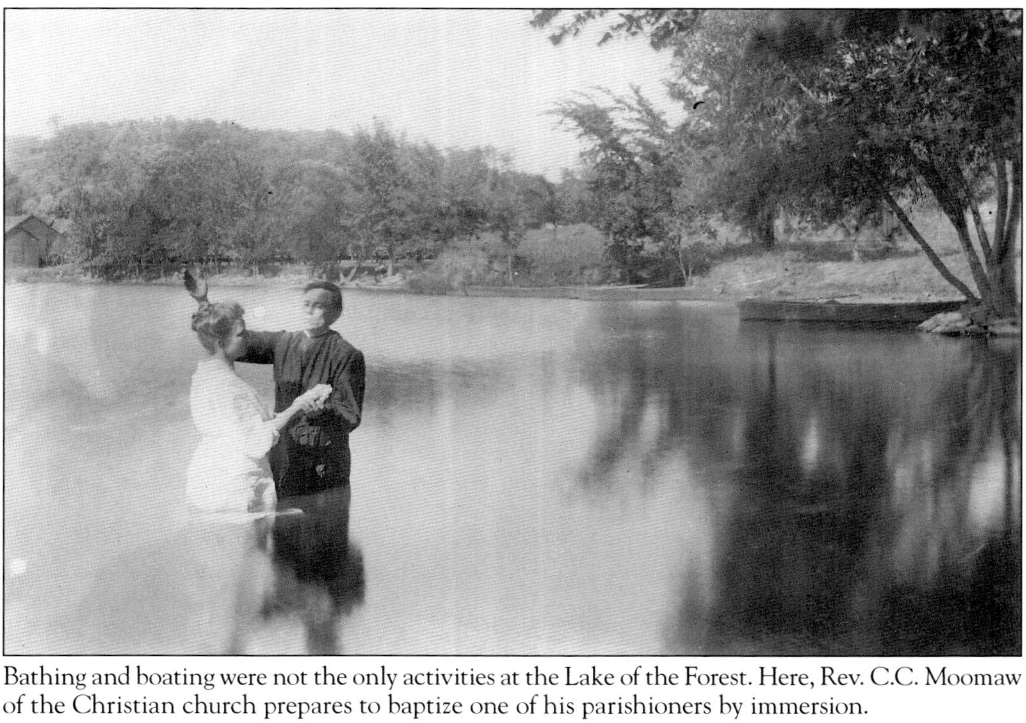

Bathing and boating were not the only activities at the Lake of the Forest. Here, Rev. C.C. Moomaw of the Christian church prepares to baptize one of his parishioners by immersion.

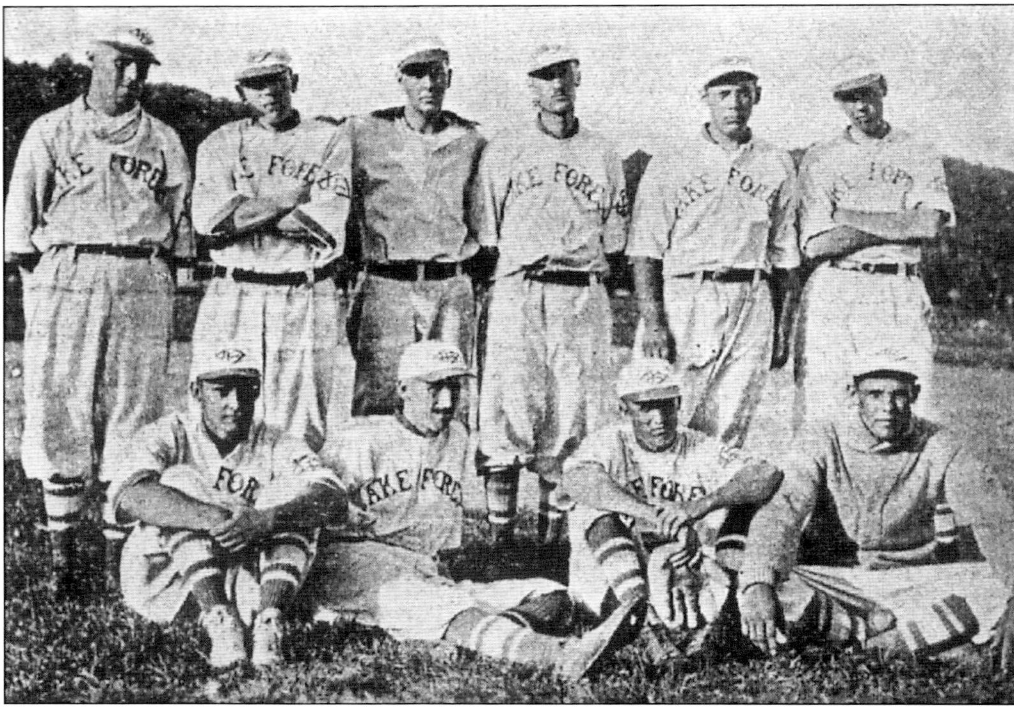

The 1912 Lake Forest baseball team includes, from left to right, (first row) Sam Hale, Dick Shofstall, Howard Shofstall, and Charles Ehrke; (second row) Bill Shofstall, Claude Vance, Bill Knapp, Bob Waters, Ham Stone, and Sam Elliot. (Courtesy of Lake of the Forest Historical Society.)

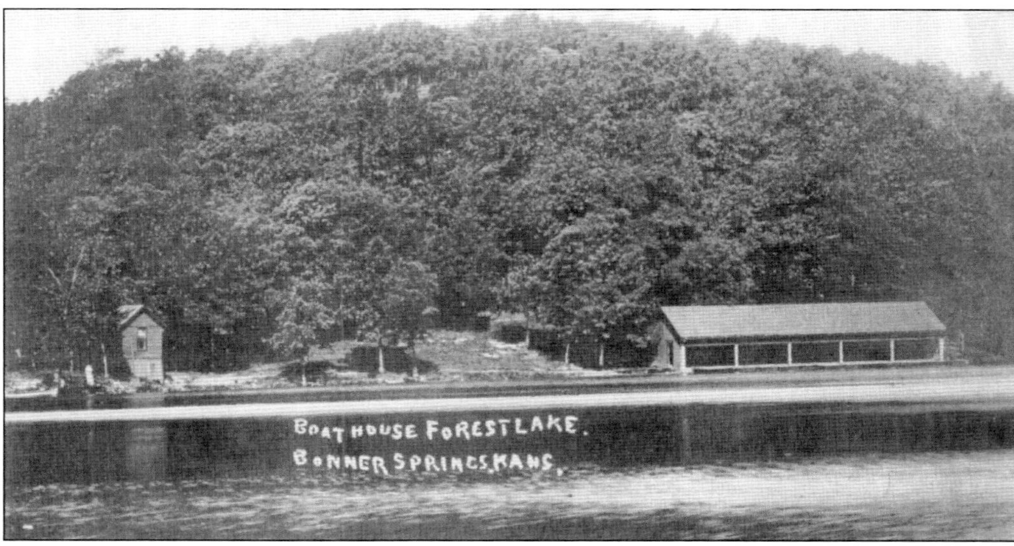

The boathouse is seen in this 1920s postcard. The price for renting a boat for a half day was 25¢.

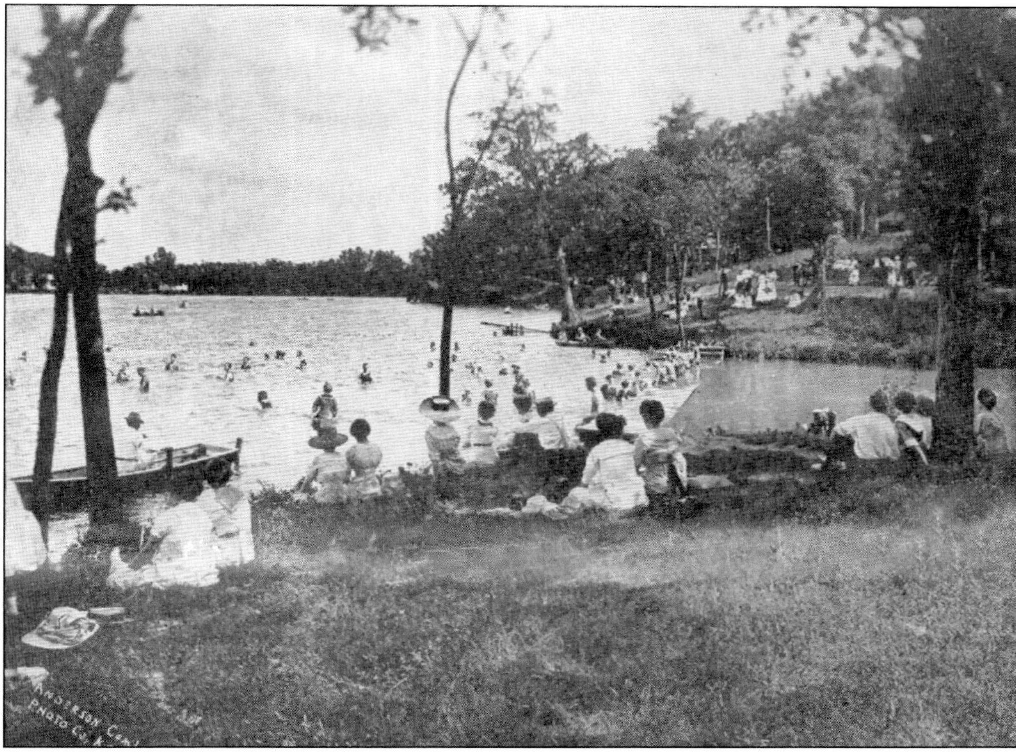

The success of J.D. Waters' vision is evident in this photograph, with many bathers, swimmers, picnickers, and onlookers enjoying a sunny day at the water's edge.

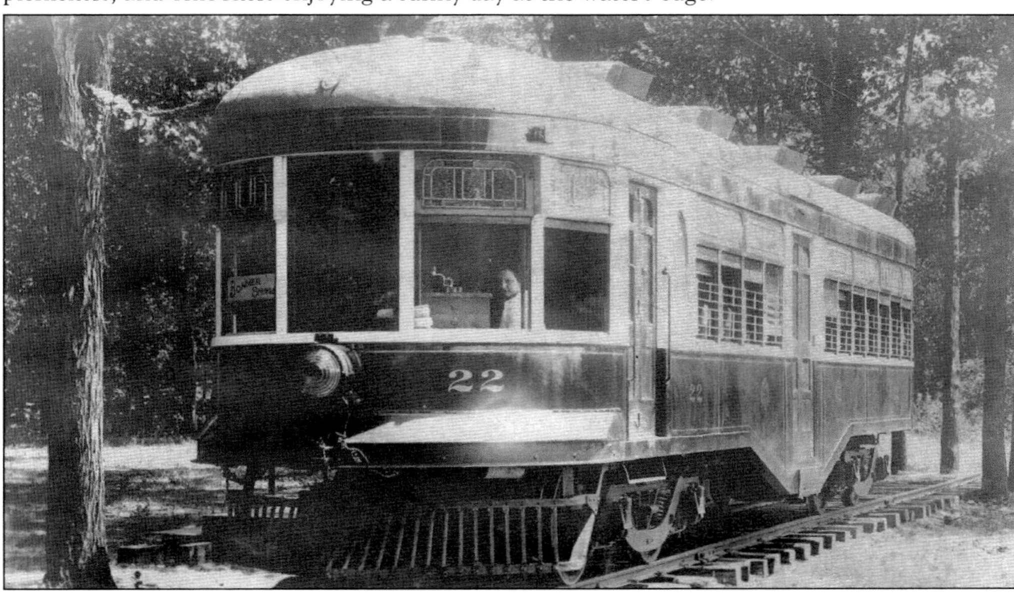

In 1912, John McDanield sold the interurban to J.D. Waters. J.J. Hein extended it to Kansas City and to Lawrence. It was completed in 1914, and two advantages were noted: it brought resort visitors to Bonner Springs, and it allowed residents to access jobs in Kansas City, making Bonner Springs a bedroom community.

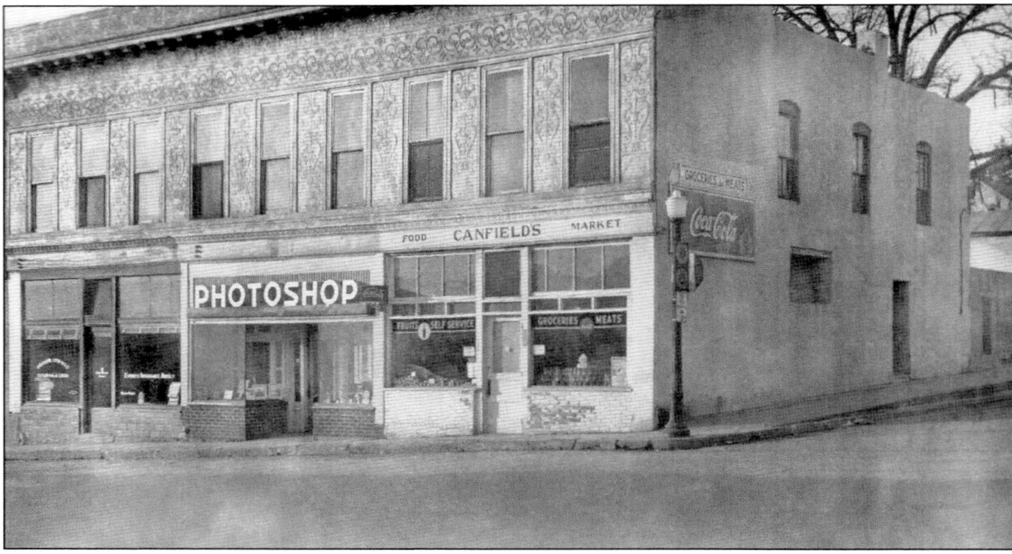

Note the gas streetlight in this photograph of Oak Street. This building was replaced by the Interstate Savings and Loan in the 1960s.

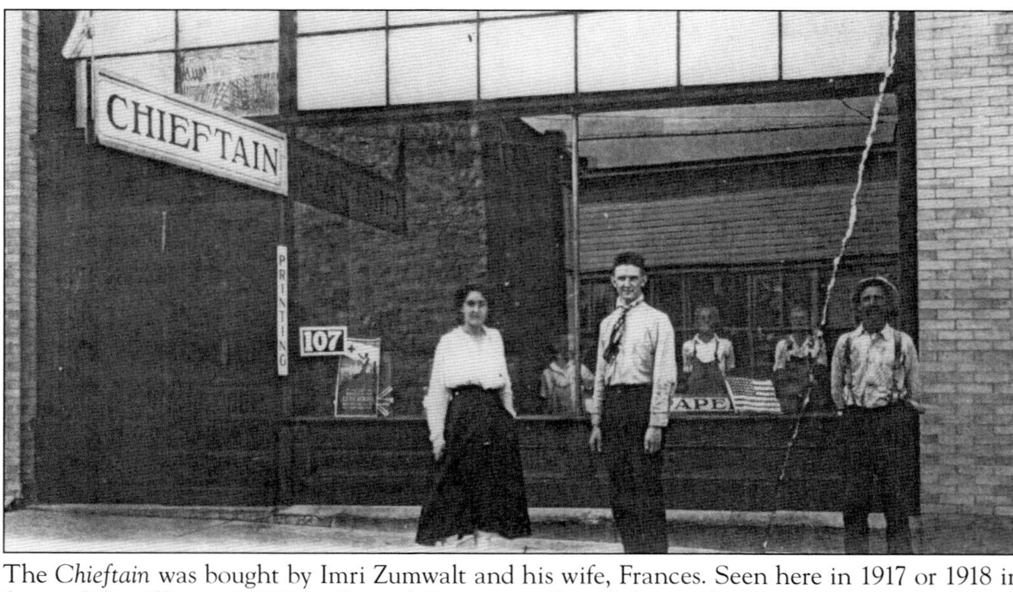

The *Chieftain* was bought by Imri Zumwalt and his wife, Frances. Seen here in 1917 or 1918 in front of the office at 107 East Second Street, are, from left to right, Frances Zumwalt, Seldon Hall, and Oscar Hyroot. The World War I poster in the window reads, "Come Across: If you can't come across with a gun, come across with your part of the Red Cross Fund."

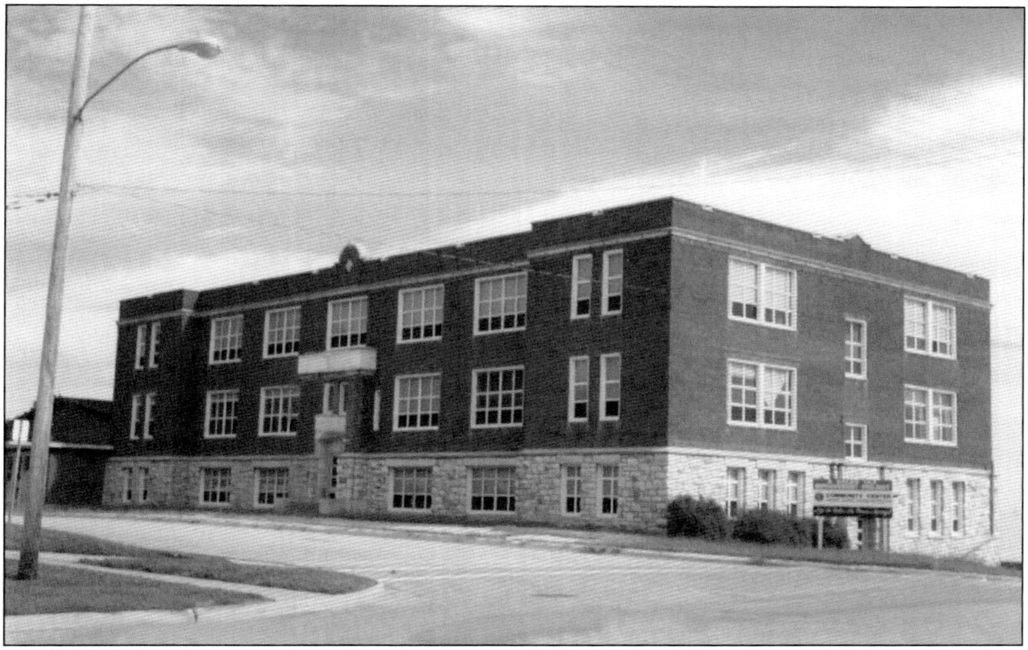

This high school was built in 1918 and was used as a junior high school after the new high school was constructed in 1960. After a new junior high school was built in 1984, this structure was abandoned. When word spread that city leaders were considering the possibility of tearing down the Bonner Springs landmark, a group led by Wendy Scheidt, Save our Skyline, began organizing. After this, Connie Harrington thought that even more should be done to preserve local history, so she founded the Bonner Springs Historic Preservation Society in 2001. The building was saved and has been undergoing renovation.

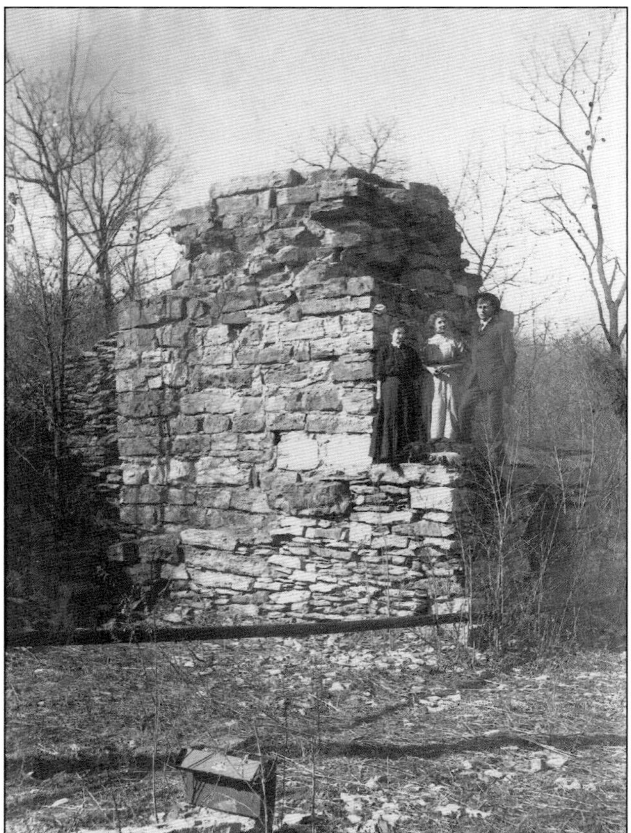

This early limekiln, in the rock quarry east of the city, was a forerunner of the cement plant that was later built at that location.

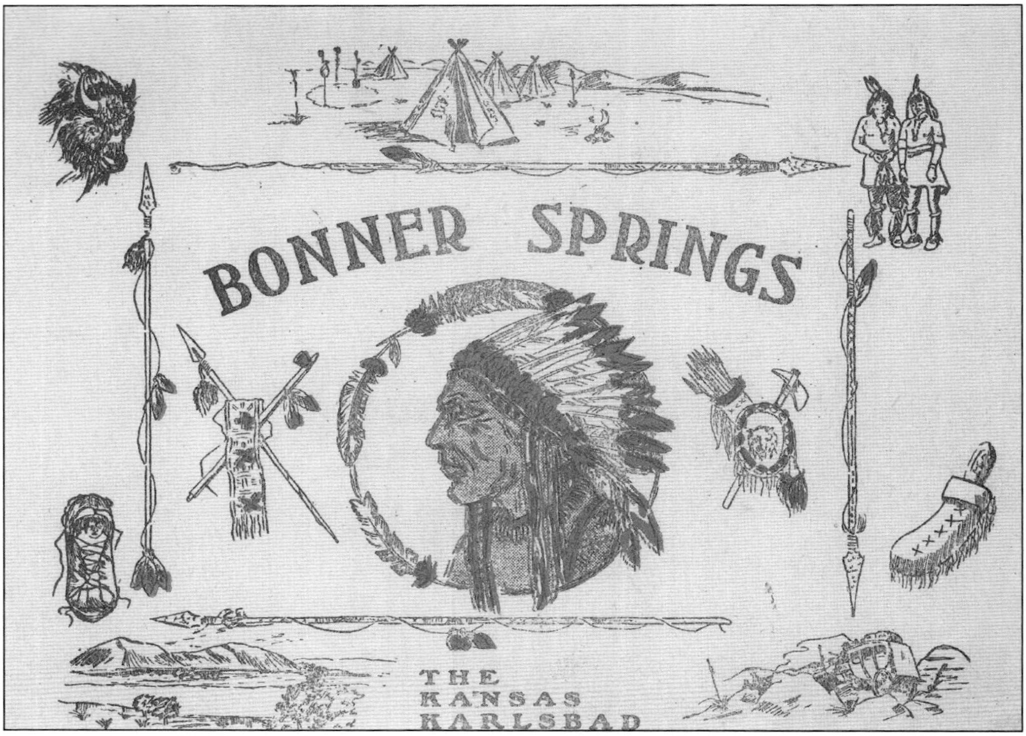

This brochure was compiled in 1917 to again promote Bonner Springs as a resort destination. Analyses of the springs, which had by then also been called Minnehaha Spring and Papoose Spring, are included in it, along with the benefits of drinking from the spring. Urbin Rudell was commissioned to photograph various scenes in the city, and those photographs were the basis of his collection of Bonner Springs images. (Courtesy of WCHS&M.)

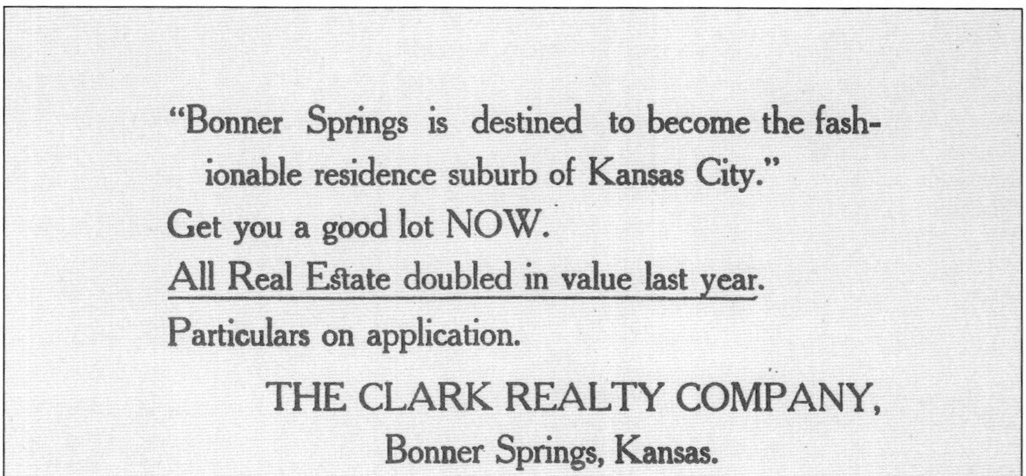

Philo Clark hoped to lure investors in the springs with this advertisement. But, again, his timing was off, as the United States was on the verge of entering World War I. (Courtesy of WCHS&M.)

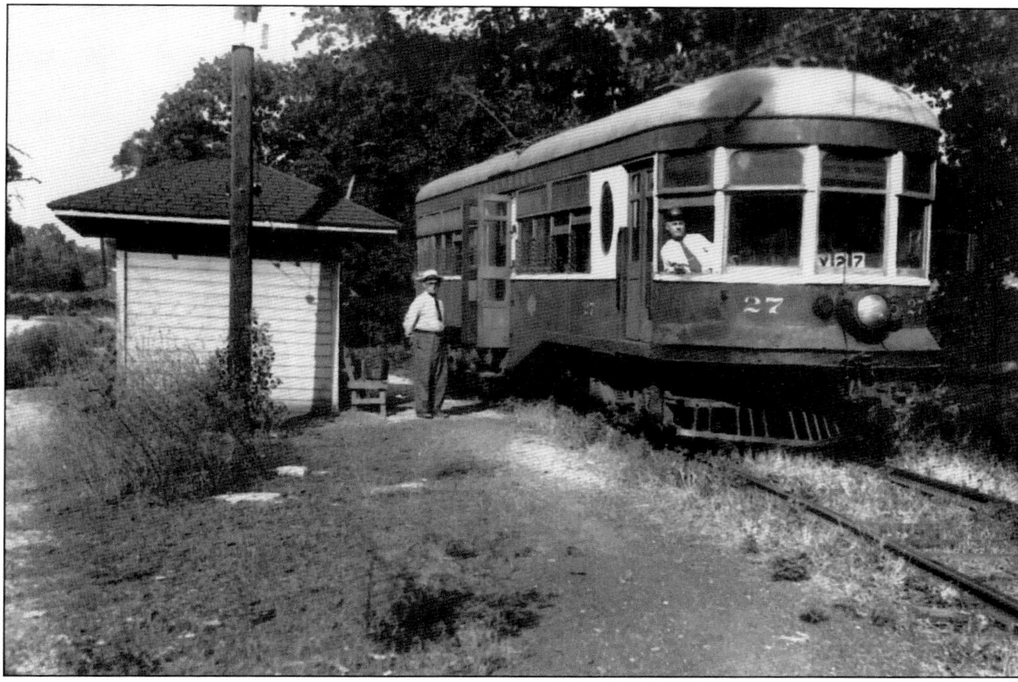

The interurban was a boon to travelers because it was convenient for travel to Kansas City. It lasted until the 1930s, when buses started regular hourly departures for Kansas City.

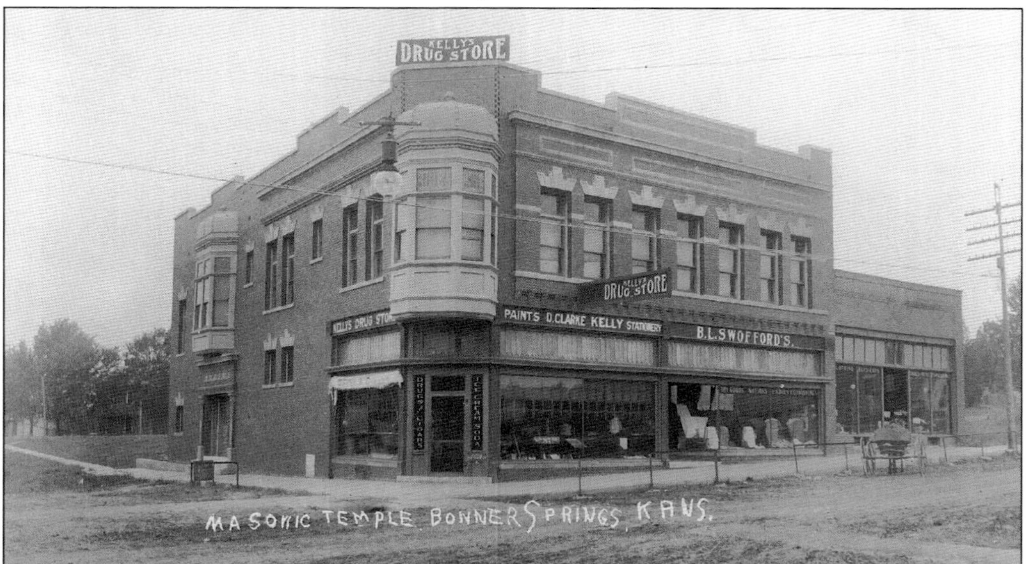

Bonner Springs Masonic Lodge No. 366 was chartered in 1904. The lodge was constructed in 1908 at a cost of $15,000. The building still stands today, although the lodge recently merged with Wyandotte Lodge No. 3. In the early days, the city had a number of societies that one could join, including the Masons, the Odd Fellows, the Rebekahs, Modern Woodmen, Royal Neighbors, Woodmen of the World, Knights of Pythias, Fraternal Aid, Ancient Order of United Workmen, Modern Brotherhood of America, and Grand Army of the Republic.

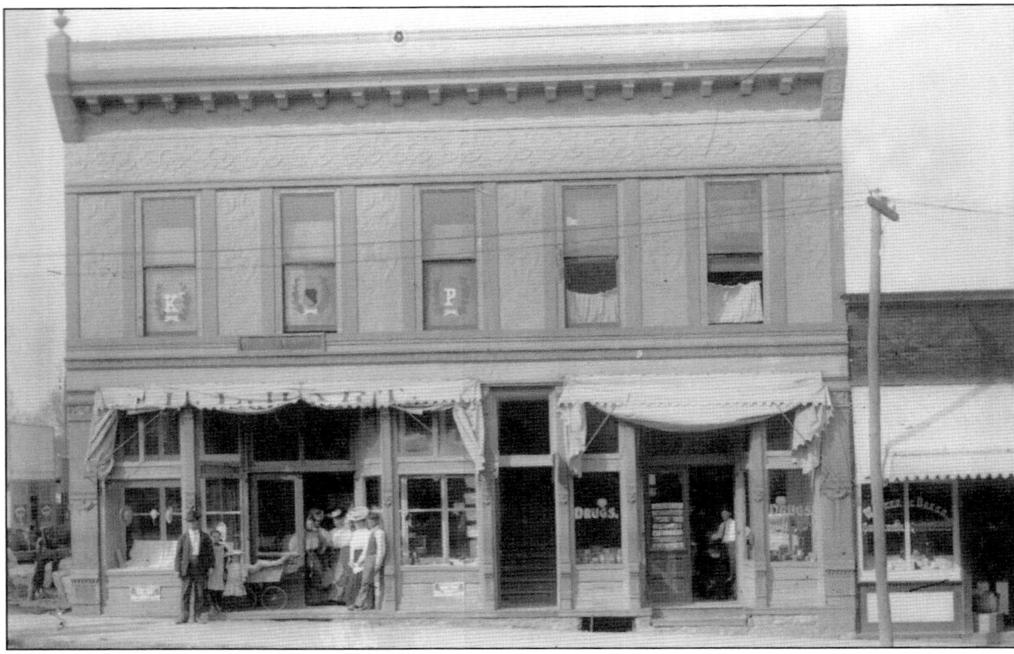

L.L. Hart (far left) stands in front of his store at the corner of Oak and Second Streets. The drugstore in the center was operated by J.V. Walker and later sold to Sam Scheffer. The Walker Bakery is on the far right. The Knights of Pythias had their headquarters on the second floor of this building. The Knights lent their meeting space to the Masons as they were organizing and while they built their own lodge.

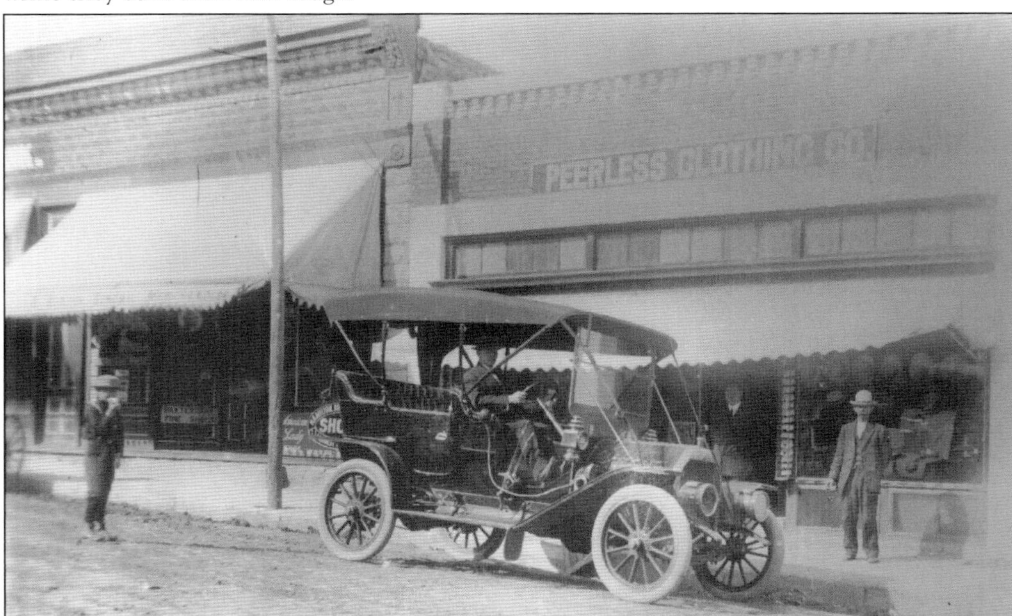

Frank Warner shows off his new Ford Model T in front of the Peerless Clothing Co., at 123 Oak Street. Oscar Hyoort (far right) looks on from the sidewalk. In 1909, the city passed its first speed law; the maximum speed was 10 miles per hour.

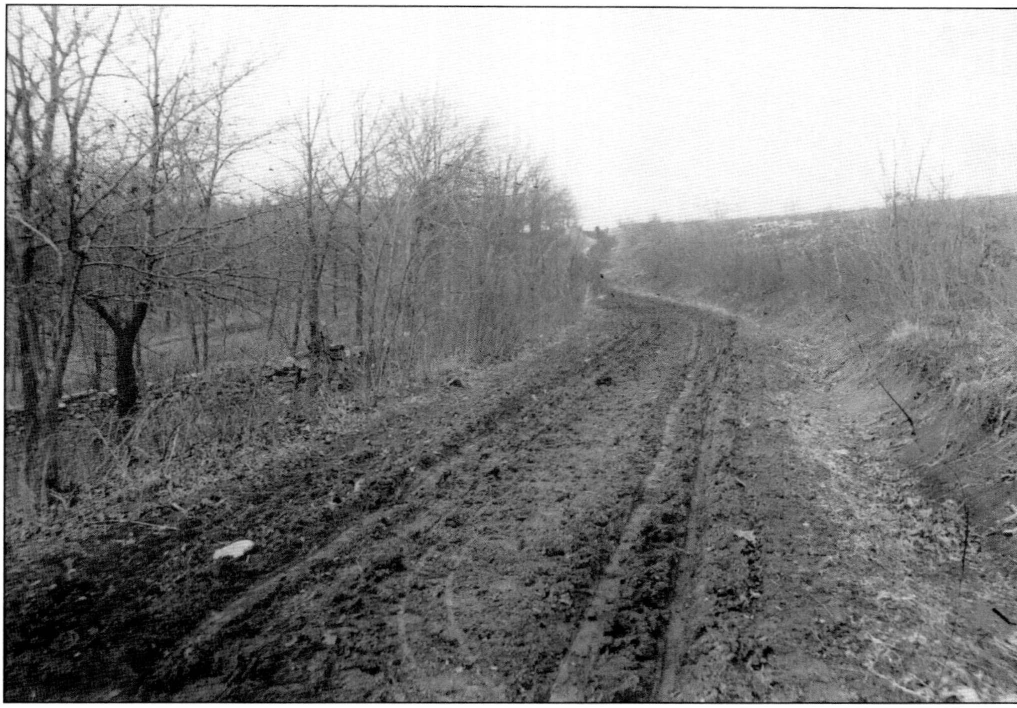

In this photograph, muddy Lakewood Road appears impassable as it heads north from Bonner Springs. When Lakewood Park was established, the road was graded and rocked, as most country roads were at that time, and still are today.

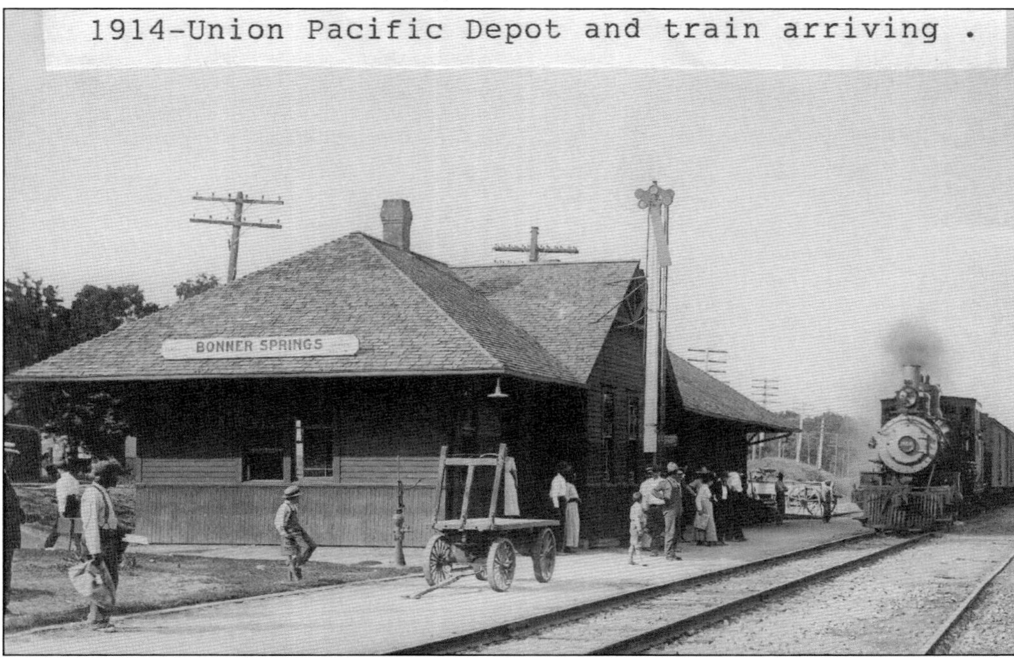

The arrival of a train was a highly anticipated event in most towns along the tracks. Mail was loaded and unloaded, as well as freight and passengers.

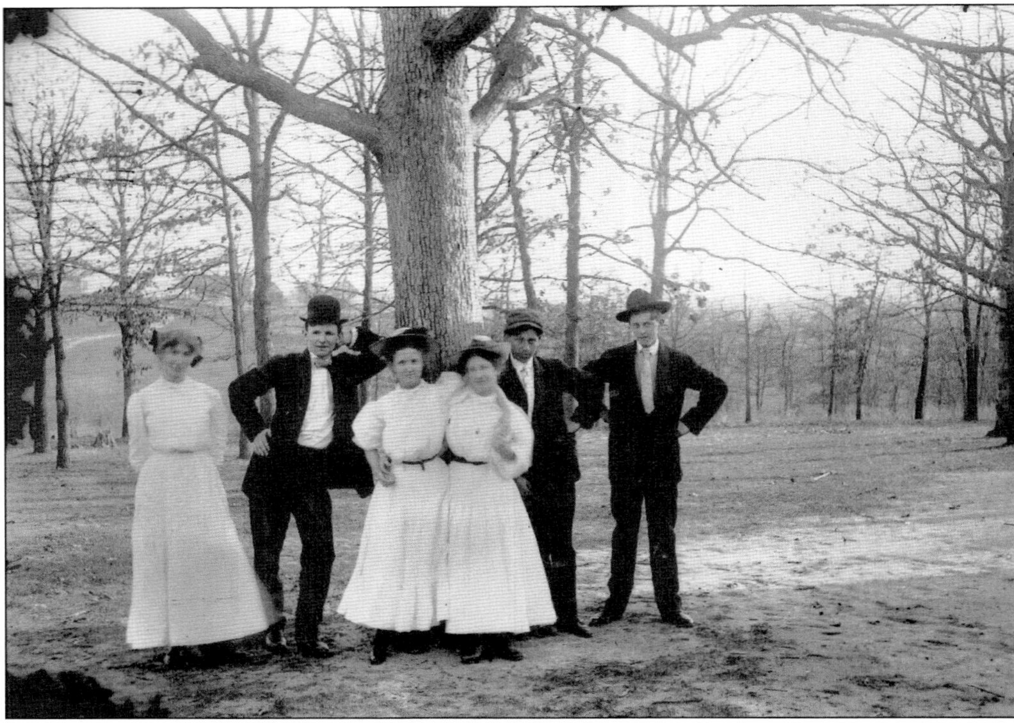

Lakewood Park, located north of Morse Avenue, was a very popular destination from 1918 until its closing in the 1950s. A spur line went directly there on the Kansas City, Kaw Valley & Western Railroad. The group seen here knew how to pose in a relaxed manner. They are, from left to right, Theo Jewett, Warner Barry, the future Trudy Bearden, Marjorie Jewett, Earl Hart, and Robert Twist.

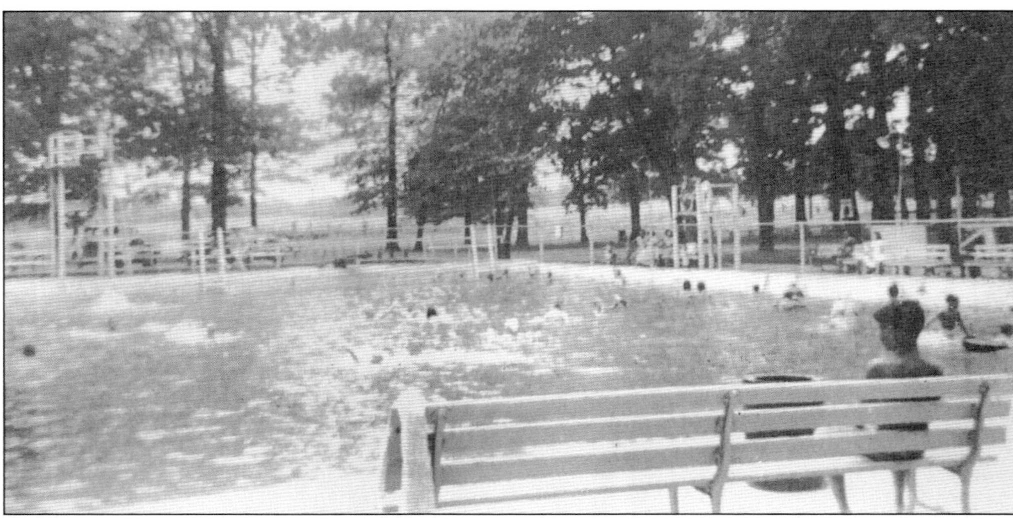

The addition of the swimming pool in 1930 gave the park yet another attraction. It was built on the foundation of a hotel and bathhouse that had been proposed in 1907 and 1908 but never materialized.

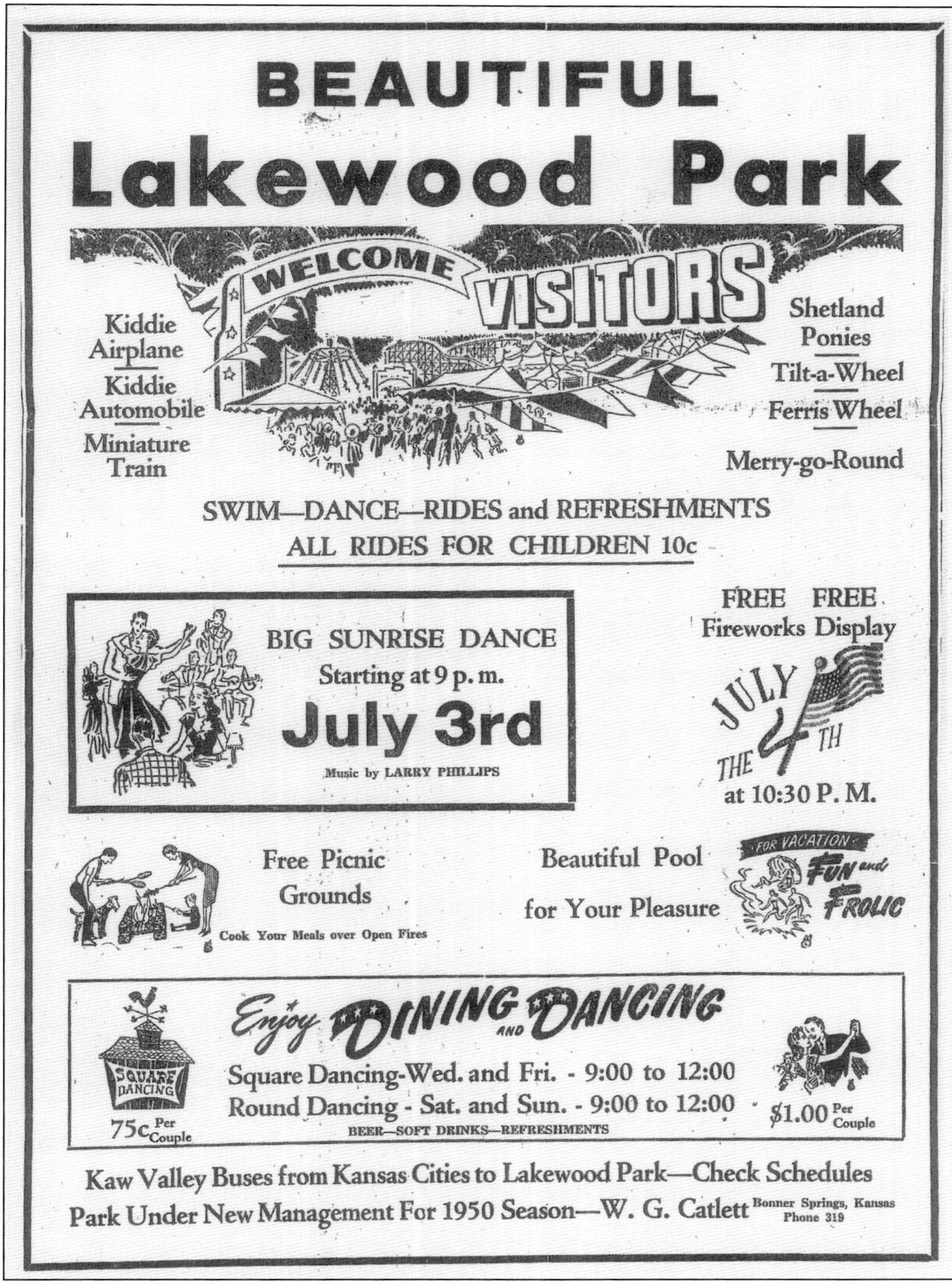

W.G. Catlett leased the park from L.D. Wiard, who purchased it in 1932 and ran it until 1949. This poster lists the many attractions available to park patrons. In the 1920s, boxing matches were a big draw.

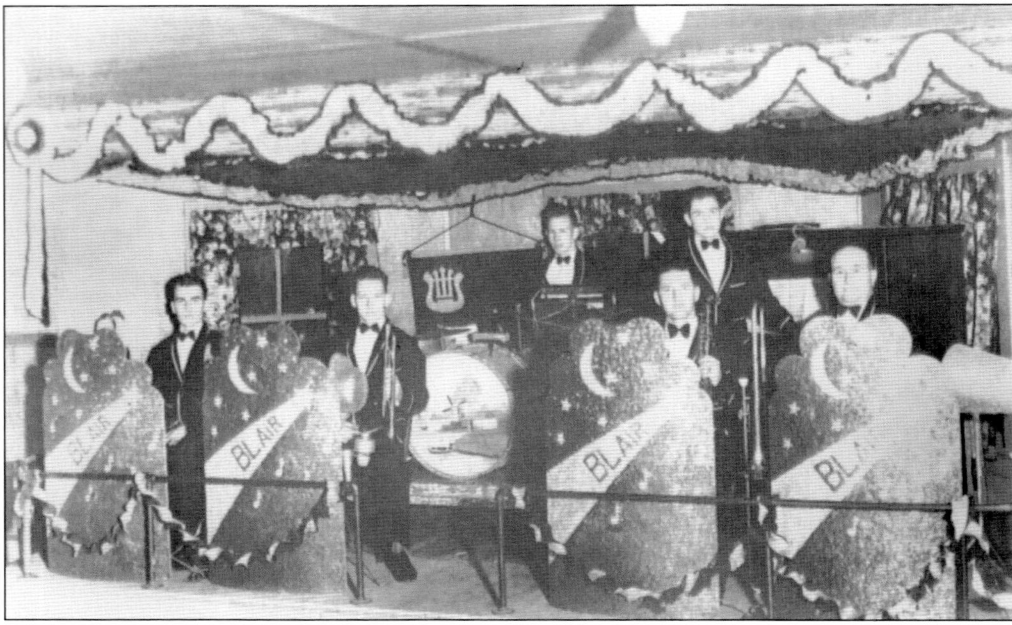

The Blair Band was a popular dance band that appeared frequently at the dance pavilion. In 1933, a season pass to the pavilion was $4.50.

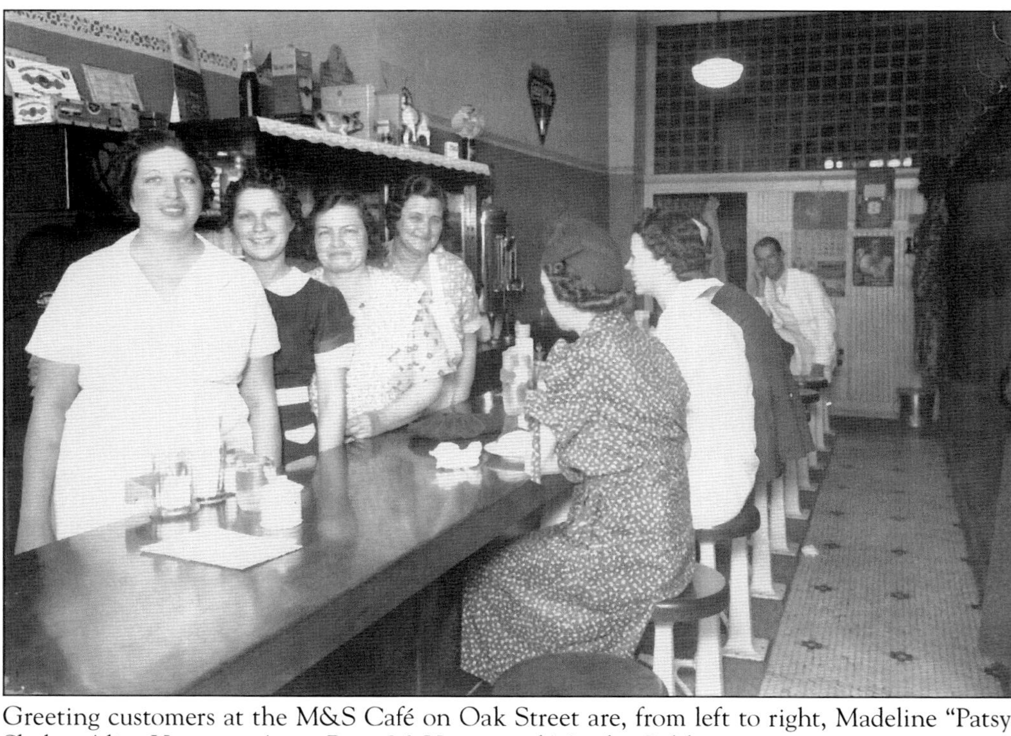

Greeting customers at the M&S Café on Oak Street are, from left to right, Madeline "Patsy" Sheley, Alice Hauetter, Anna Ryan McHenry, and Maudie Colsb.

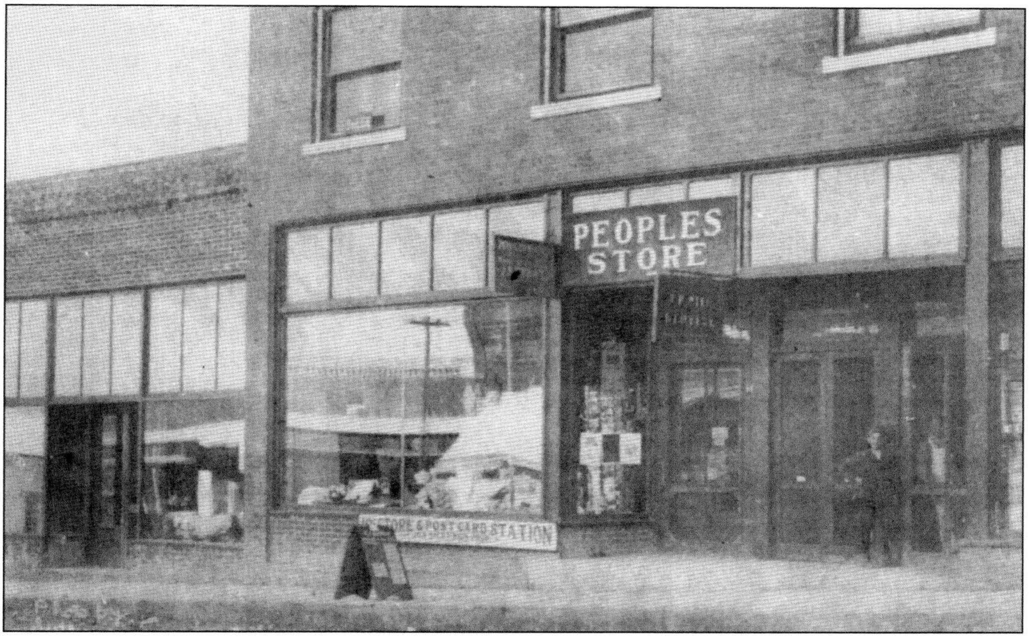

The location of the Peoples Store is unknown. Most stores at that time were general stores, selling groceries, clothing, and household items.

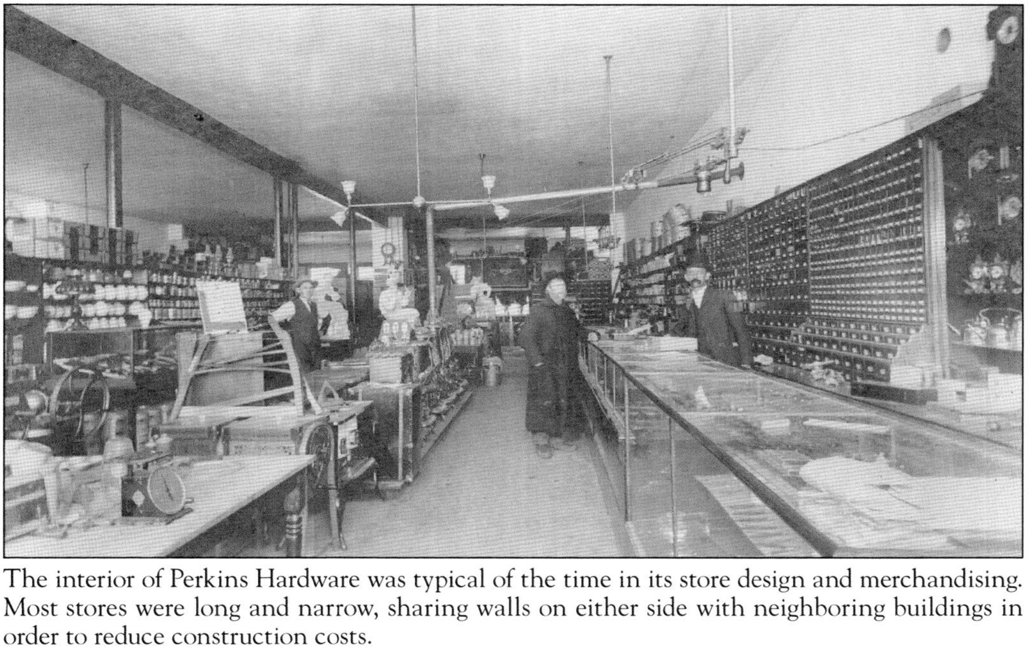

The interior of Perkins Hardware was typical of the time in its store design and merchandising. Most stores were long and narrow, sharing walls on either side with neighboring buildings in order to reduce construction costs.

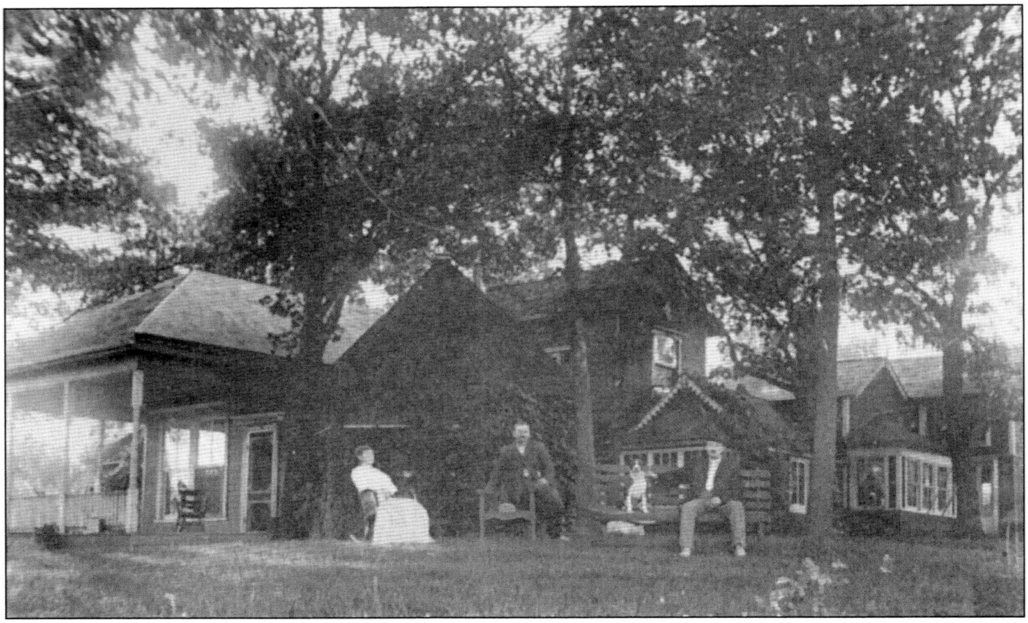

The home of S.D. Harlow, known as Red Gables, was between Cornell and Warner Streets. Harlow's granddaughter Harlean Carpenter visited them in the summers during her youth. She lived in Kansas City and attended Barstow School, a private school for young ladies. In 1921, her parents divorced and her mother took her to Los Angeles, where she enrolled in the Hollywood School for Girls. She went on to become the movie star Jean Harlow.

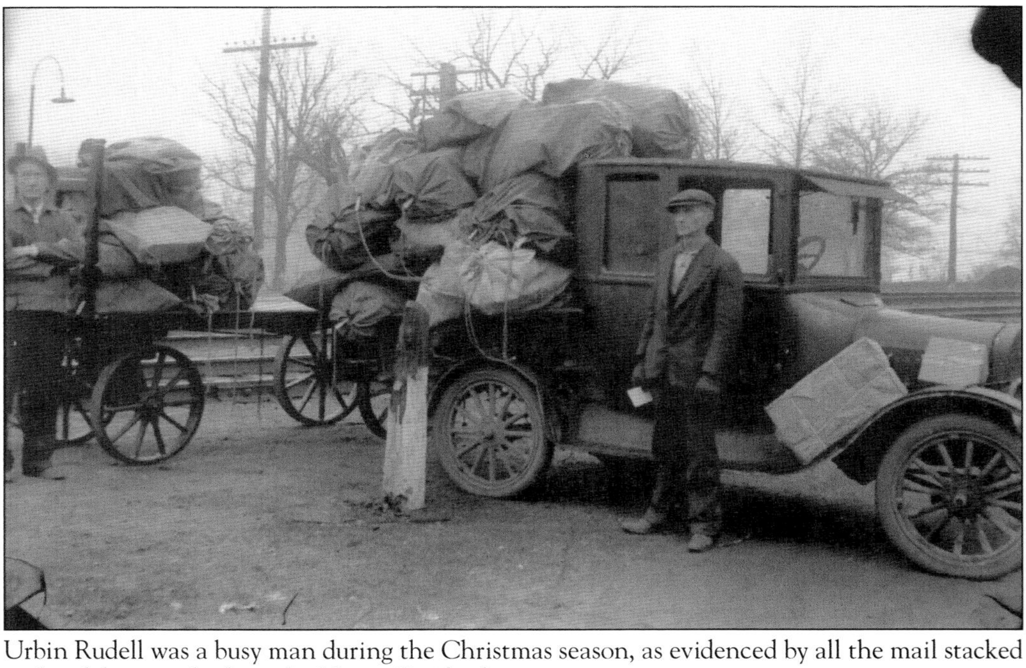

Urbin Rudell was a busy man during the Christmas season, as evidenced by all the mail stacked on his delivery vehicle at the Union Pacific depot.

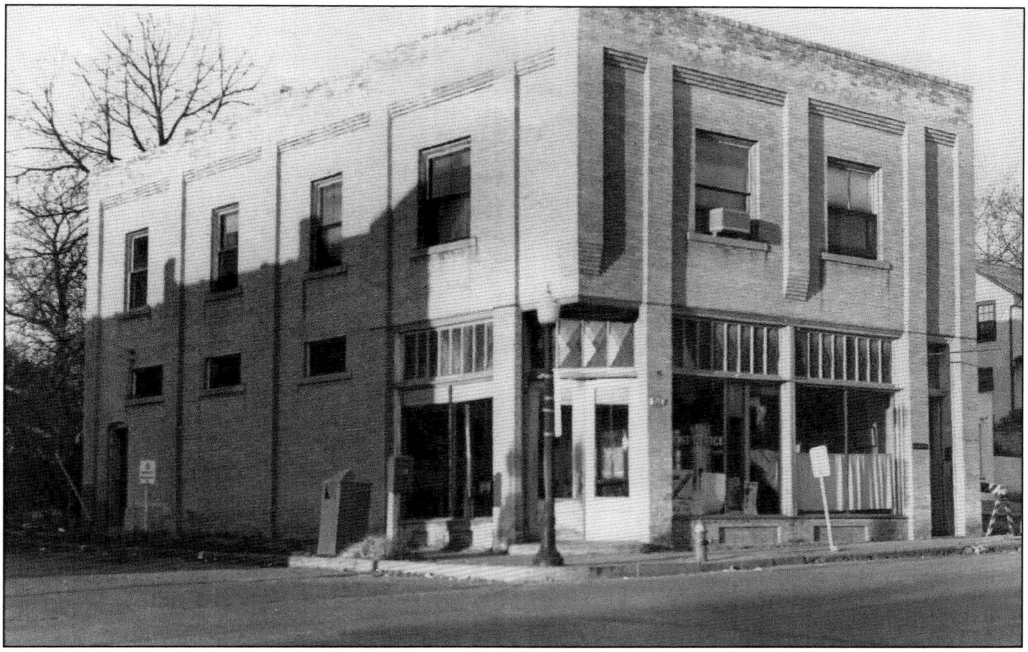

Located on the southwest corner of Oak and Second Streets, this two-story building still stands and has been occupied continuously since it was built. The photograph shows a fire hydrant, a trash receptacle, a streetlight, and even an air conditioner in the upper window of the building.

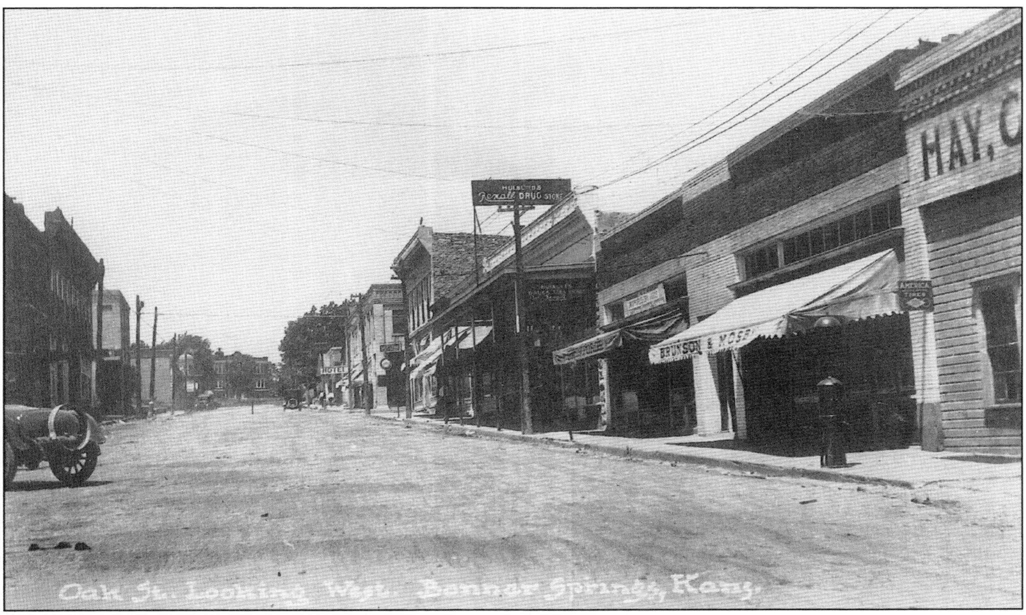

This photograph of Oak Street shows the recently opened Rexall store and hotel.

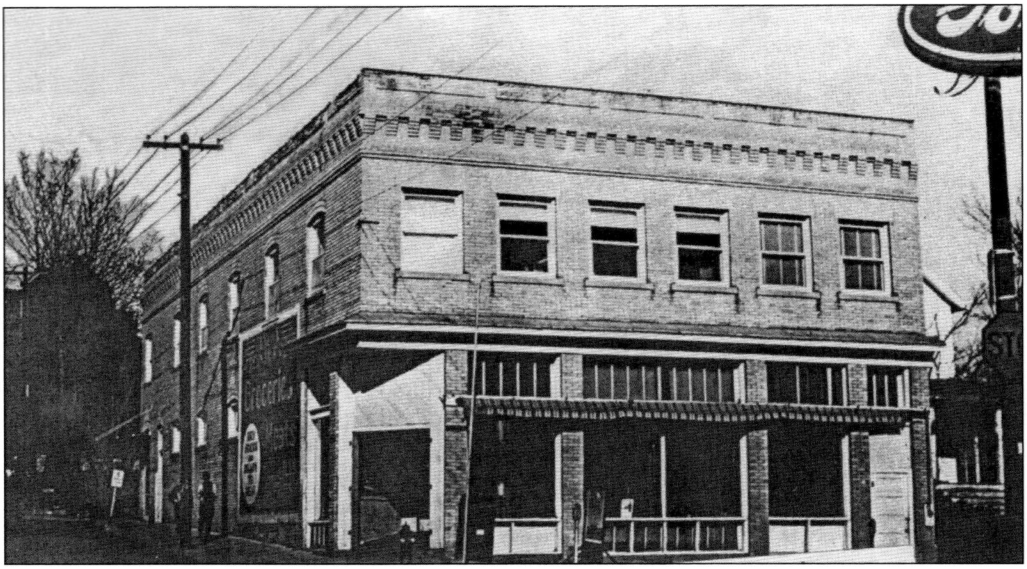
The Olsen building housed Ed Olsen's grocery on the first floor. The second floor was used as a schoolroom for the overflow of students from the high school a block away.

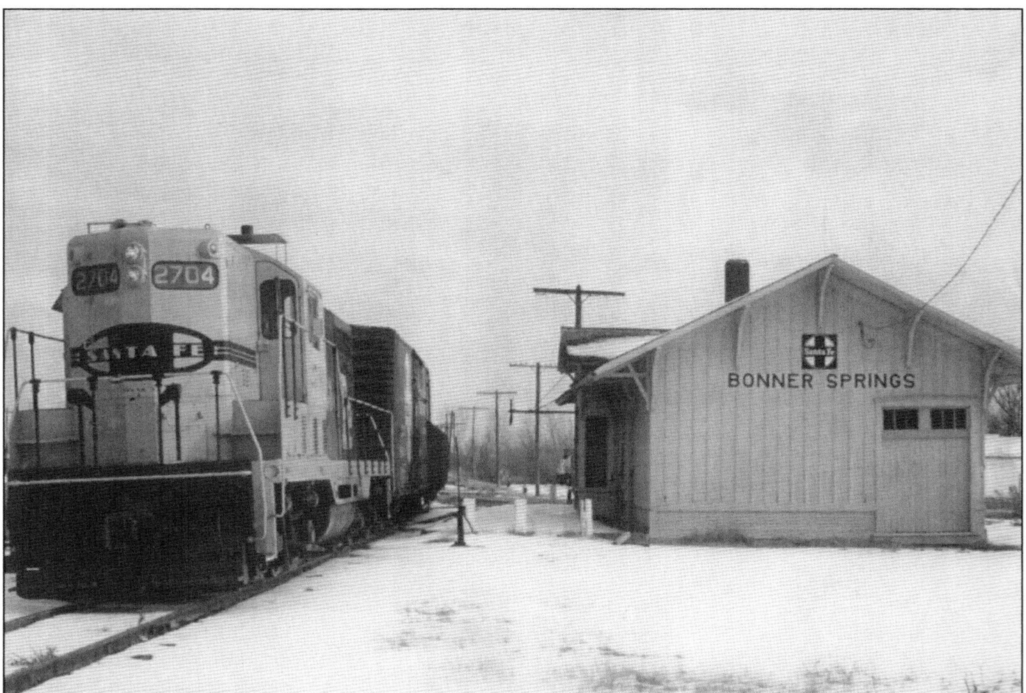

The Santa Fe depot was on the south side of Bonner Springs. Both the Union Pacific and Santa Fe depots were razed in the 1960s, after Bonner Springs was no longer a stop on either line.

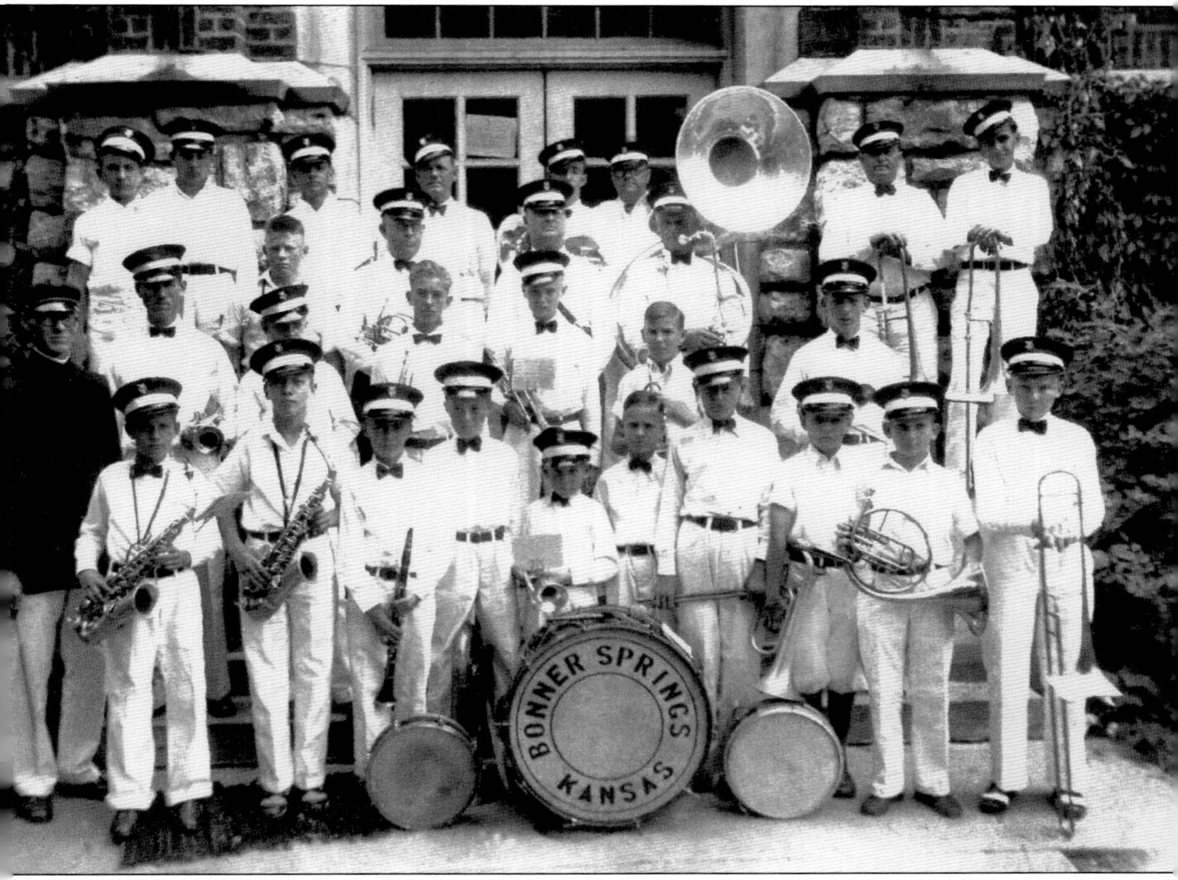

The Bonner Springs City Band gathered for this group photograph in 1932. The band includes, from left to right, (first row) Albin Holmquist Jr., John Stubbs, J. Stotts, George Mize, Paul Mize, Jimmy Gerhardt, Lloyd Campbell, C. Small, Frank Schirmer, and Junior Jewett; (second row) bandleader Albin Holmquist, J. Campbell, C. Williamson, Edwin Baglin, ? Brown, unidentified, and Ernest Rudell; (third row) Frank Lamb, ? Dunwell, Bill Orr, and Oscar Hyroot; (fourth row) ? Burgess, ? Cronemeyer, W. Brown, ? Morgan, unidentified, Hall DeWeese, ? Blair, and ? Bundy.

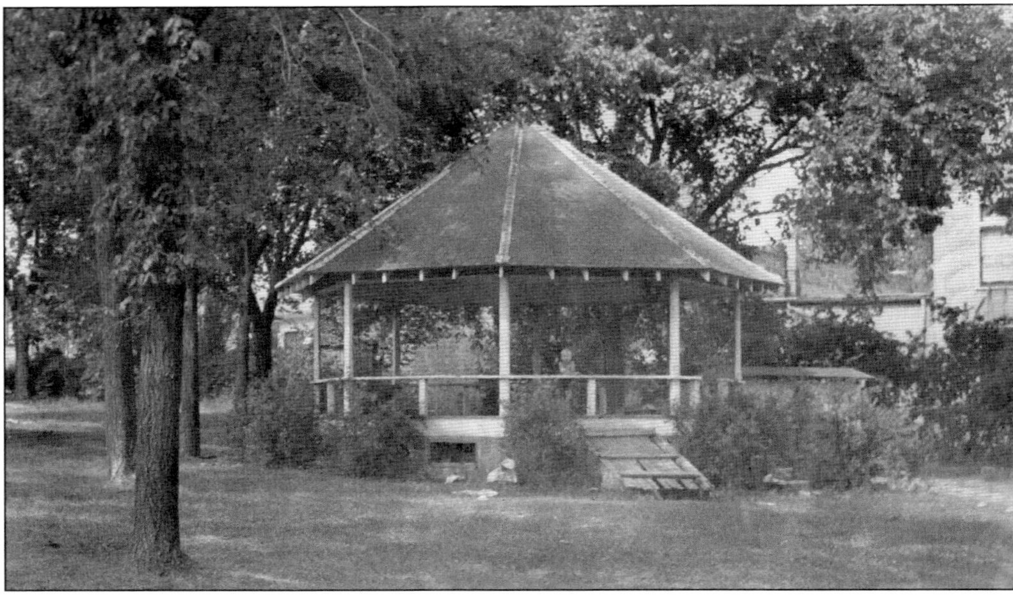

This bandstand was built in 1927 in a little park behind the Masonic lodge, at South Nettleton Avenue and Third Street. After it became too unsafe to use, plans were made to move it to the grounds of the National Agricultural Center & Hall of Fame, but it was too far gone.

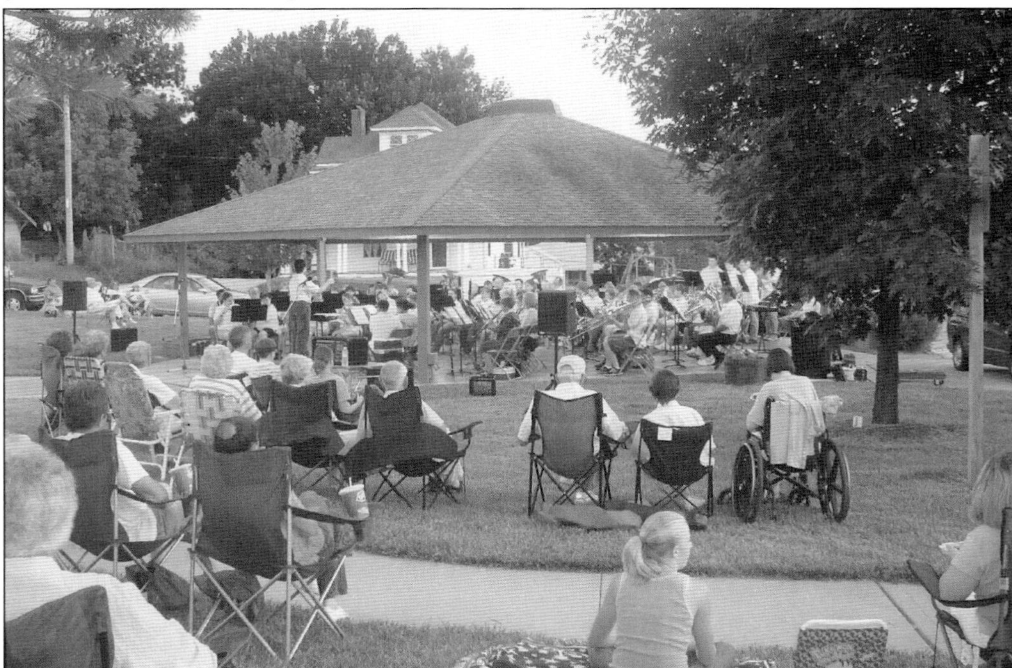

The current Bonner Springs City Band presents eight regular Thursday evening concerts in the band pavilion at Kelly Murphy Park during the summer. It also plays special concerts for the Fourth of July festivities and Tiblow Days. The park and the band concert area were built in 1986 and named in honor of a young Bonner Springs police officer killed in the line of duty. It is located at Elm and Second Streets. (Courtesy of City of Bonner Springs.)

Five

AFTER THE DEPRESSION

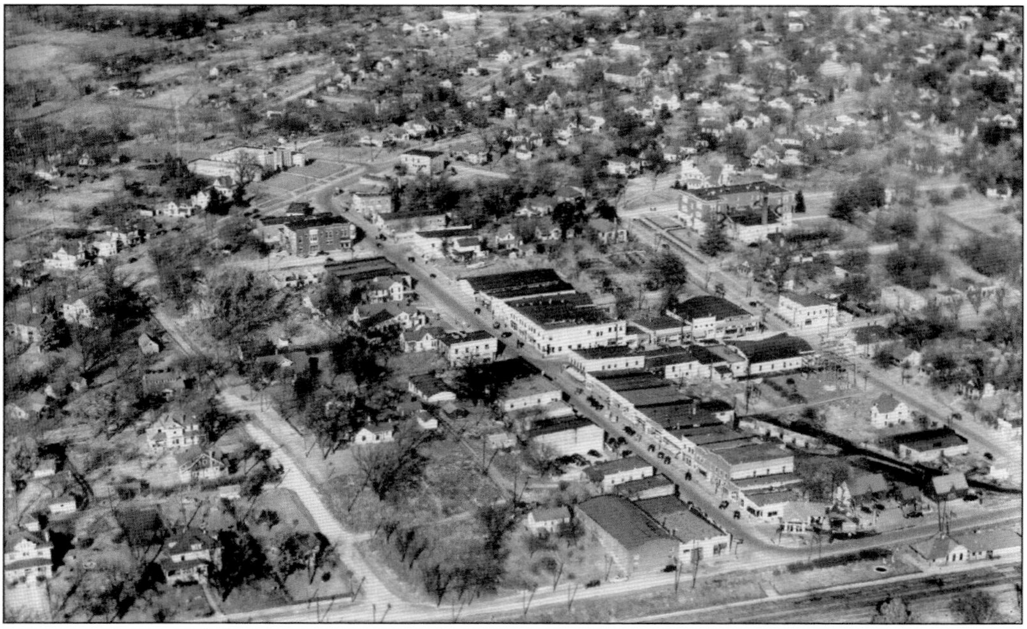

This aerial view of the downtown area shows Oak Street (center) fairly full of businesses. The haphazard parking on only one side did not last very long, as increased traffic volume resulted in the installation of parallel parking on both sides of the street shortly after this photograph was taken.

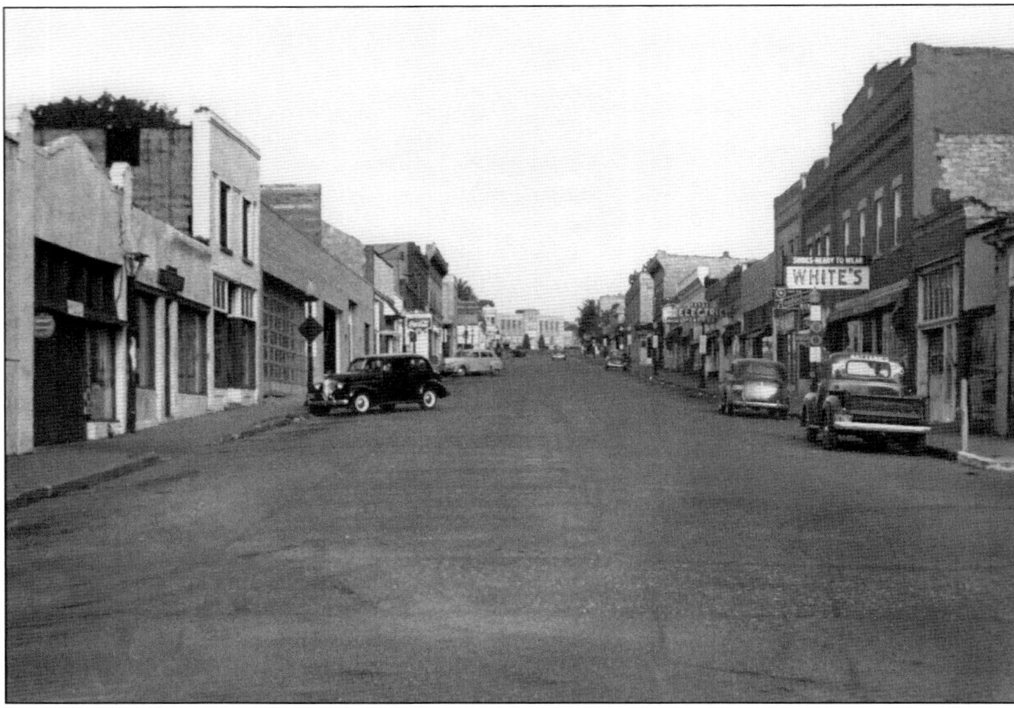

This view up Oak Street in the 1940s looks very clean compared to earlier photographs of muddy streets.

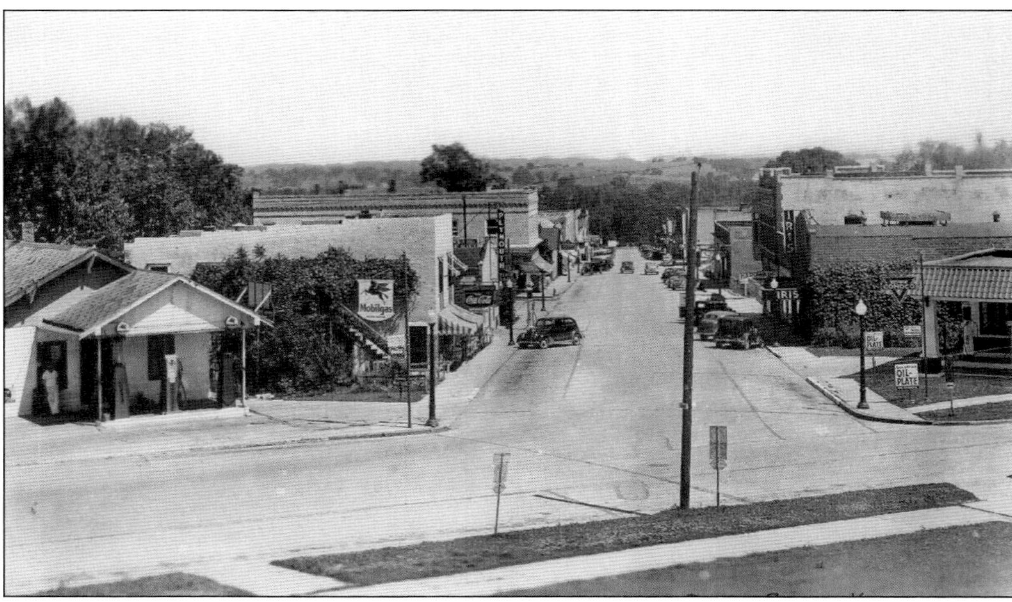

This photograph of the view looking down Oak Street highlights the importance of the automobile, as there are gas stations on the two corners opposite one another. The Iris Theater (right) was purchased in 1934 by the Orear family, who managed it for 14 years. When a large, new 9-foot-by-12-foot screen was installed, it was a big news item in the paper.

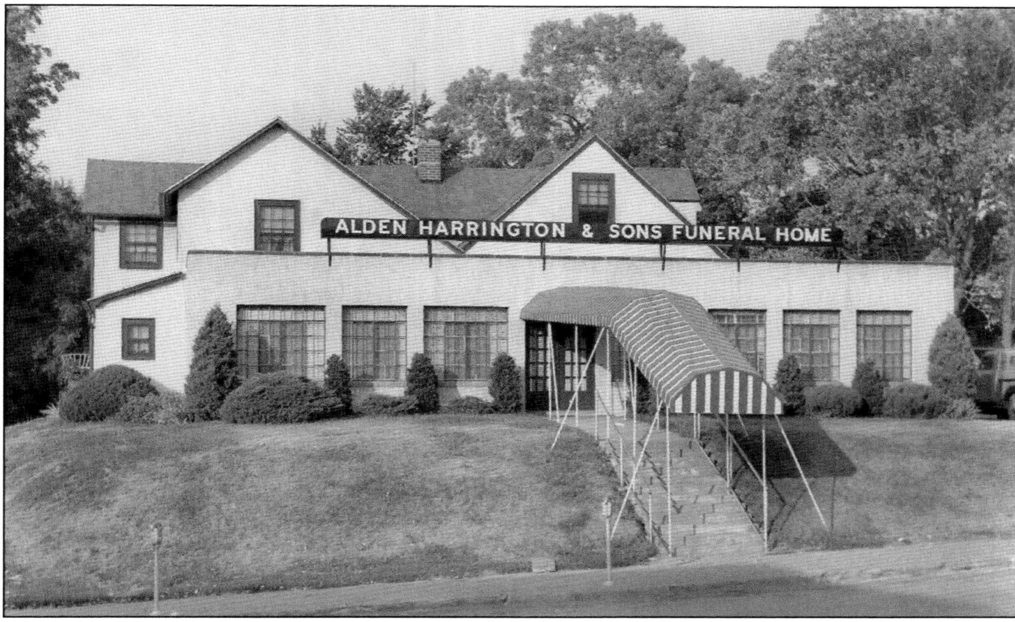

The Alden-Harrington Funeral Home has been in the same family for over 100 years. Frank Alden originally purchased it from W.S. Twist. Alden's daughter Irene then married Ward Harrington, and their son John and grandsons Jeff and Bradley operate the business today.

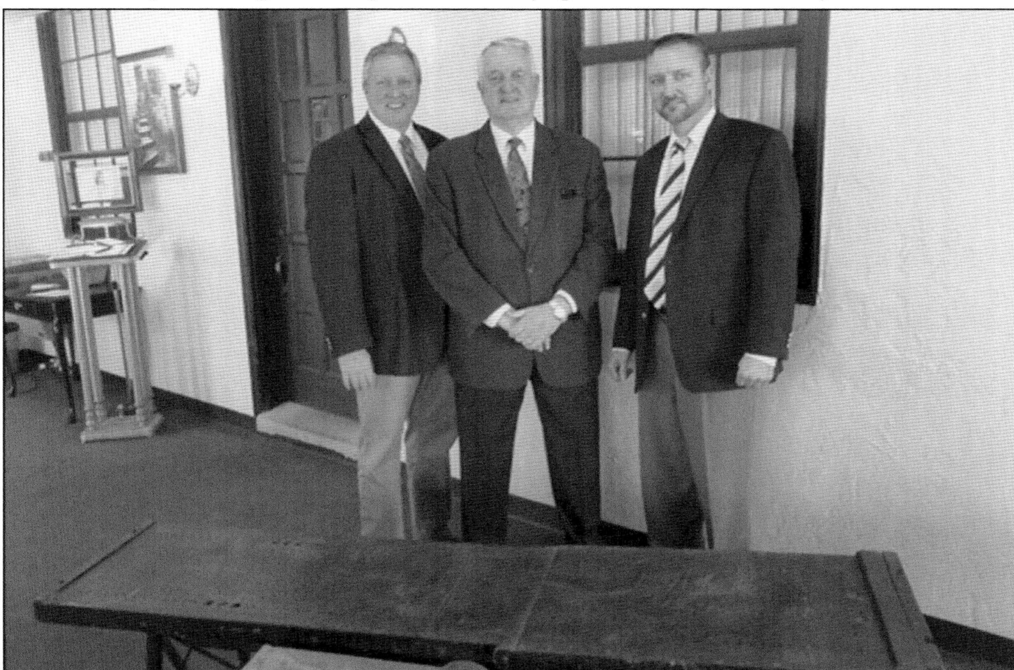

Until funeral homes were established, most embalming was done in the home of the deceased. The portable table in the foreground was used to rest the body upon while the process was accomplished. Brothers Jeff (left) and Bradley Harrington are seen here flanking their father, John Harrington.

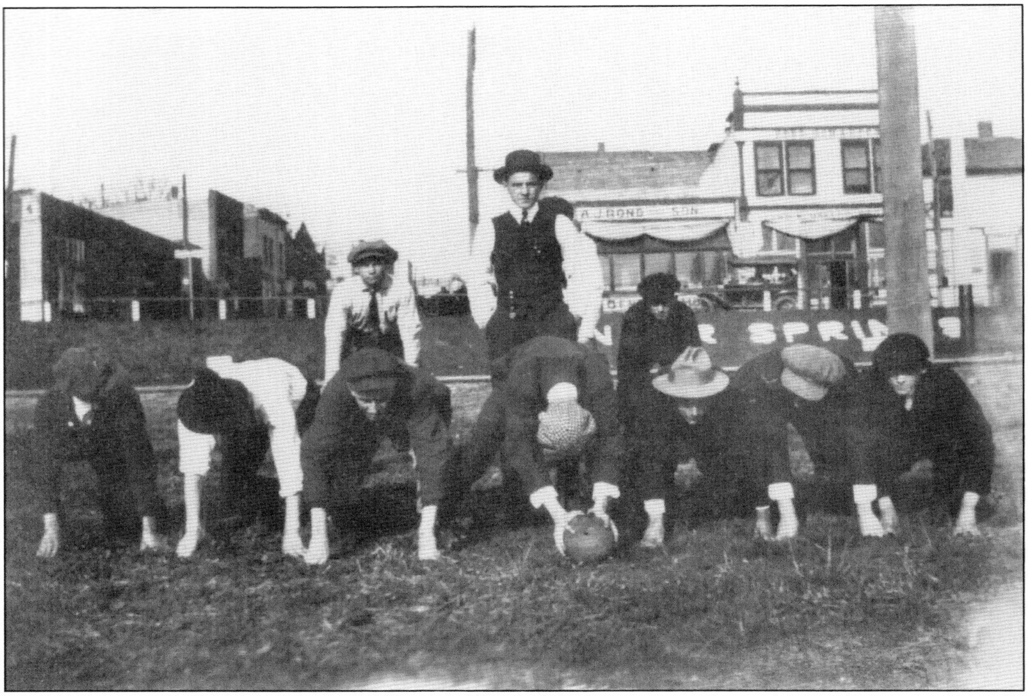

Before the highly organized sports leagues of today, most towns had their own sports team. These football players are likely preparing for a game with a rival town.

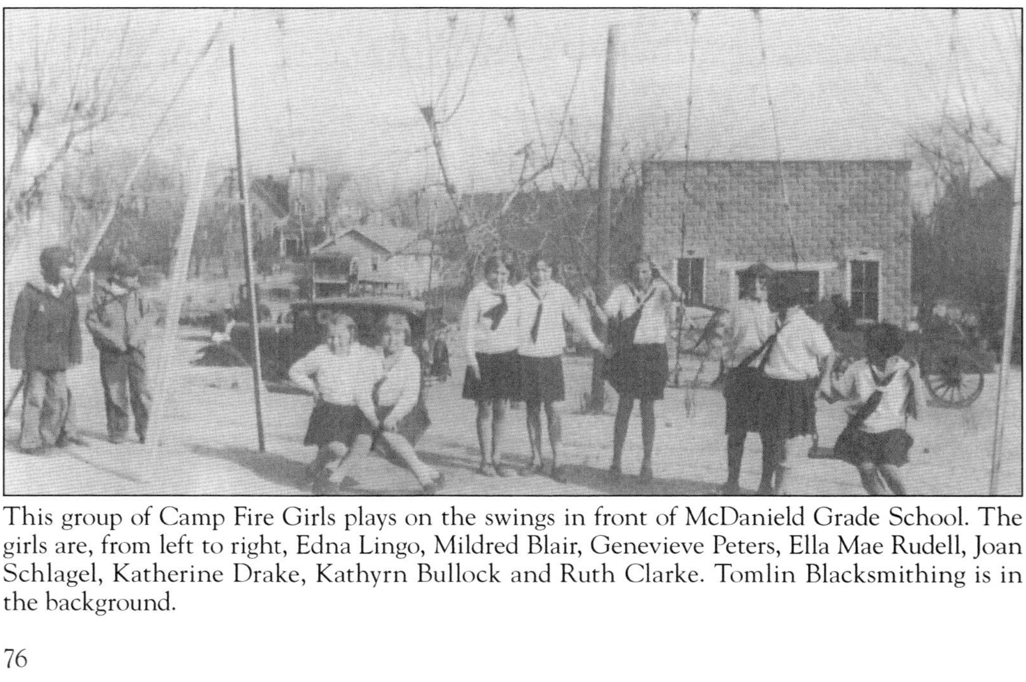

This group of Camp Fire Girls plays on the swings in front of McDanield Grade School. The girls are, from left to right, Edna Lingo, Mildred Blair, Genevieve Peters, Ella Mae Rudell, Joan Schlagel, Katherine Drake, Kathyrn Bullock and Ruth Clarke. Tomlin Blacksmithing is in the background.

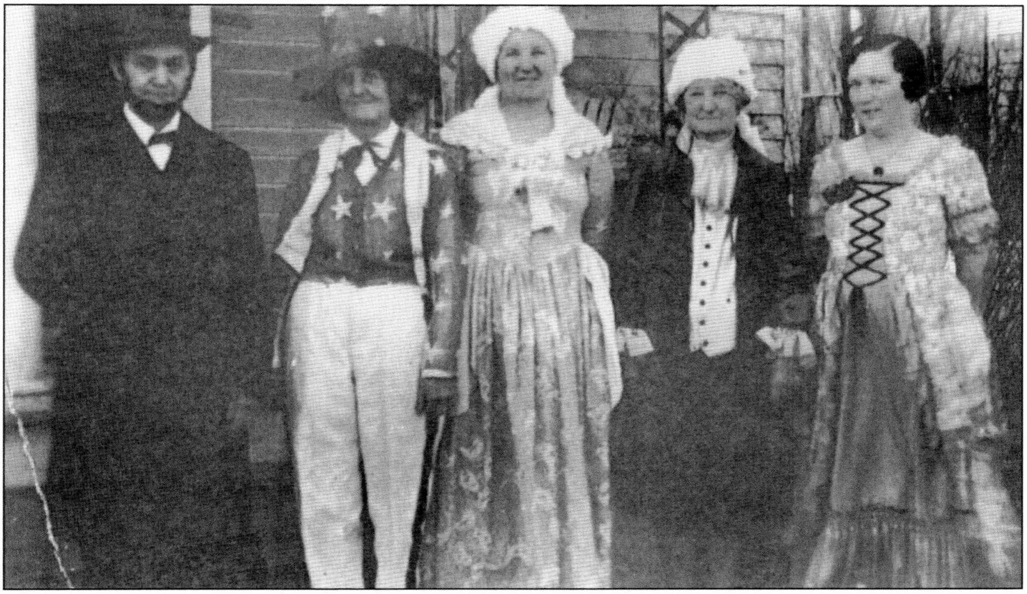

In 1935, the Women's Relief Corps held a silver tea at the home of Mrs. George Washburn on South Nettleton Avenue. They are identified from left to right as follows: Jennie Gallagher is dressed as Abraham Lincoln, Mrs. Milton Penrod as Uncle Sam, Mrs. S.D. Harlow as Martha Washington, Mrs. Washburn as George Washington, and Mrs. ? Carlson as a Colonial lady.

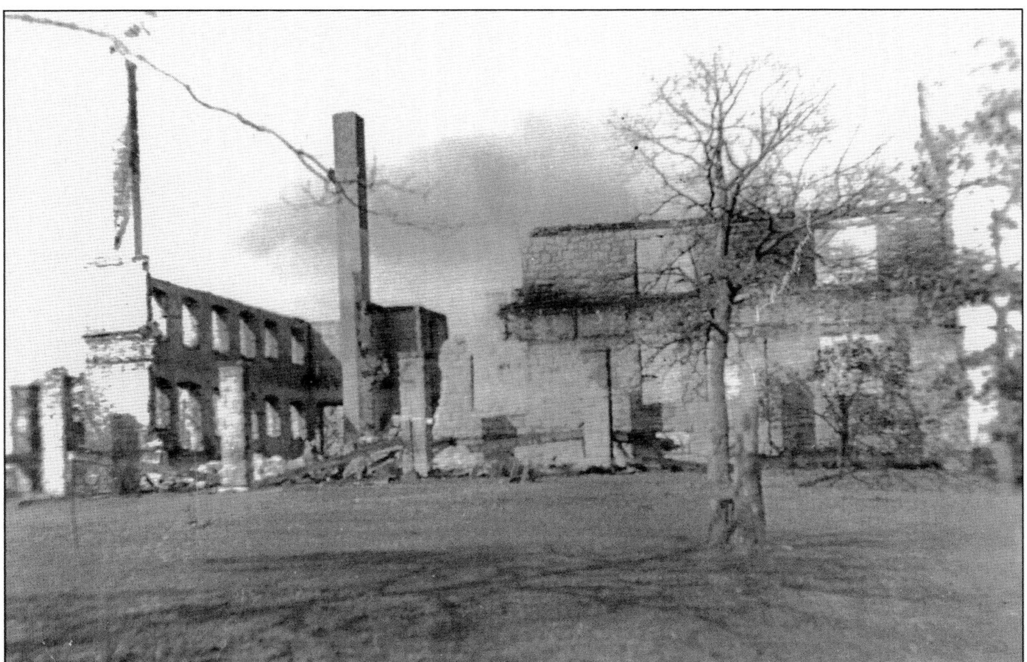

The Bonner Springs Sanitarium had been abandoned for some time when it burned in 1944.

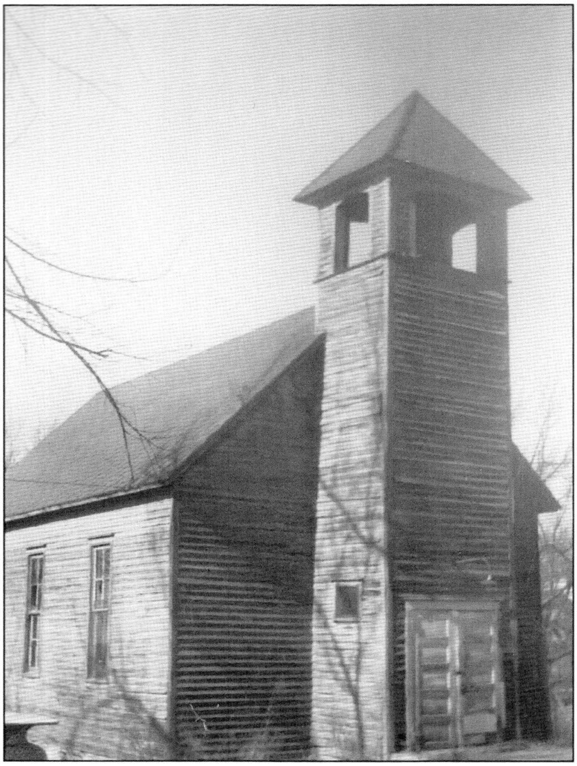

The first Sacred Heart Catholic Church was purchased from the Christian church and converted into a Catholic church.

The new Sacred Heart Catholic Church was built on Spring Street in 1921, along with a rectory for the priest and the nuns who taught at Sacred Heart School. It suffered an arson fire in 1996 and had to be demolished.

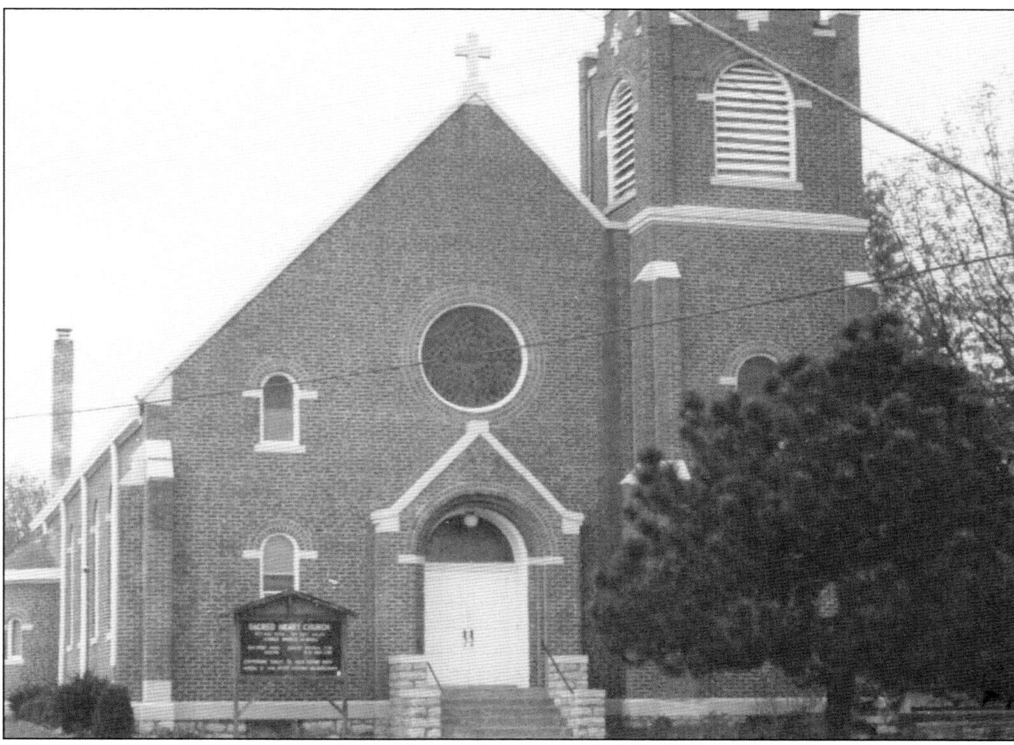

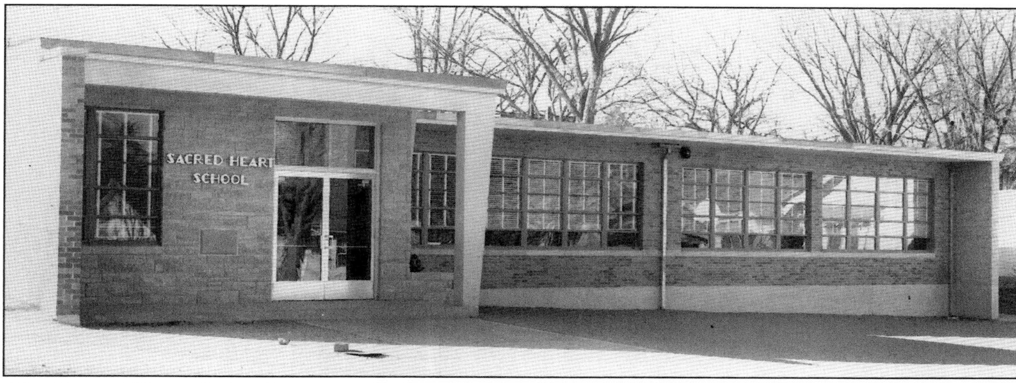

The Sacred Heart School consisted of grades one through eight. When the church burned down in 1996, parishioners continued meeting until the new church building was constructed in Johnson County. (Courtesy of WCHS&M.)

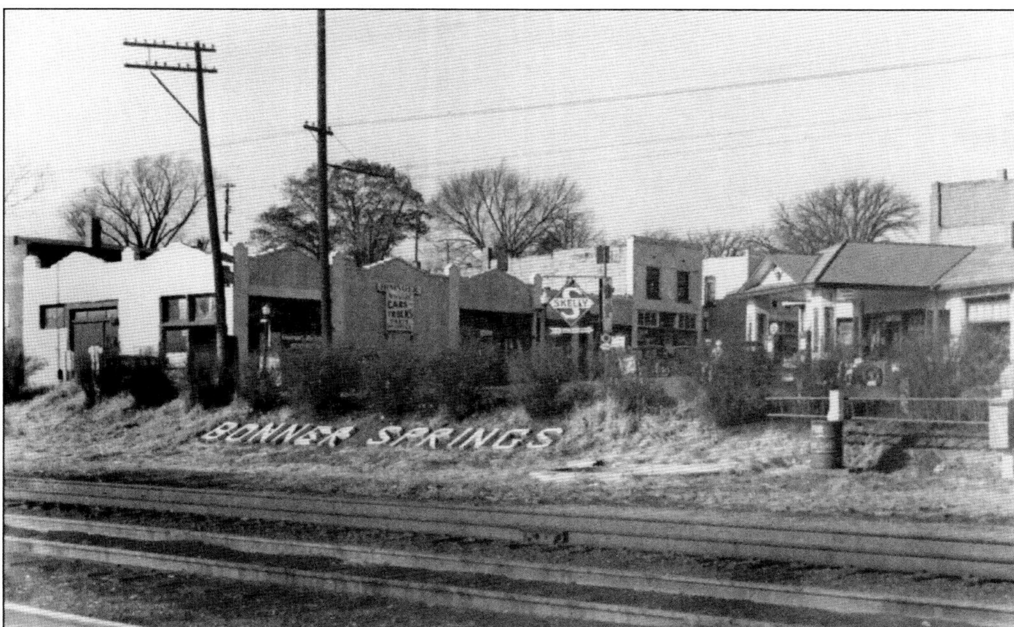

After the trains no longer stopped in Bonner Springs, the landscape was not cared for as it had been. The letters welcoming the passengers even became overgrown. They were eventually buried in the dirt, and were only rediscovered when the station agent began poking around one day. The Jaycees then moved them to the edge of the high school football field.

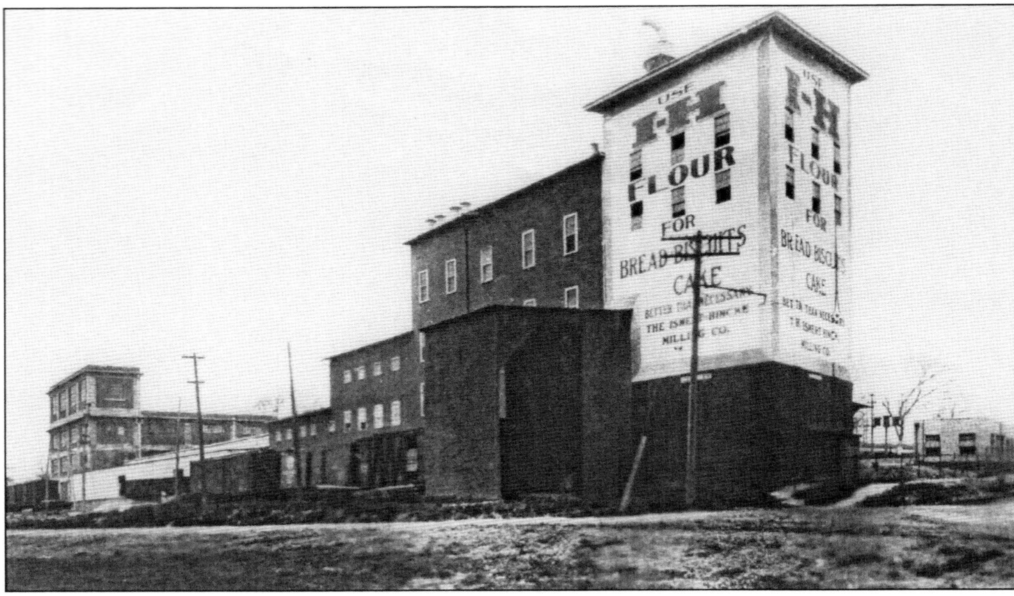

This cereal plant was once a thriving division of Safeway that made the pancake flour for every Safeway store in America. One of the first projects of the newly formed chamber of commerce, in 1966, was to have the freight zone that ended at the east boundary of the city extended to include the cereal plant, which saved the plant quite a bit in freight fees.

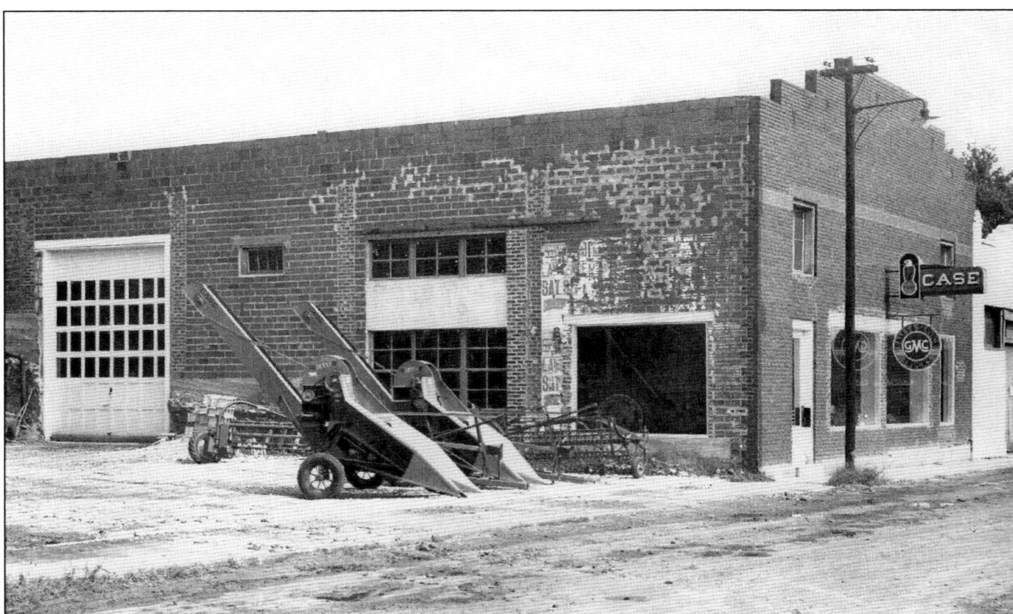

Coleman Coal & Feed was started in 1940 by Jim Coleman. The business moved into this building on Oak Street in 1952. Being a farmer, Coleman understood the need for farm machinery, repair, and parts, and changed the name to Coleman Equipment.

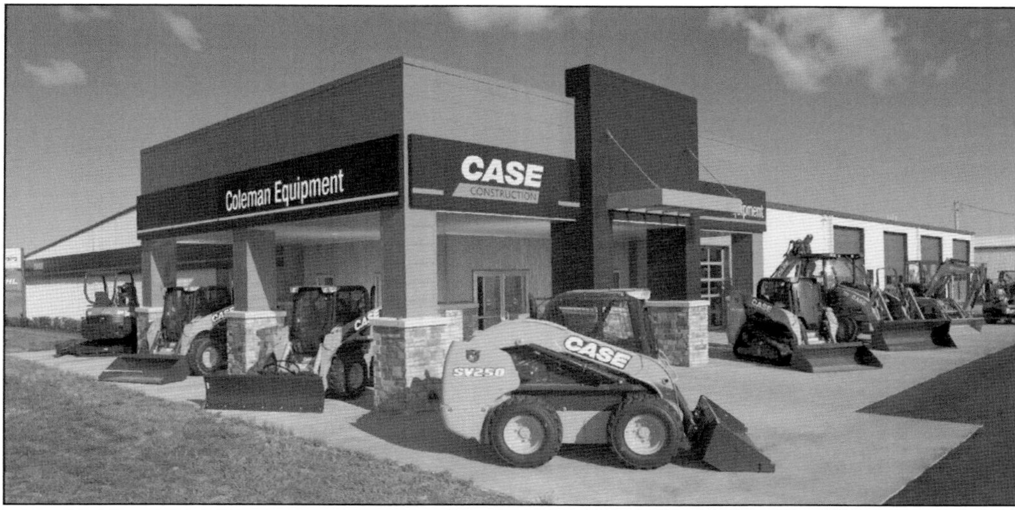

Coleman Equipment is now on Kansas Highway 7, on the south side of the Kansas River. It moved from downtown Bonner Springs when urban renewal took its building. While it still supplies farm machinery, it has also shifted to light construction needs, as seen here. Using the power of the Internet to display its catalog of machinery, equipment, and parts, the firm now ships out between 100 and 150 parcels per day to customers all over the United States and overseas. (Courtesy of Coleman Equipment.)

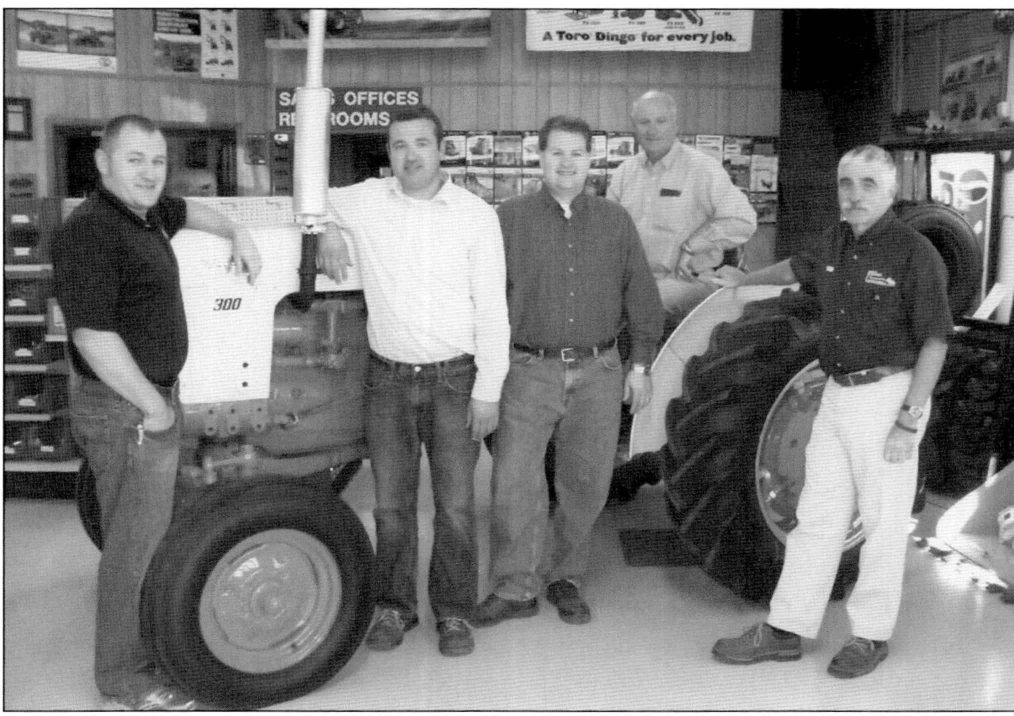

The second and third generations to run Coleman Equipment have adapted the business to grow while keeping its focus on customer service. Seen here, from left to right, are Jim Coleman's grandsons Jason, John, and Chris Coleman and his sons Del and Bruce Coleman. (Courtesy of Coleman Equipment.)

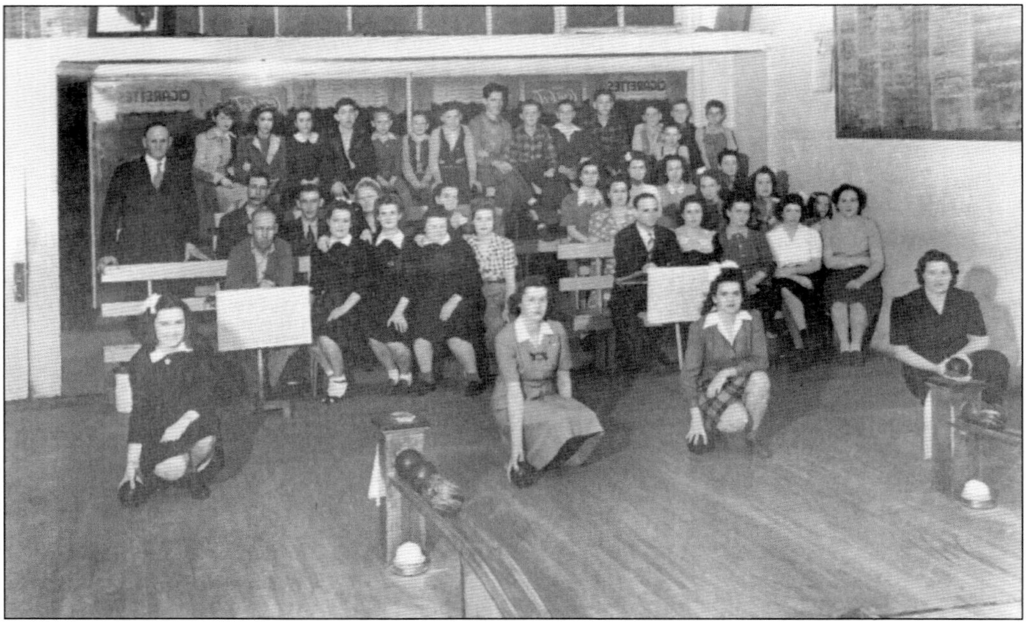

Play Well Lanes, a duckpin bowling alley, was a popular spot for bowlers of all ages. The alley, at 208 Oak Street, was operated by Pete Kindred. This photograph of the ladies' league was taken in 1944. Duckpin bowling was somewhat hazardous, as pins sometimes flew back up the short alley after the stronger bowlers powered the ball down the lane.

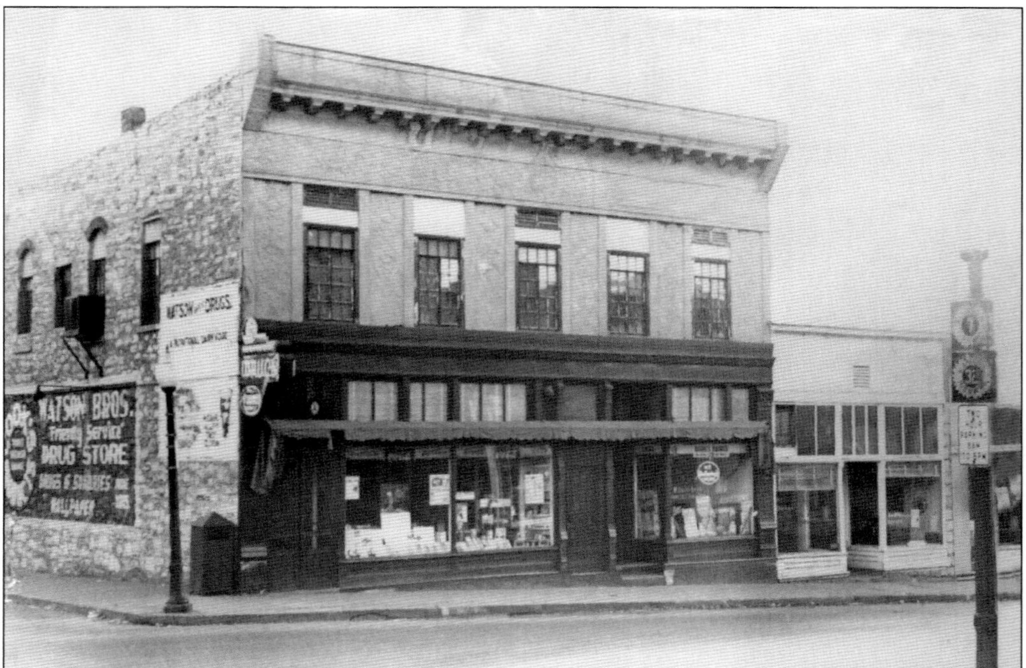

Watson Brothers Drug Store was a fixture for many years in the Knights of Pythias building on the northeast corner of Oak and Second Streets. As evidenced by the highway signs, both Kansas Highway 7 and Kansas Highway 32 pass through downtown Bonner Springs.

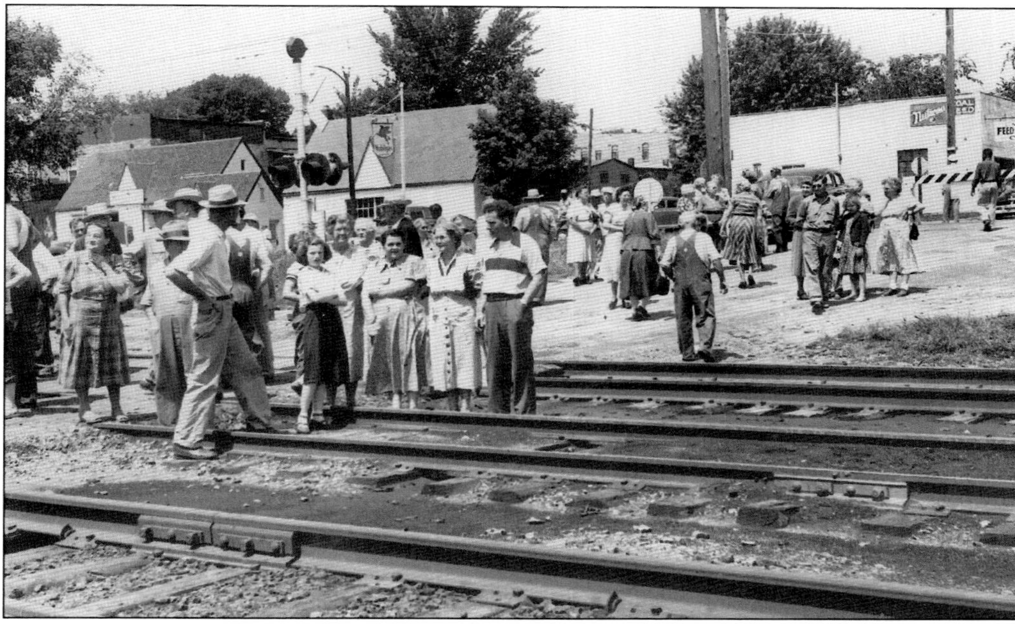

On July 11, 1951, the Kansas River crested at Bonner Springs. While it flooded all the bottomland, it did not reach the railroad tracks along Front Street. This group of curious onlookers gathered to watch what became the worst flood of the Kansas River ever. It did terrific damage to the entire Kansas City area.

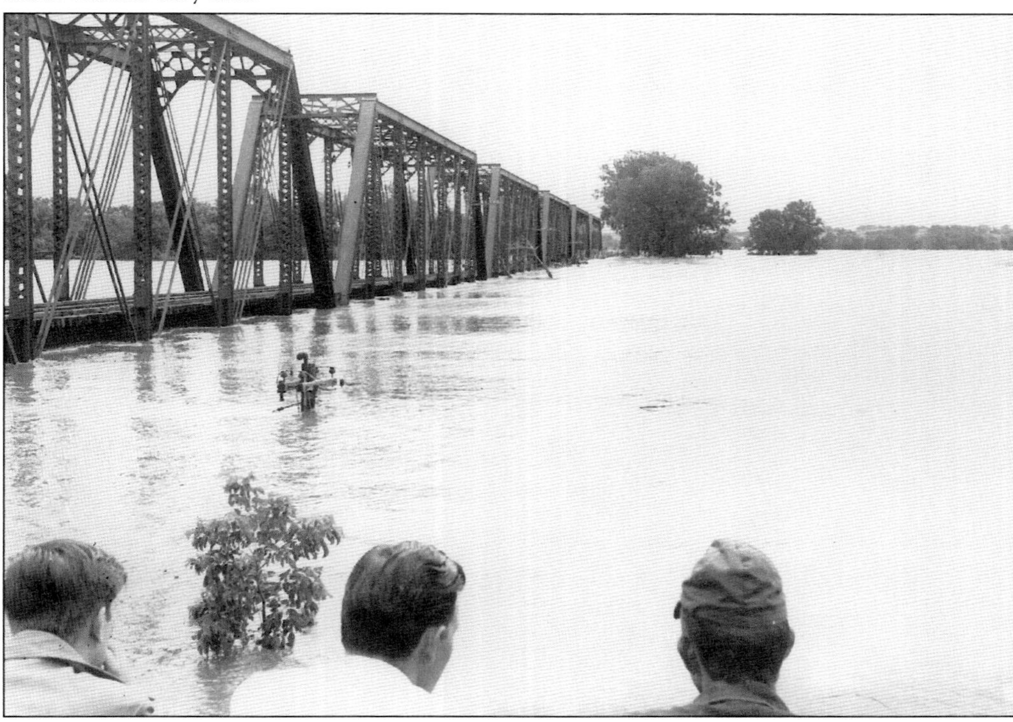

The river came dangerously close to taking out the wagon bridge connecting Bonner Springs with Johnson County on Kansas Highway 7.

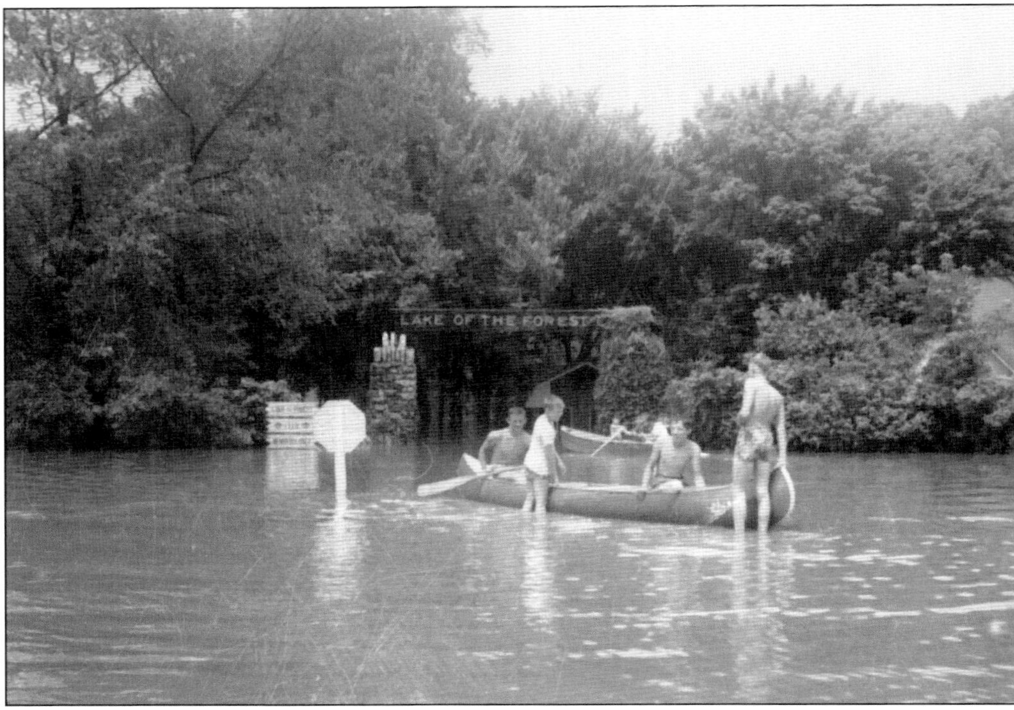

Canoeing after the flood are, from left to right, Tom Klotz, Bob White, Bob Klotz, and Jack Pearman.

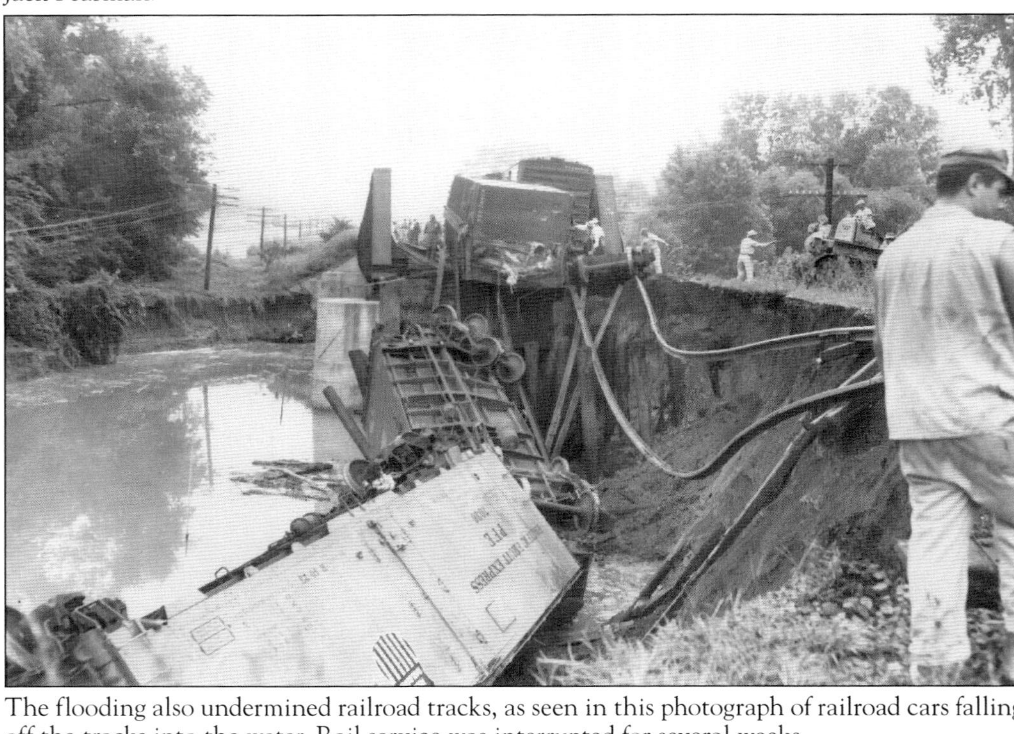

The flooding also undermined railroad tracks, as seen in this photograph of railroad cars falling off the tracks into the water. Rail service was interrupted for several weeks.

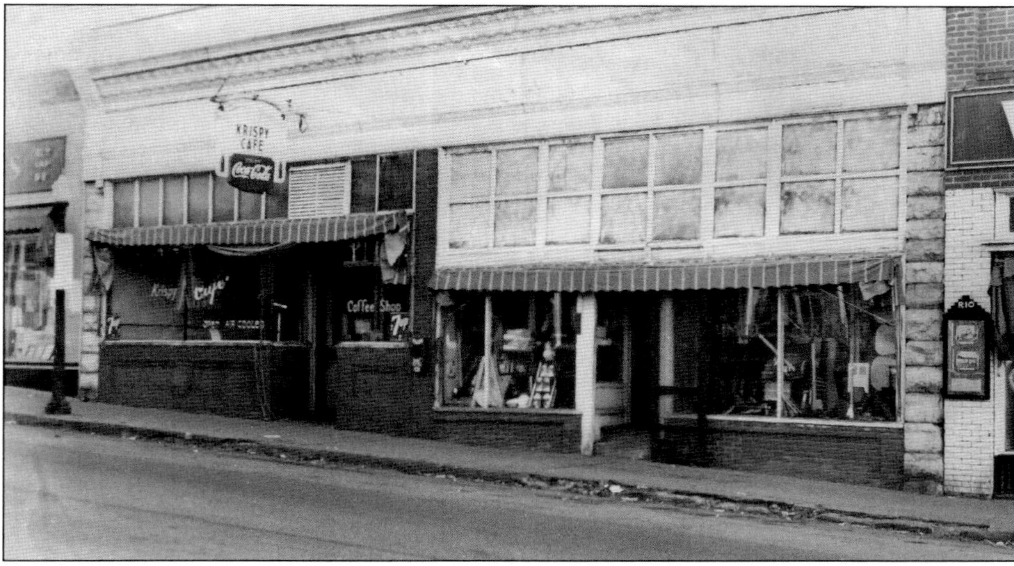

The Krispy Café was a staple on Oak Street for many years. It is seen here at its original location in the 100 block of Oak Street. It moved to a new building in the early 1950s.

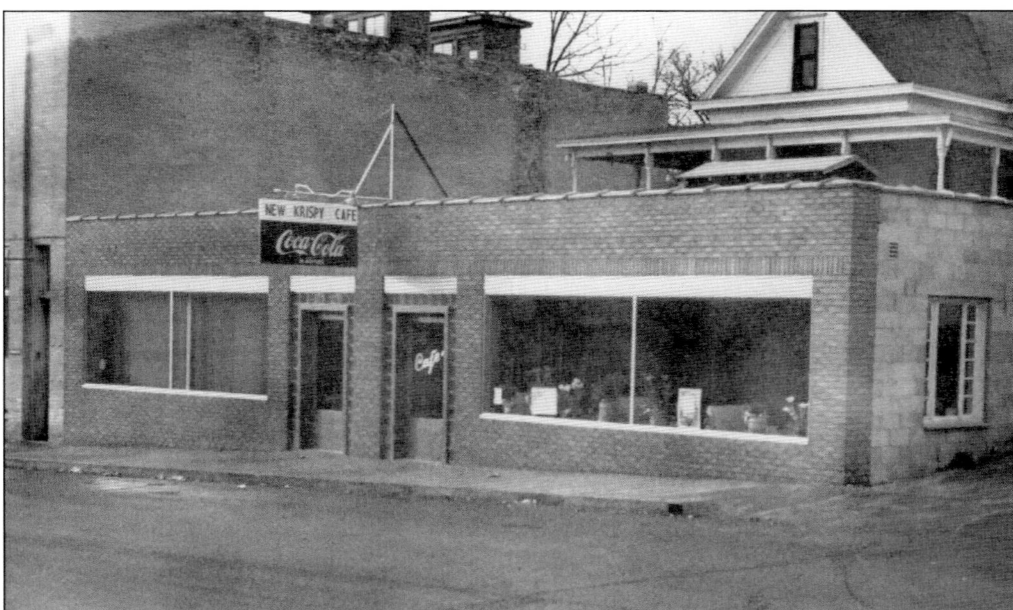

The New Krispy Café was built in front of the house at 202 Oak Street. The restaurant was owned by Roland and Faye Mapes. Faye's mother, Mae Pine, lived in the house behind the café and helped with the cooking.

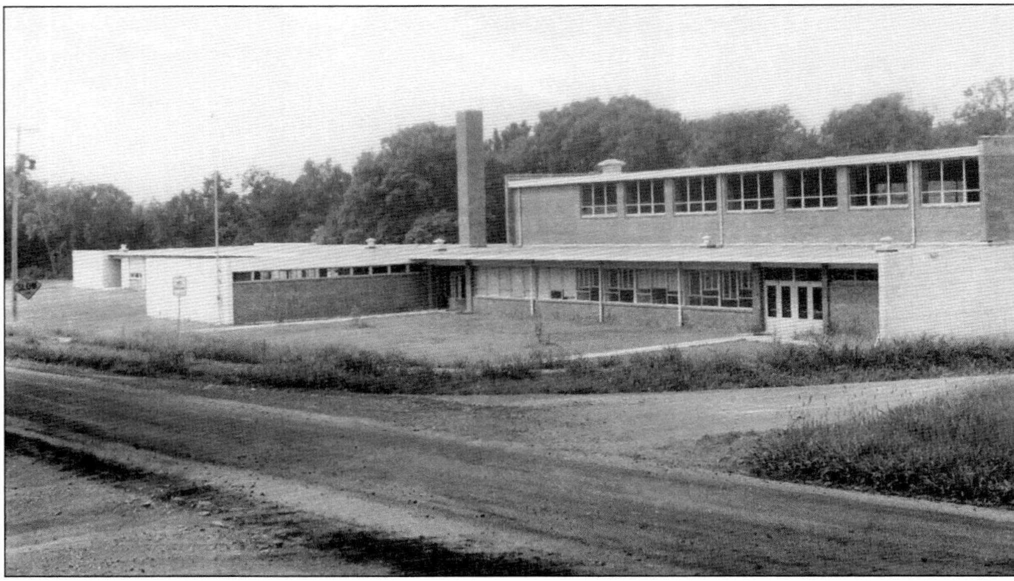

Southwest School was built in 1954 at the corner of Neconi Avenue and Shadyside Street, an area that had been used as a football field for many years. By that time, the high school football team played in the new Lions Park.

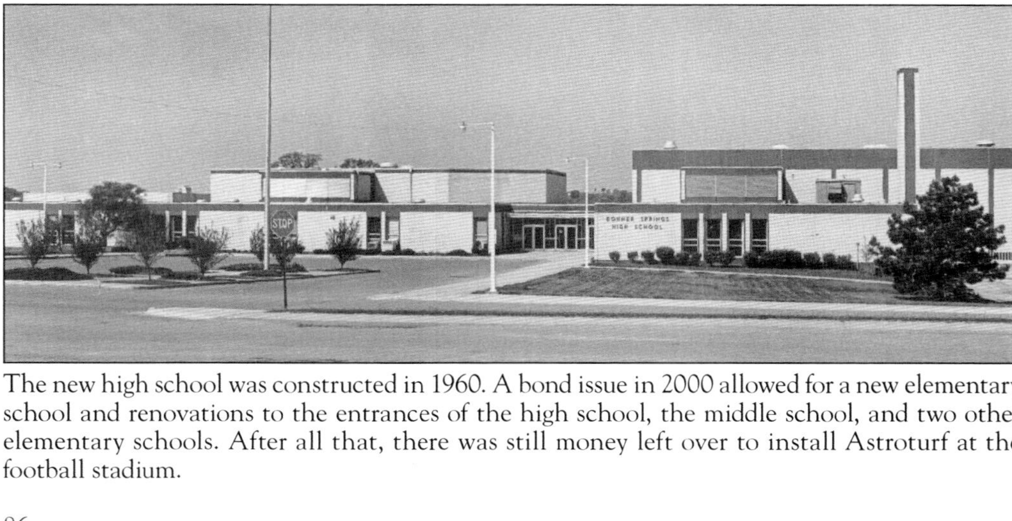

The new high school was constructed in 1960. A bond issue in 2000 allowed for a new elementary school and renovations to the entrances of the high school, the middle school, and two other elementary schools. After all that, there was still money left over to install Astroturf at the football stadium.

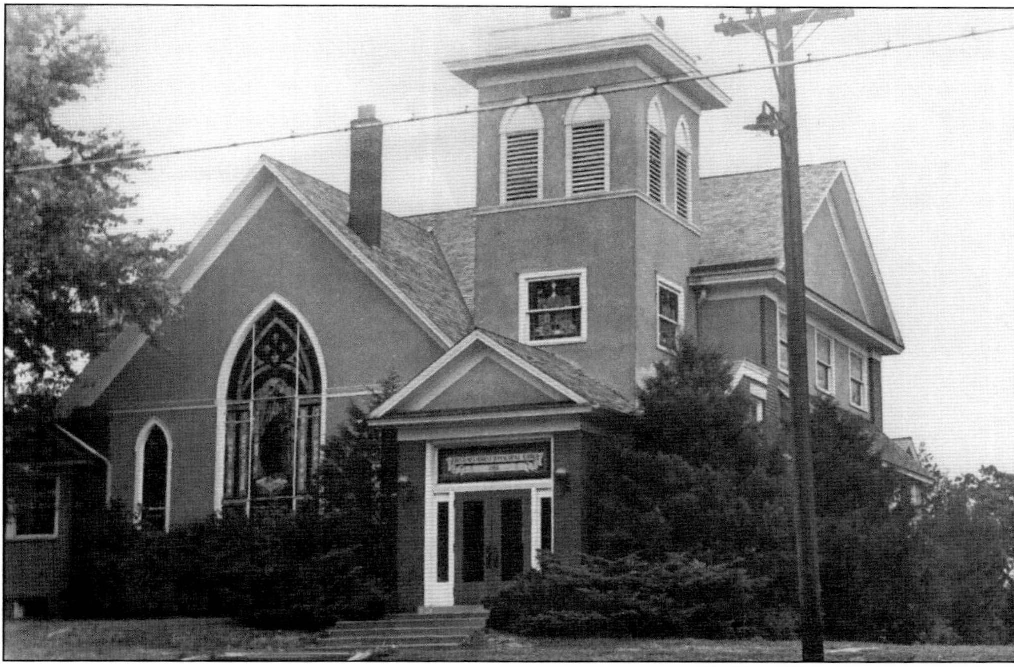

The second Methodist church (above) was built on the corner of Kump and Neconi Avenues. An educational wing was added to the north. It was sold to the Assembly of God congregation when a new church (below) was built at 415 West Morse Avenue in 1965. An assembly hall and kitchen were added later to the new church, with much of the work done by the congregation.

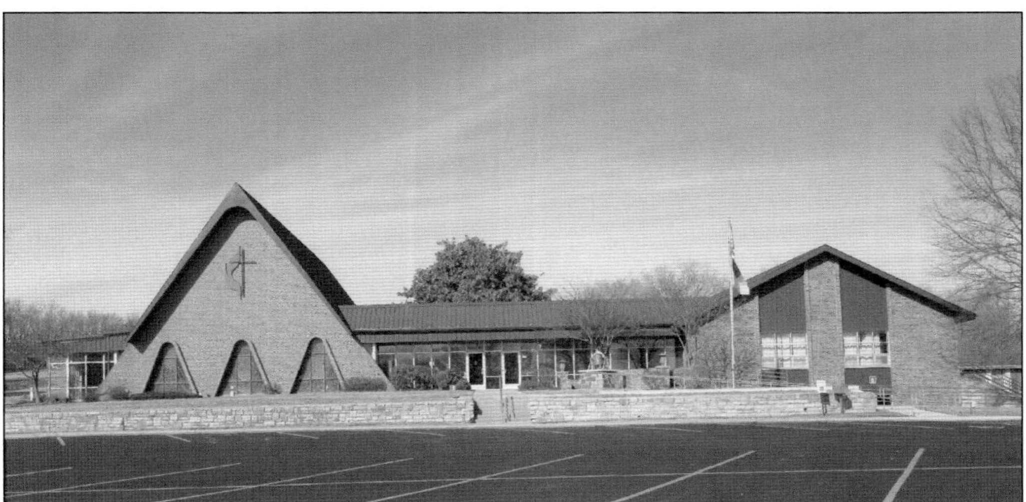

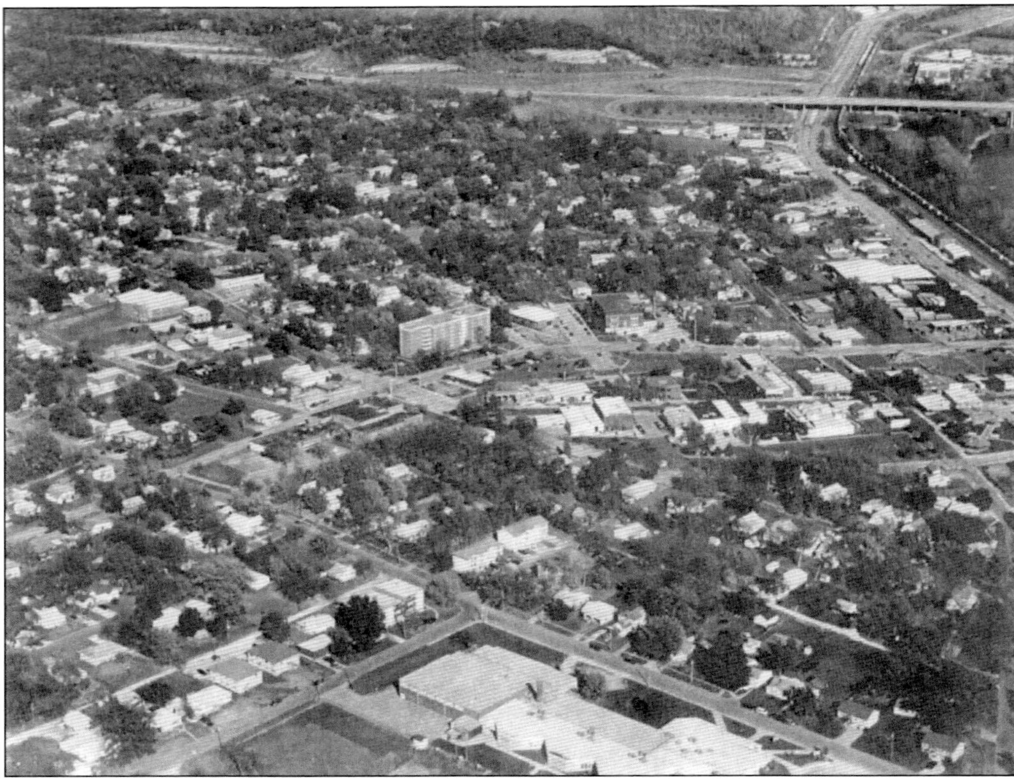

The new bridge over the Kansas River, completed in 1960, was a welcome addition to the city, although traffic did not go directly downtown anymore.

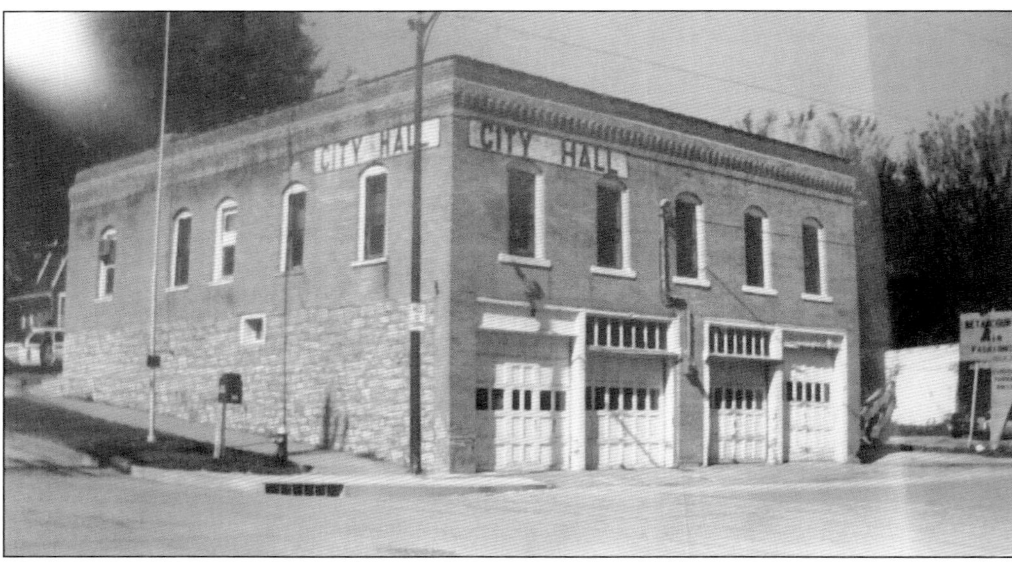

The old city hall housed the city library and the city offices on the second floor. The fire equipment was kept on the ground level.

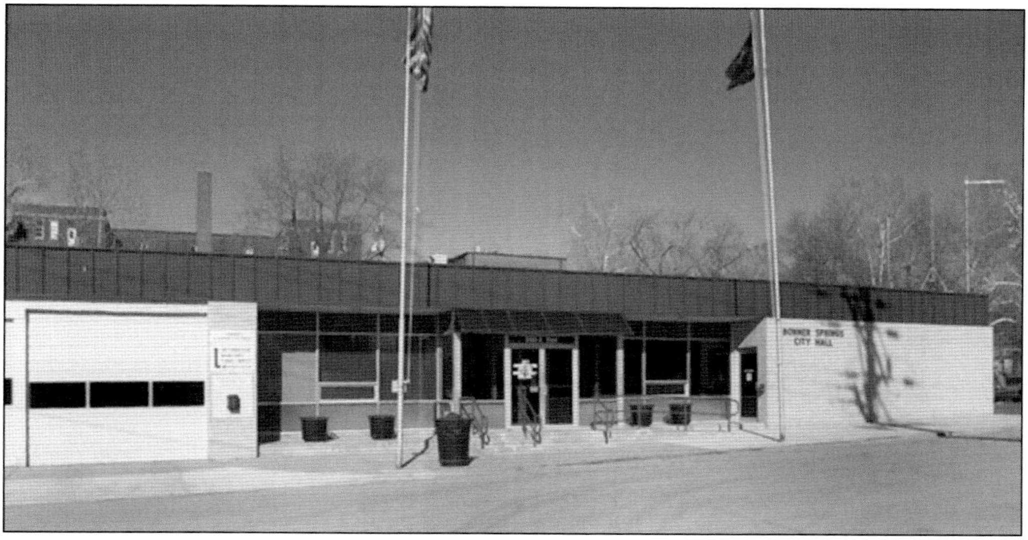

The new city hall was dedicated in 1963. It housed the fire department as well as the EMS headquarters, which was added as an outgrowth of the department.

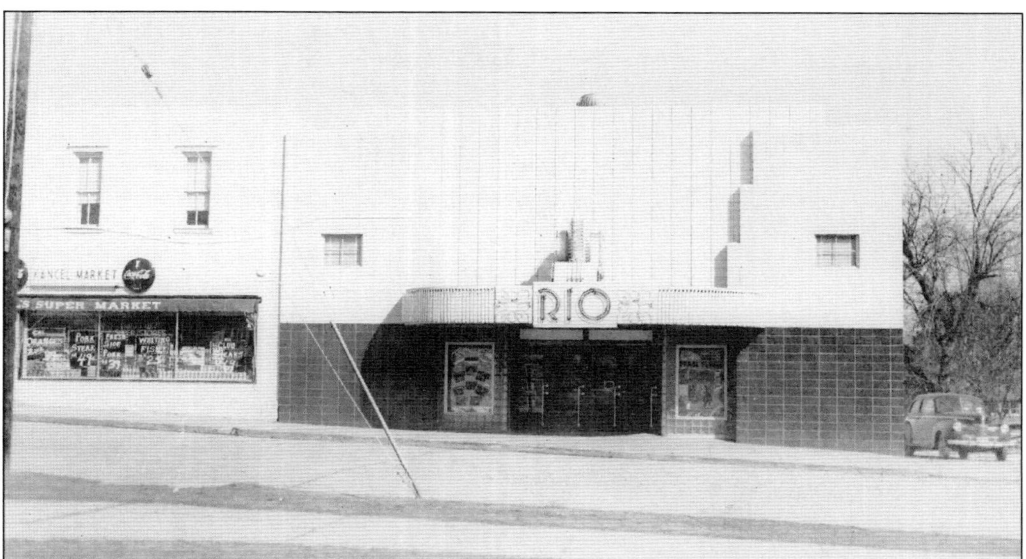

The Rio movie theater was located at Nettleton and Kump Avenues. It burned in 1969 and was never replaced.

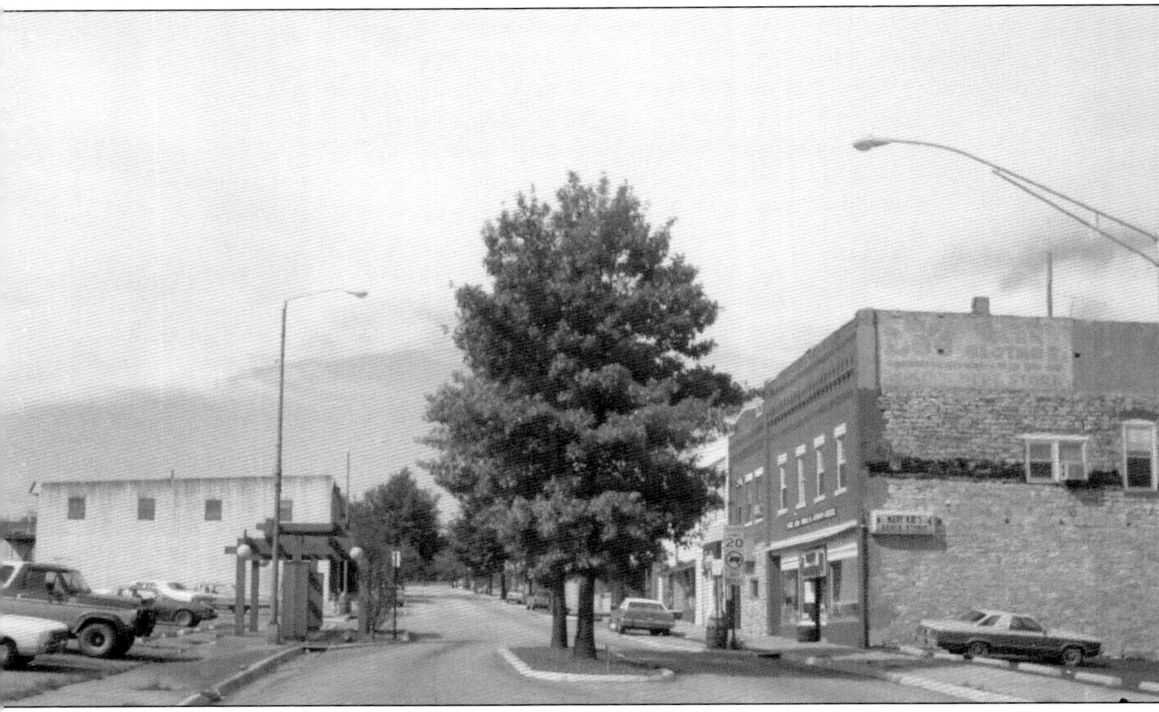

In 1969, urban renewal projects began tearing down parts of the downtown business district. The plan was to beautify the area with islands, trees, and kiosks. Most businesses updated and improved their stores. The kiosk seen here on the left was one of several on Oak Street. The kiosks were removed after a few years.

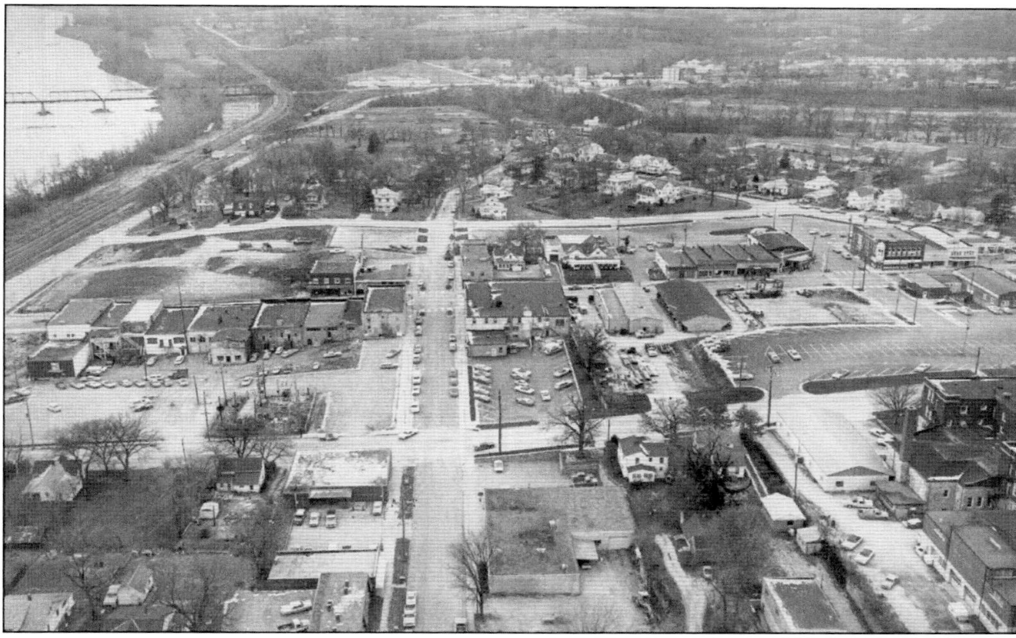

A total of 16 buildings were removed to make room for the enlarged parking lots behind the Oak Street buildings, as seen in the center of this photograph. The businesses that did not have rear access to their shops soon adapted.

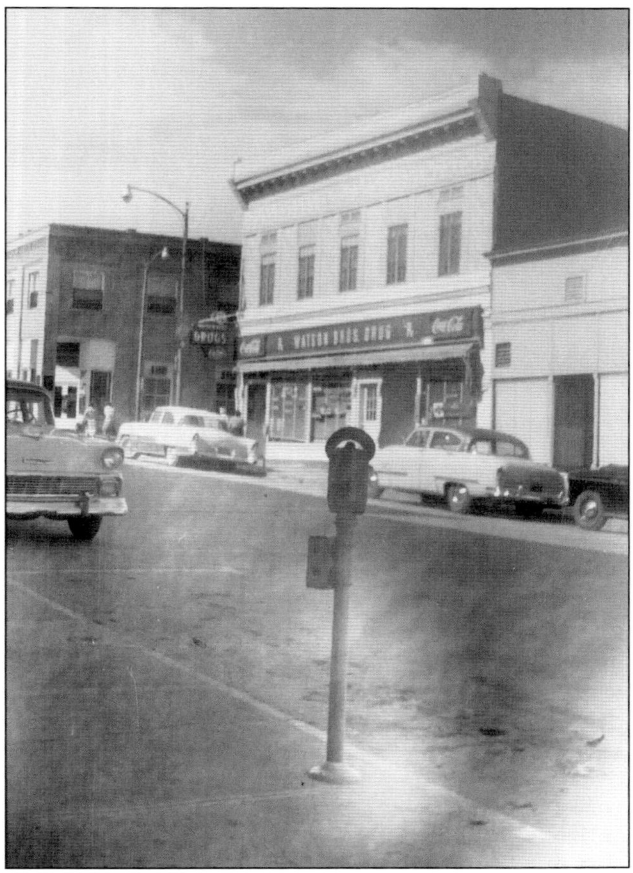

Another ill-fated project was the installation of parking meters on Oak Street. They only lasted a few years.

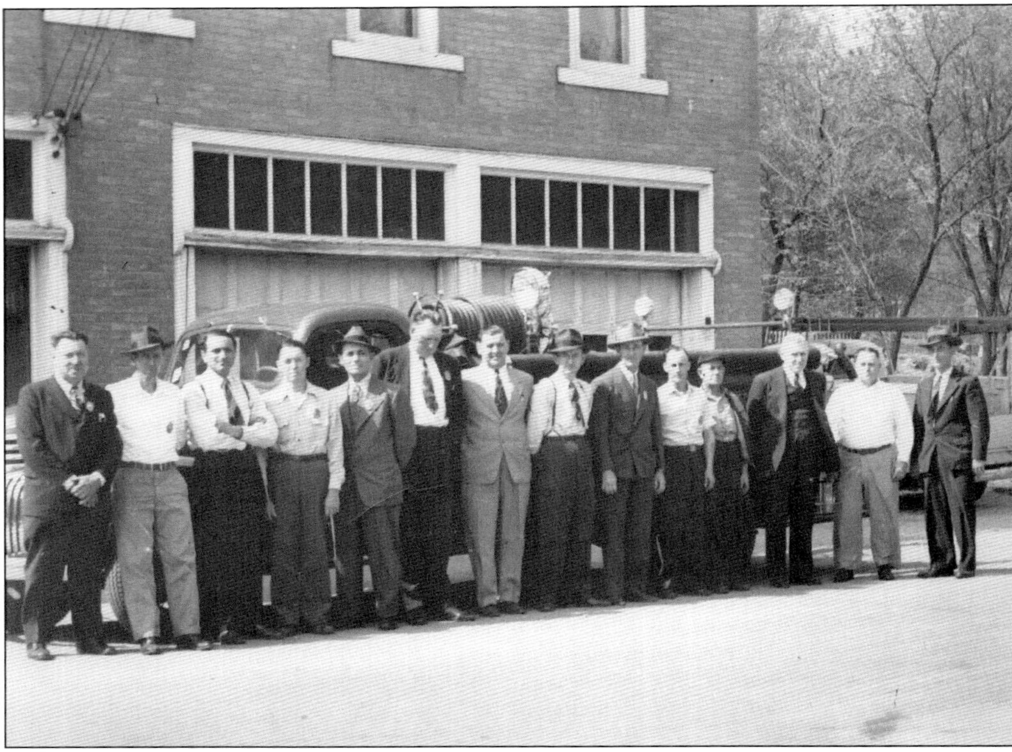

Proud members of the Bonner Springs Volunteer Fire Department pose in front of their new 1941 Chevrolet Pumper fire truck. They are, from left to right, George Haugh, Walter Honeywell, Floyd Johnson, Harold Meredith, Frank Stempges, Ed Poulsen, Joe Woolf, Gerald Powell, Gene Sheley, George Gardner, George Hyoort, Albert Kuchenthal, Otis Tice, and Harley Martinek.

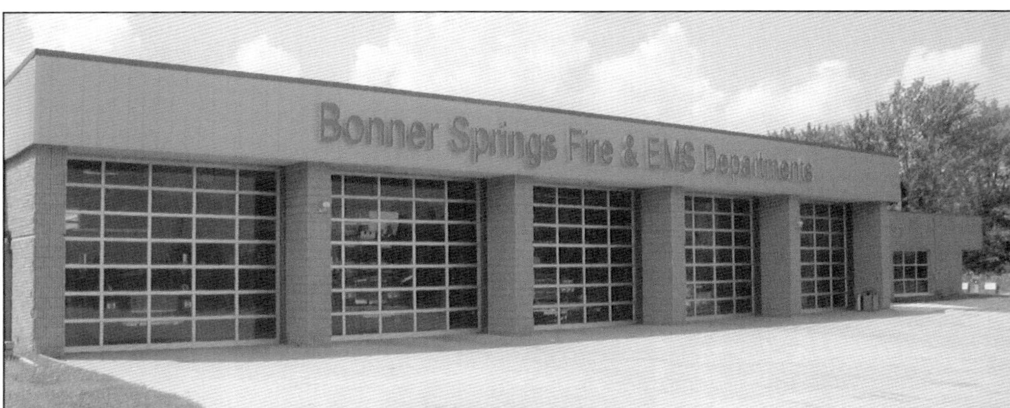

The new fire and EMS station is on a high rise on North Nettleton Avenue to make for a quicker getaway when a fire call comes in. Longtime fire chief Tony Dusil advocated emergency medical training for the department, and that became a reality in 1975. The fire department and ambulance service were made into two departments in 1976. Both departments have contributed heavily to fire prevention education in the schools and in the entire community. (Courtesy of City of Bonner Springs.)

Six

Attractions, Celebrations, and Organizations

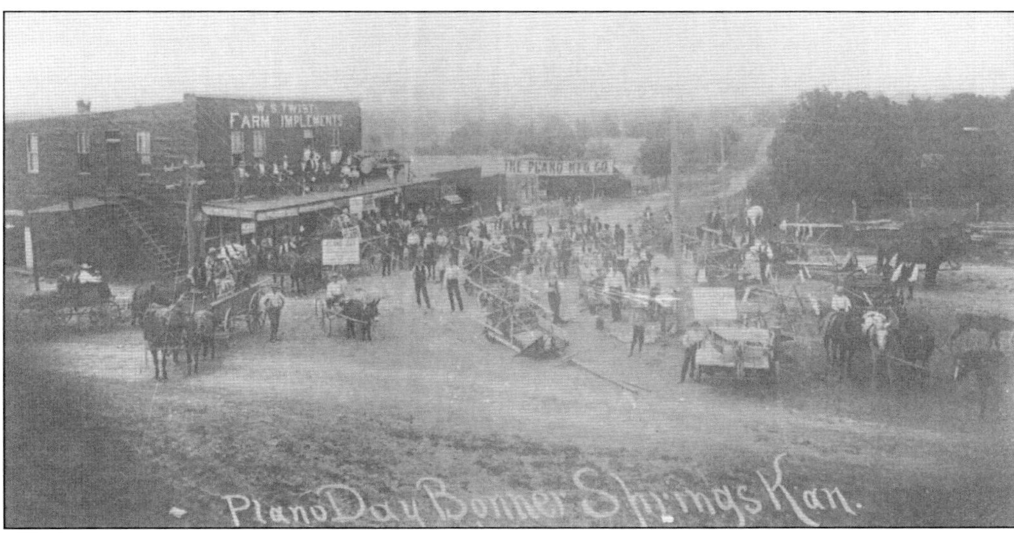

In early Bonner Springs, Plano Days brought implement manufacturers to town to display the latest in farm machinery. It was sponsored by W.S. Twist's farm implement company (left).

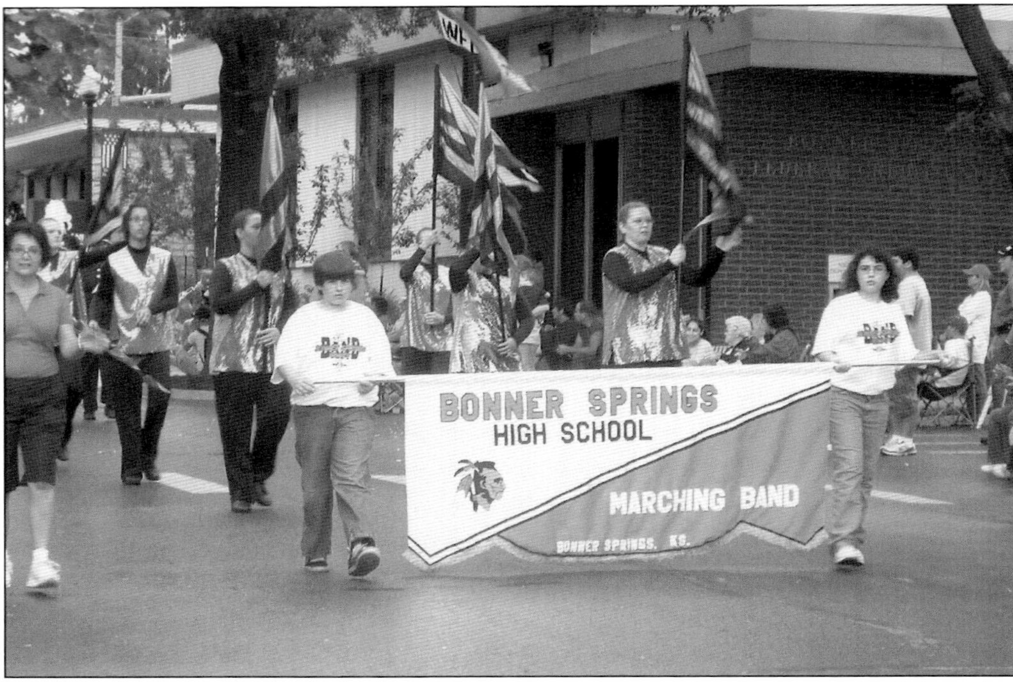

Since 1958, Bonner Springs has celebrated Tiblow Days. The weekend event brings thousands to town for a parade, concerts, various shopping booths, and a car show. The Bonner Springs High School band leads the parade. (Courtesy of City of Bonner Springs.)

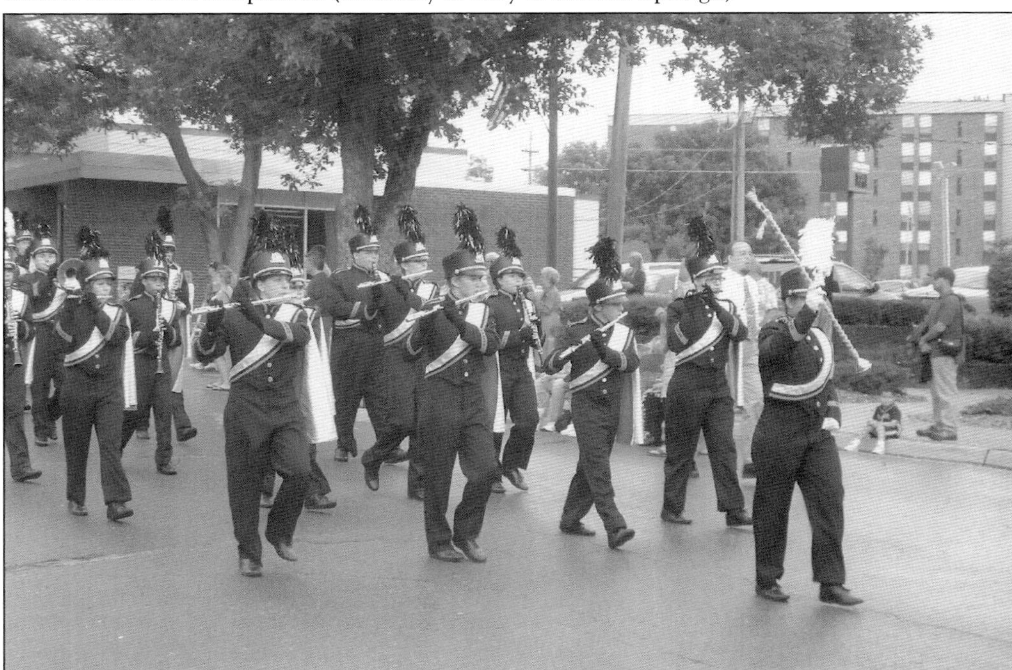

The marching band leads the lively Saturday morning parade during Tiblow Days. (Courtesy of City of Bonner Springs.)

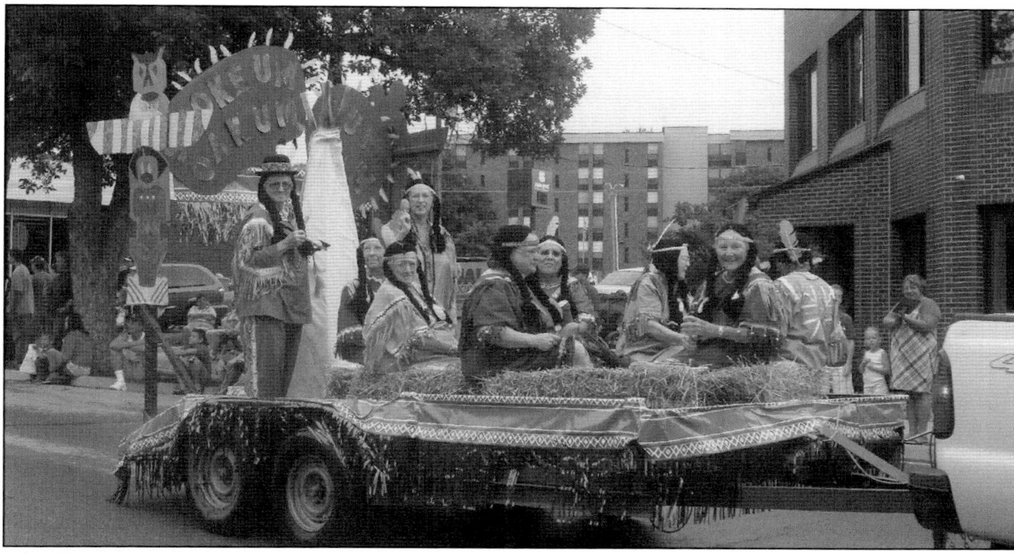

The floats created by the senior citizens' group usually win prizes. This particular year, their float had an Indian theme. (Courtesy of City of Bonner Springs.)

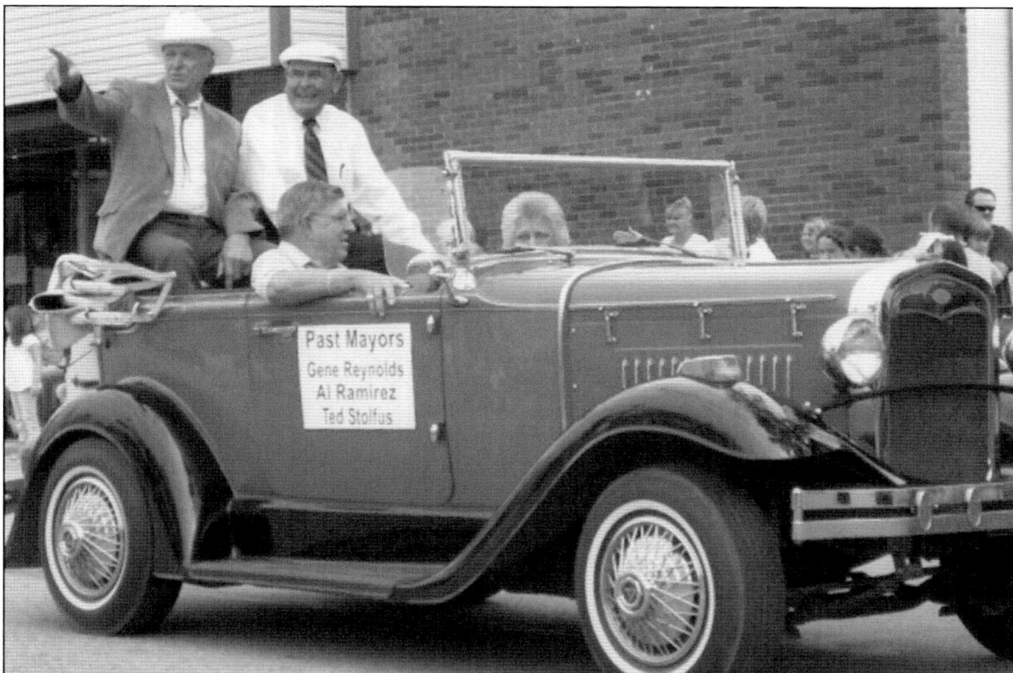

The Tiblow Days weekend starts on Thursday evening with the Mayor's Banquet. Besides honoring the living past mayors of Bonner Springs, the banquet is when the annual Vaughn-Trent Award is presented for community service. The award is named for Marion Vaughn, a prominent former mayor of Bonner Springs, and Lindy Trent, a former mayor of Edwardsville. Both men served their communities honorably for a long time. Here, past mayor Ted Stolfus points to the crowd as fellow past mayor Al Ramirez looks on beside him. Seated in the front are another past mayor, Gene Reynolds, and driver Kathy Ramirez. (Courtesy of City of Bonner Springs.)

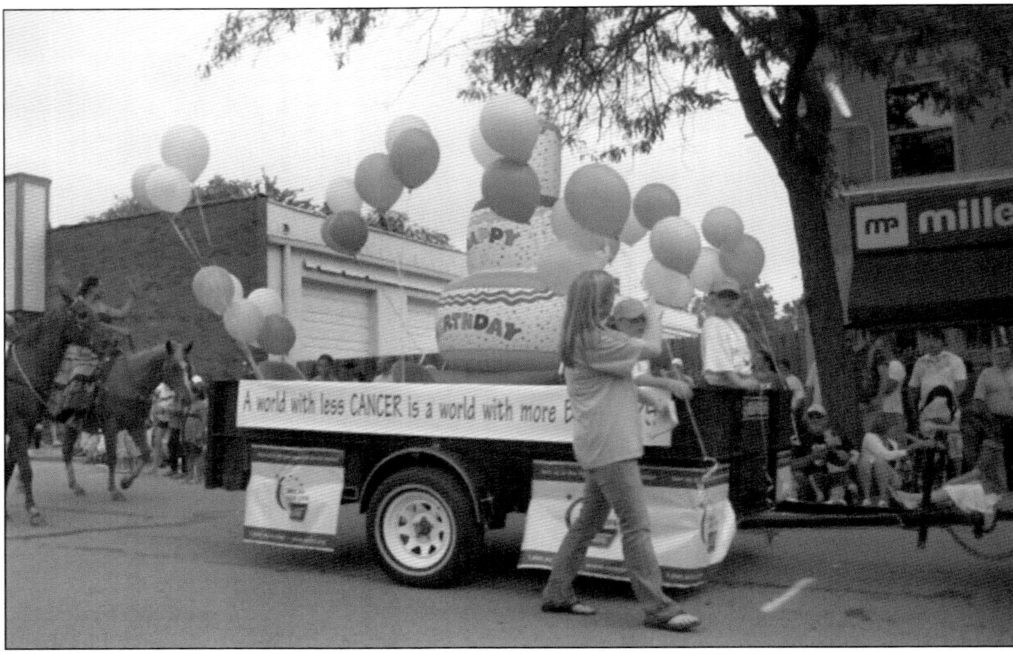

Relay for Life is a cancer fundraiser that usually raises over $100,000 at its annual event in Bonner Springs, held at the high school football field. The parade is likely nearing its end, as the saddle clubs are usually the last entries. (Courtesy of City of Bonner Springs.)

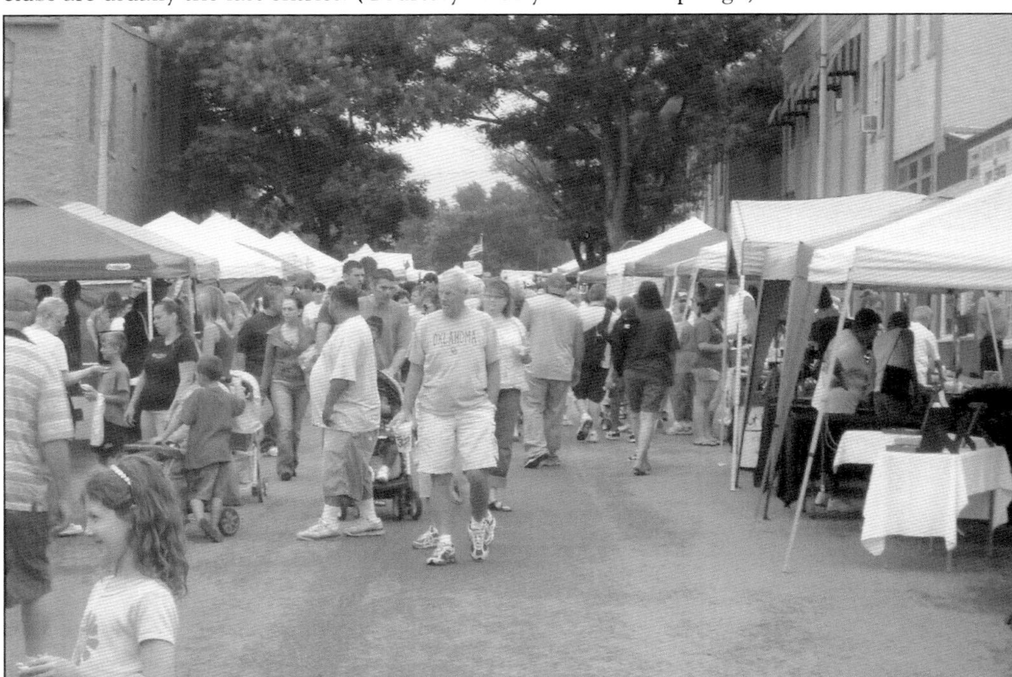

The streets are crowded with folks visiting the displays during Tiblow Days, which feature food, community action organizations, and crafts. (Courtesy of City of Bonner Springs.)

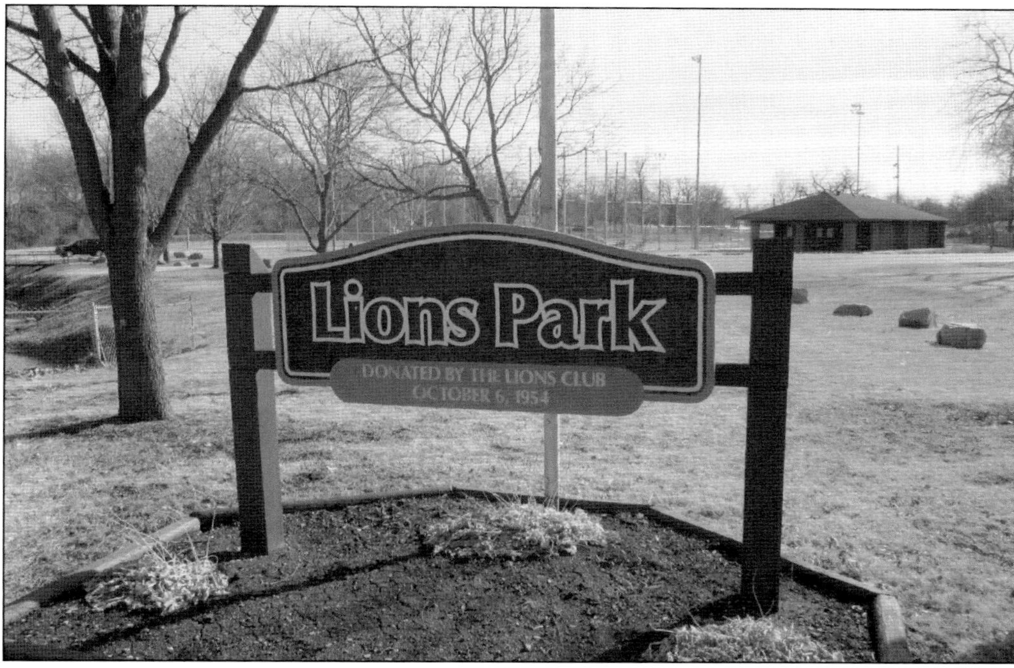

Lions Park was donated to the city by the Bonner Springs Lions Club in 1954 after the club purchased the land from the Rehm family farm. The park included a football field until the high school was built, and it now has several baseball diamonds, a concession stand, and a playground area.

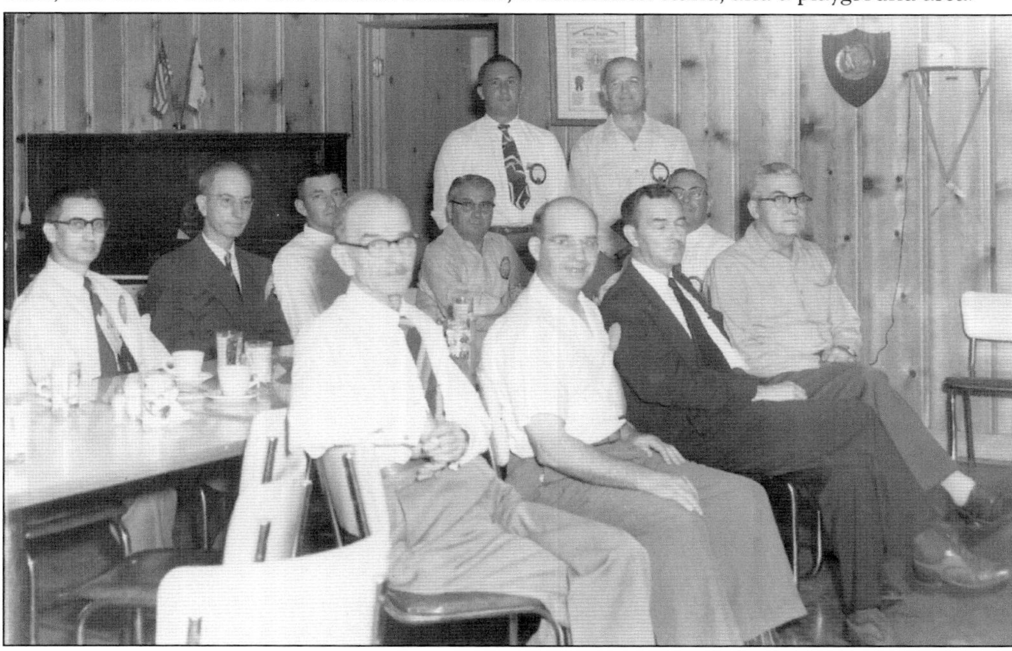

The Lions Club, represented by Clarence Boyer Jr. and Ward Harrington (standing, background), formally presented the deed to Lions Park to the city at this meeting, attended by, from left to right, (first row) Bernard ? (auditor), Herschel Walker, Lee Weeks, and Bill Cunningham; (second row) Lawrence Hayden, Harley Martinek, Bruce Wasson, Bill Hestand, and Milt Penrod.

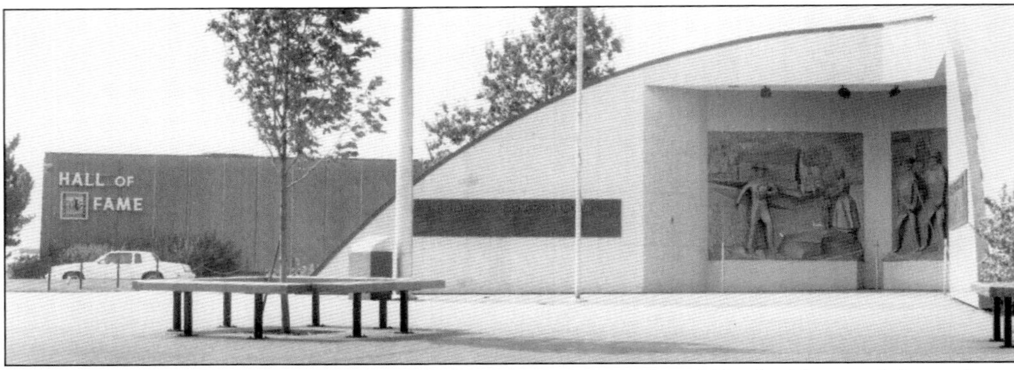

Created by Congress with a rare federal charter on August 31, 1960, the National Agricultural Center & Hall of Fame is located on 126th Street, across from the Wyandotte County Park. Even though it was created by a charter, it receives no federal funds and was constructed with donations from the farming community and its suppliers. (Courtesy of WCHS&M.)

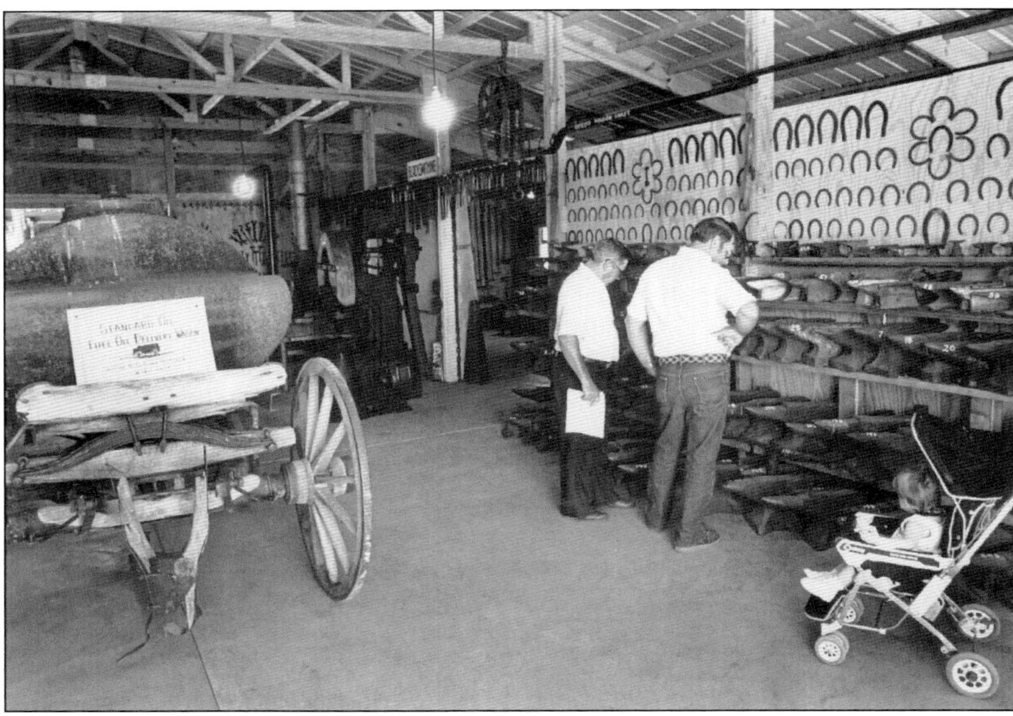

Displays of the history of farming and recognition of Hall of Fame recipients occupy several buildings. A miniature steam railroad carries visitors to the freestanding old schoolhouse, a typical early farmhouse, and other attractions. (Courtesy of WCHS&M.)

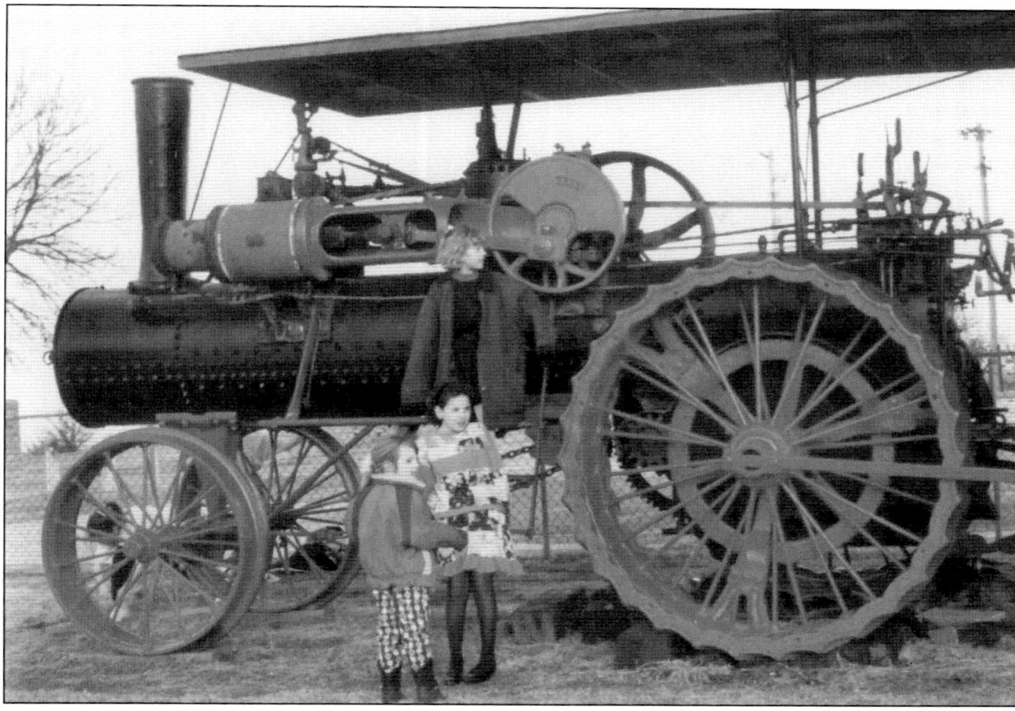

School groups especially enjoy seeing the old steam tractors and the other machinery used in the early days of farming. (Courtesy of WCHS&M.)

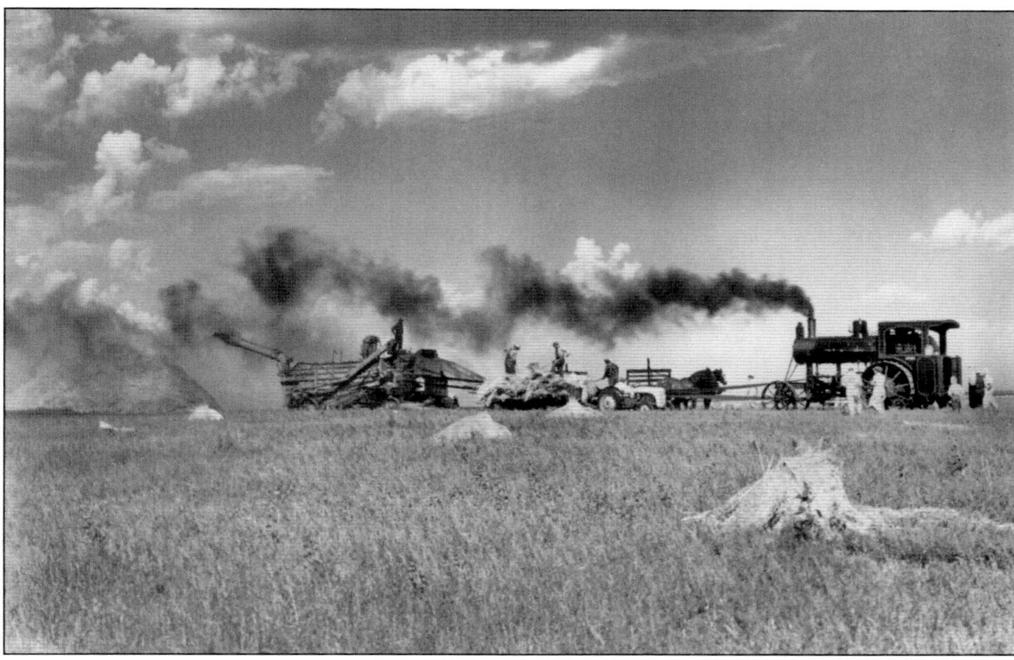

One of the highlights of the National Agricultural Center & Hall of Fame is an old-fashioned threshing bee, using the steam tractors of the day. The event draws many owners of the still-operating machines, who participate for an appreciative crowd of onlookers. (Courtesy of WCHS&M.)

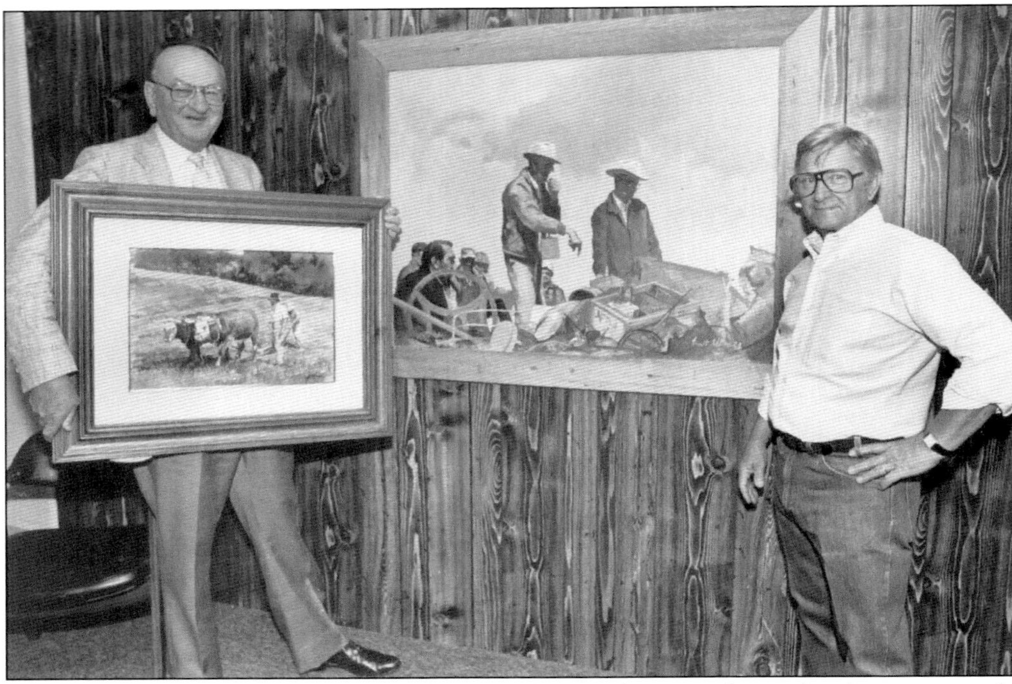

Renowned artist Ernst Ulmer (right) of Bonner Springs donates a farm-related painting to the National Agricultural Center & Hall of Fame. Accepting is Frank Corbett of the board of directors. (Courtesy of WCHS&M.)

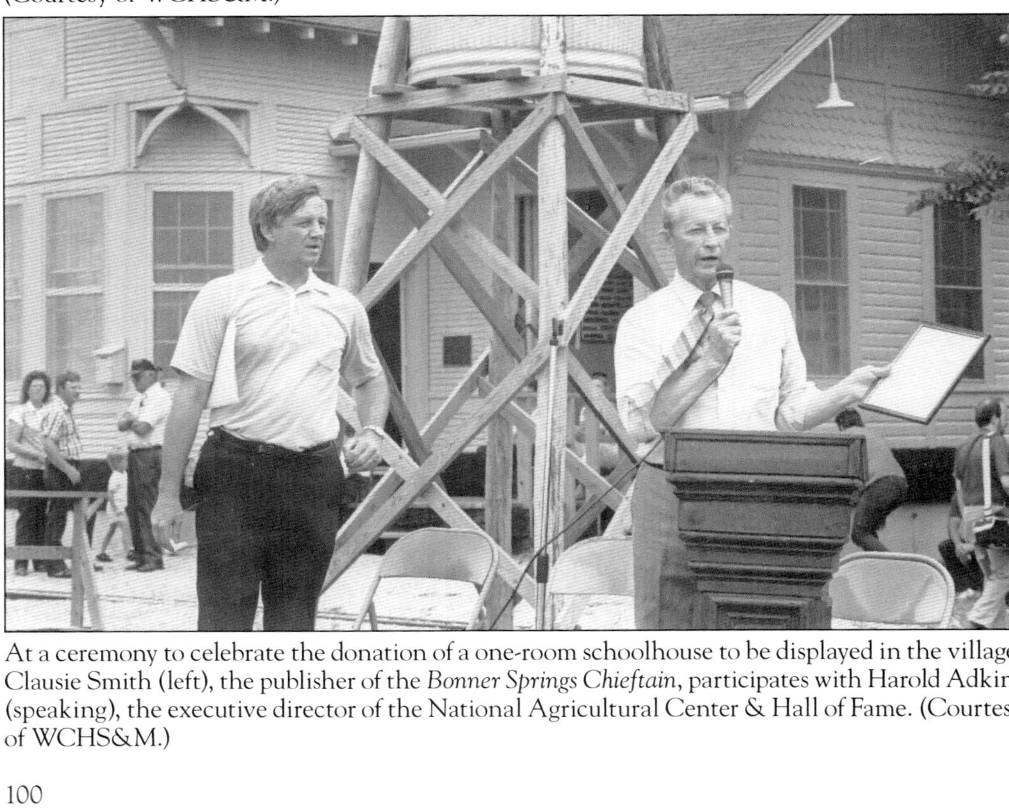

At a ceremony to celebrate the donation of a one-room schoolhouse to be displayed in the village, Clausie Smith (left), the publisher of the *Bonner Springs Chieftain*, participates with Harold Adkins (speaking), the executive director of the National Agricultural Center & Hall of Fame. (Courtesy of WCHS&M.)

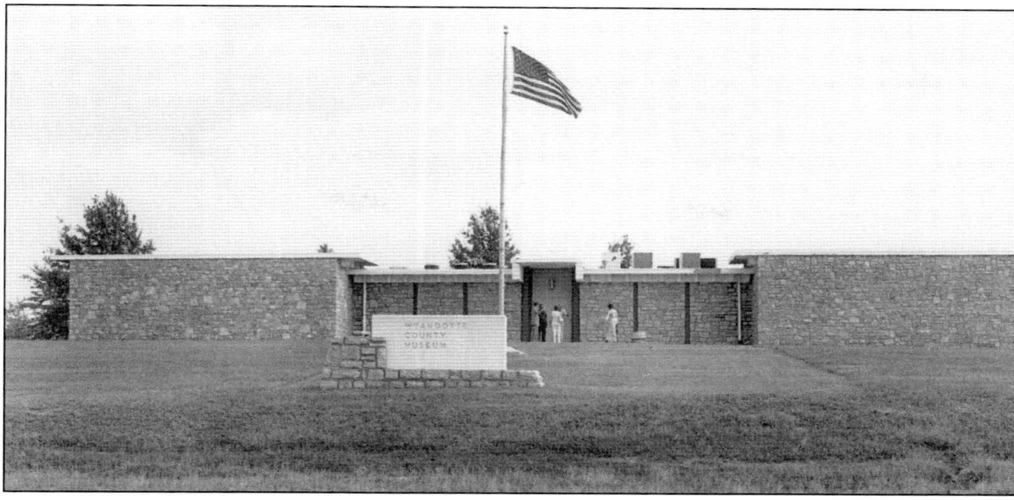

The Wyandotte County Museum is located in Wyandotte County Park and houses collections and displays that focus on the history of the county. The original structure was built in 1964, and the Trowbridge Addition, named for renowned amateur archaeologist Harry Trowbridge, was added later. (Courtesy of WCHS&M.)

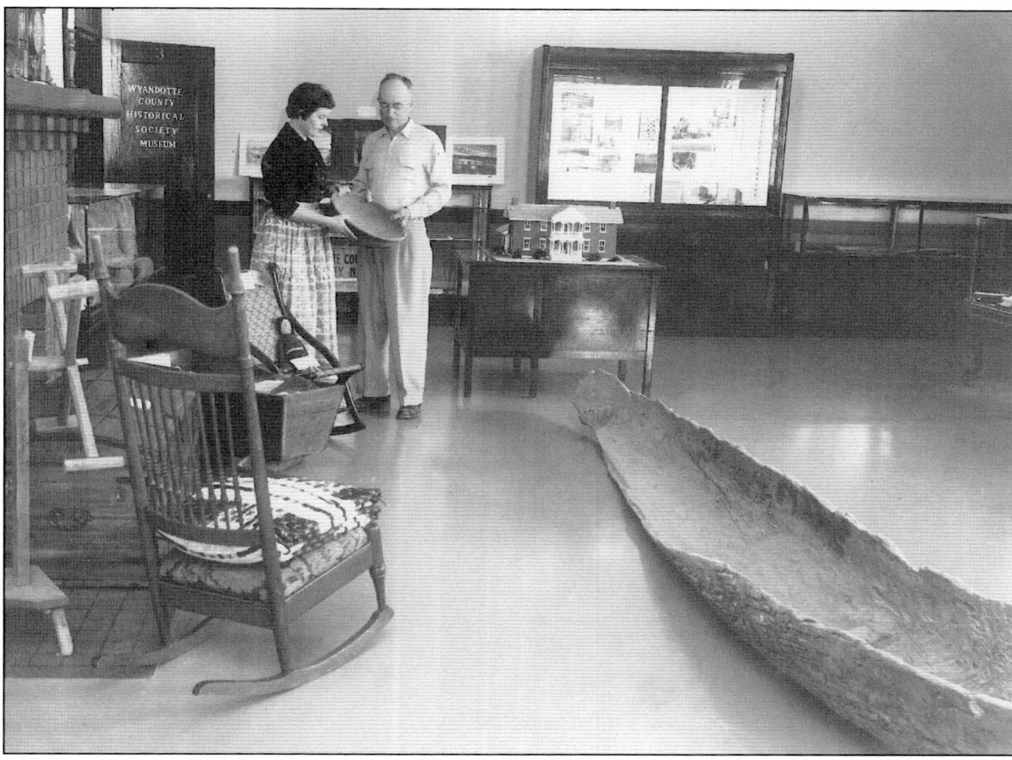

The Wyandotte County Historical Society, under the leadership of Virginia Glandon (left), was given space on the second floor of Memorial Hall in Kansas City, Kansas, for the start of a museum. Artifacts had already been donated, especially by Harry Trowbridge (right), who had discovered remnants of a Hopewell culture settlement on his farm in Wyandotte County. The dugout canoe on the floor was uncovered at the mouth of the Kansas River. (Courtesy of WCHS&M.)

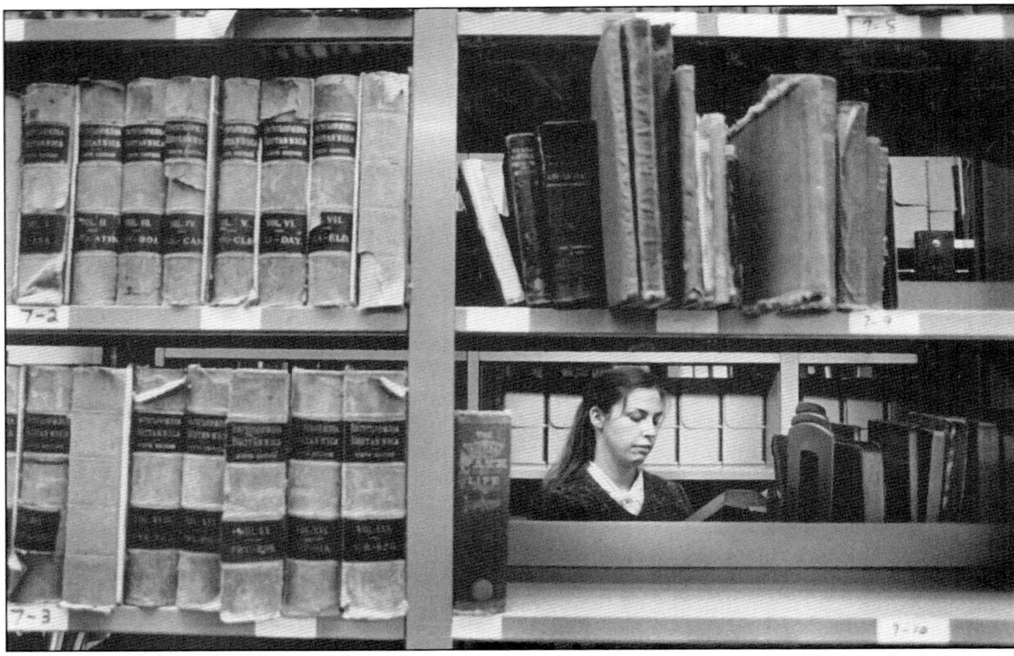

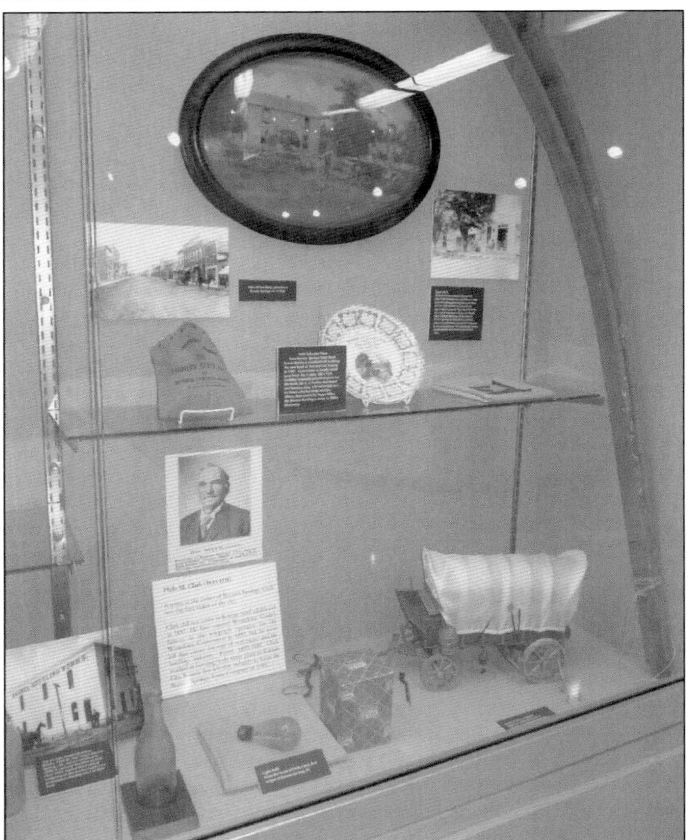

The museum has an extensive collection of records, books, maps, photographs, and newspapers that assist researchers seeking information on history, genealogy, cemeteries, or almost anything pertaining to the past of Wyandotte County. (Courtesy of WCHS&M.)

Bonner Springs is featured in this display, which includes artifacts from the bottling works and other businesses as well as a history of the town.

The museum recently underwent an upgrade of many of its displays, and this medicine man costume is an example of the detail involved. The costume was authentically made, using early methods to tan the hide, dye the feathers, and sew the beading.

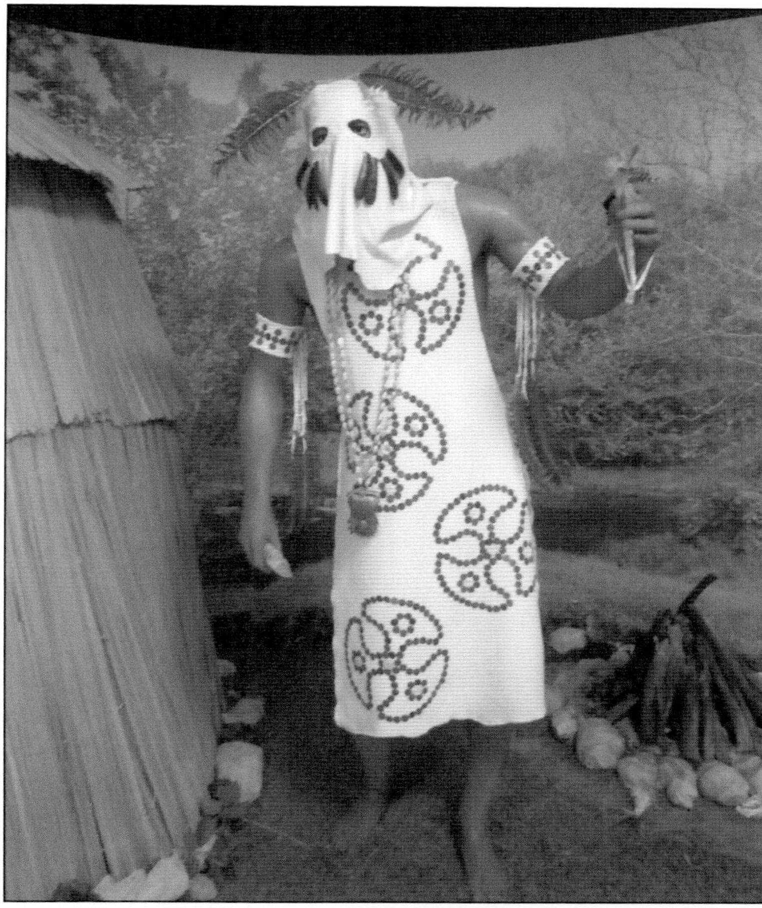

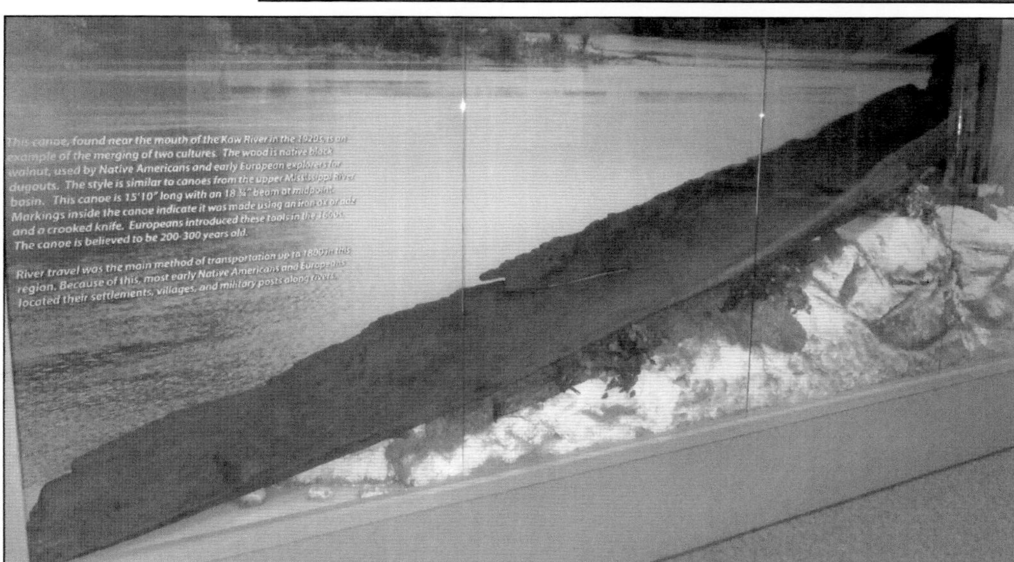

This dugout canoe is displayed in another authentic setting, along with panels of explanation.

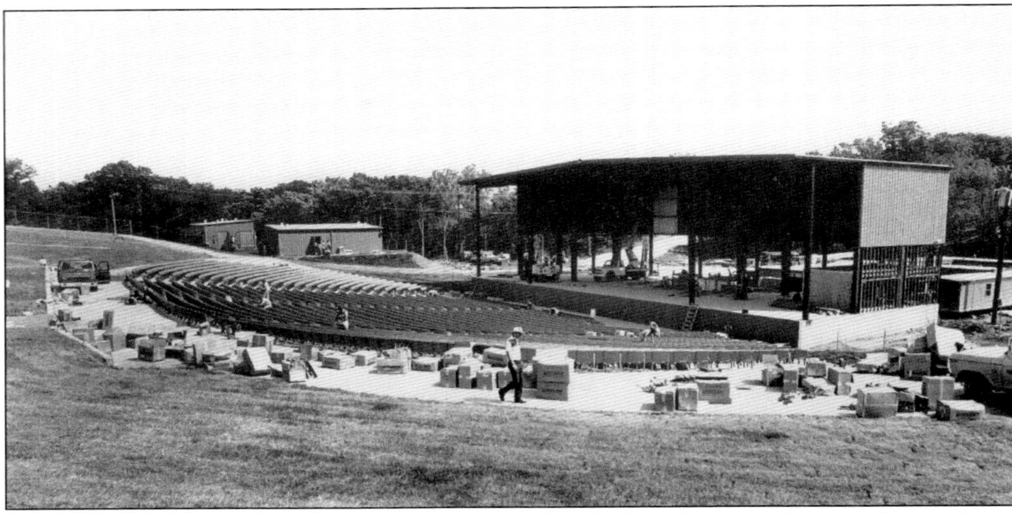

One of the benefits of the city's annexation endeavors in the 1970s was the availability of open land for housing and recreational opportunities. Sandstone (now Cricket Wireless) Amphitheater was conceived to provide a concert setting surrounded by the natural flora and fauna. It was built in 1984. (Courtesy of WCHS&M.)

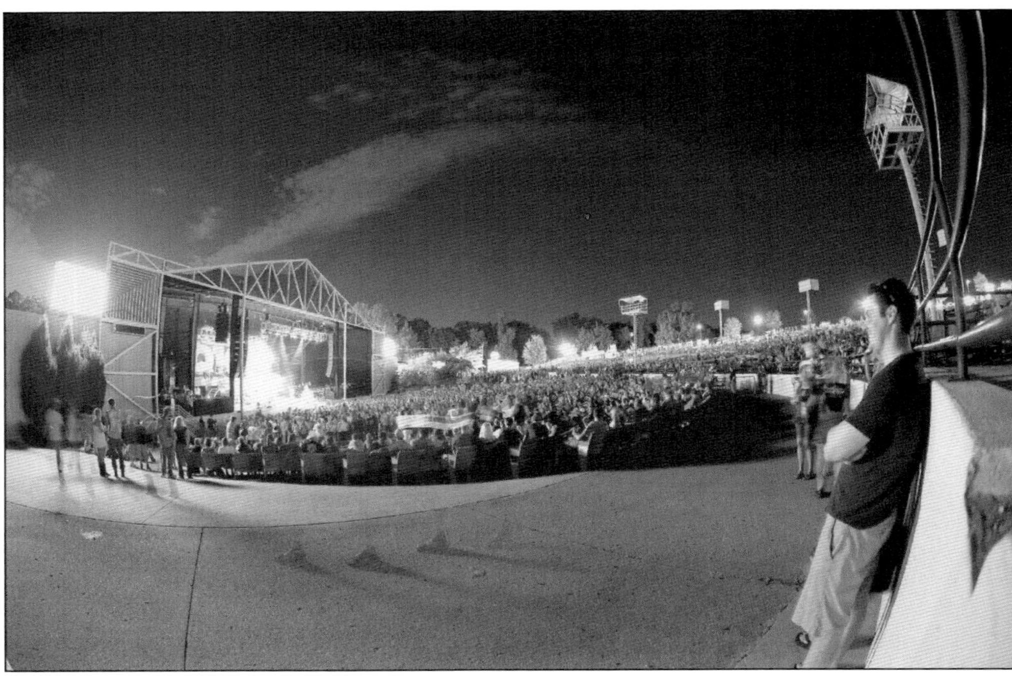

A big crowd enjoys a concert at Cricket Wireless Amphitheater. The capacity for concerts is 18,000, with 3,100 seats and boxes. The remainder of the crowd sits on the sloping ground. (Photograph by Paul'luc Chokota, courtesy of Cricket Wireless Amphitheater.)

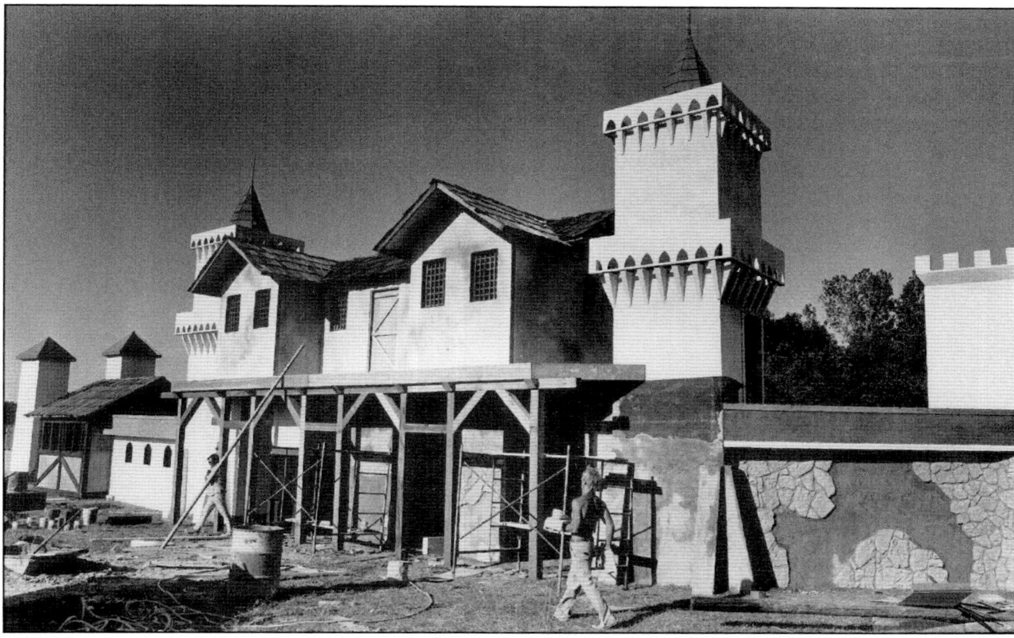

The Kansas City Arts Institute leased land north of the National Agricultural Center & Hall of Fame and began building a site to be used for a Renaissance festival. From a modest beginning in the fall of 1976, it has grown into a 16-acre area with permanent buildings and 13 stages. (Courtesy of WCHS&M.)

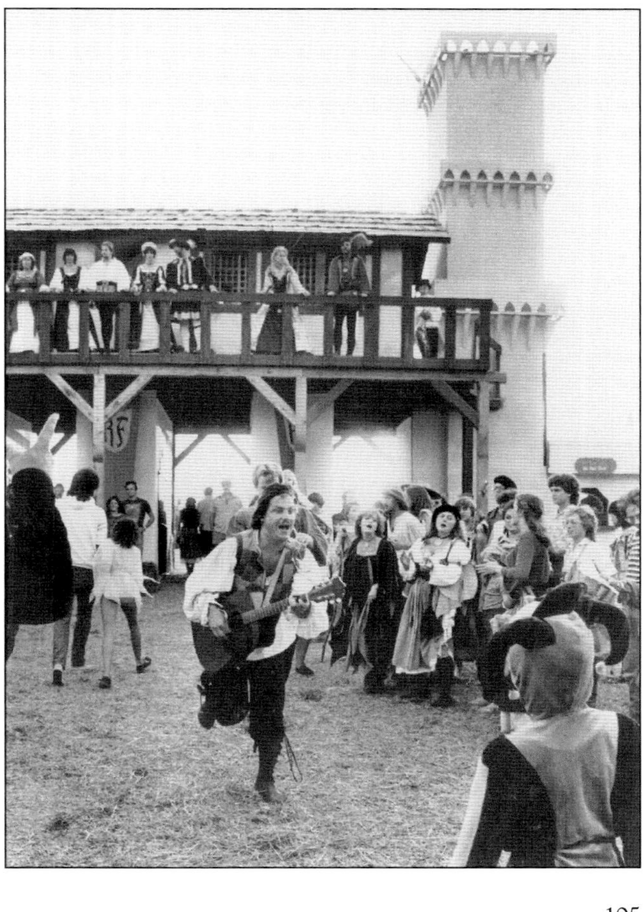

The Kansas City Renaissance Festival is held on weekends beginning on Labor Day weekend and ending in mid-October. More than 100 performers participate, providing everything from face-painting to fencing and jousting to juggling. Among the various foods available is the turkey leg, which has been a mainstay from the start. (Courtesy of WCHS&M.)

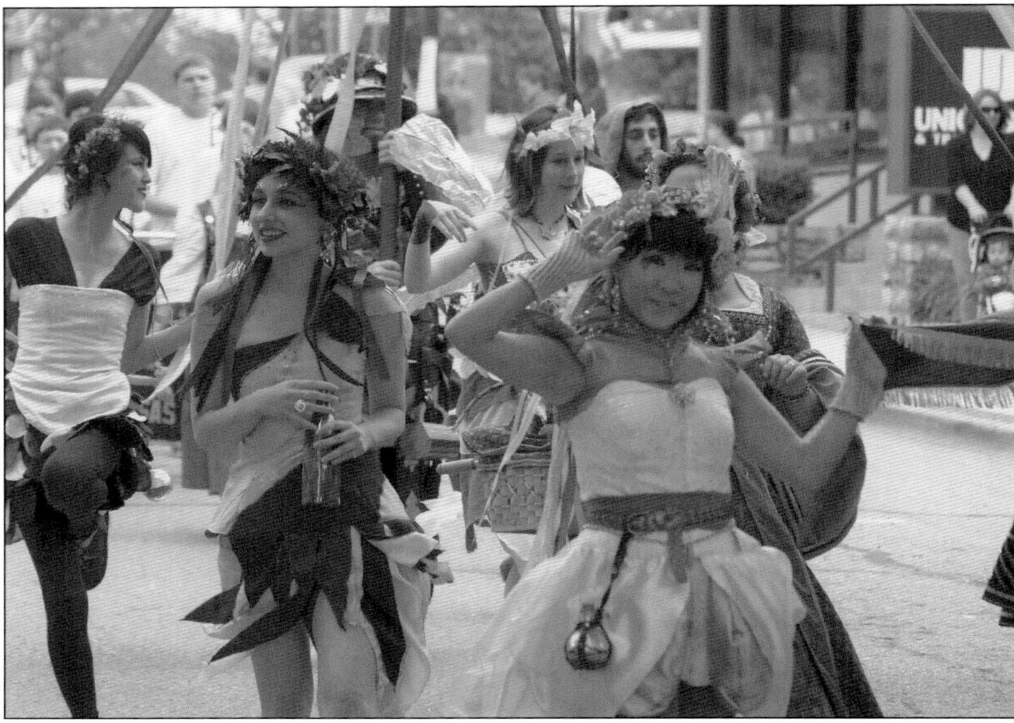

Performers from the Renaissance festival parade down Oak Street at the Marble Days parade. This event, which started recently, encourages downtown merchants to offer fun events and games at their businesses to attract children. (Courtesy of City of Bonner Springs.)

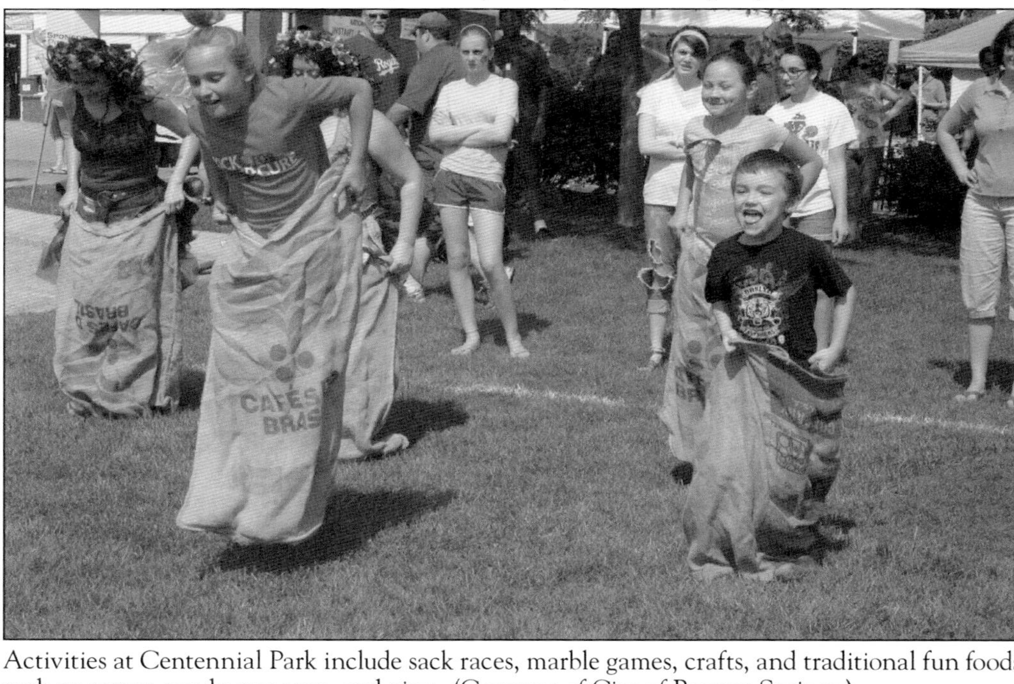

Activities at Centennial Park include sack races, marble games, crafts, and traditional fun foods such as cotton candy, popcorn, and pizza. (Courtesy of City of Bonner Springs.)

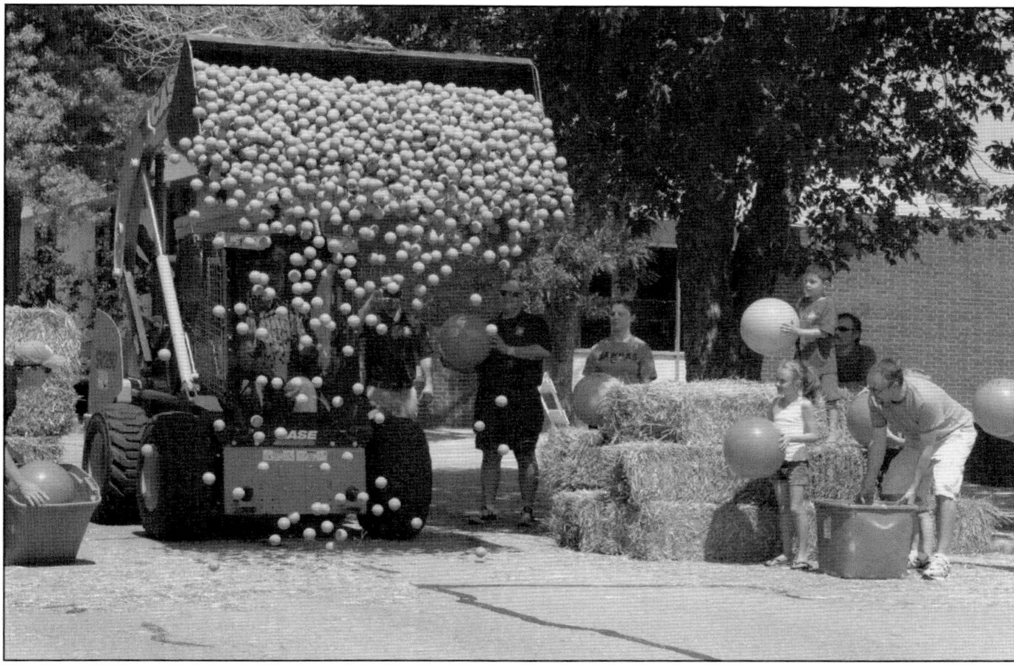

The highlight of Marble Days is the Running of the Pinkies, in which numbered pink balls are purchased from local merchants, with the proceeds going to a chosen charity. A maze is constructed on Oak Street with hay bales, buckets, and other obstacles. The balls are unloaded, as seen here, and off they go down the street. The first few through the gate at the bottom are the winners.

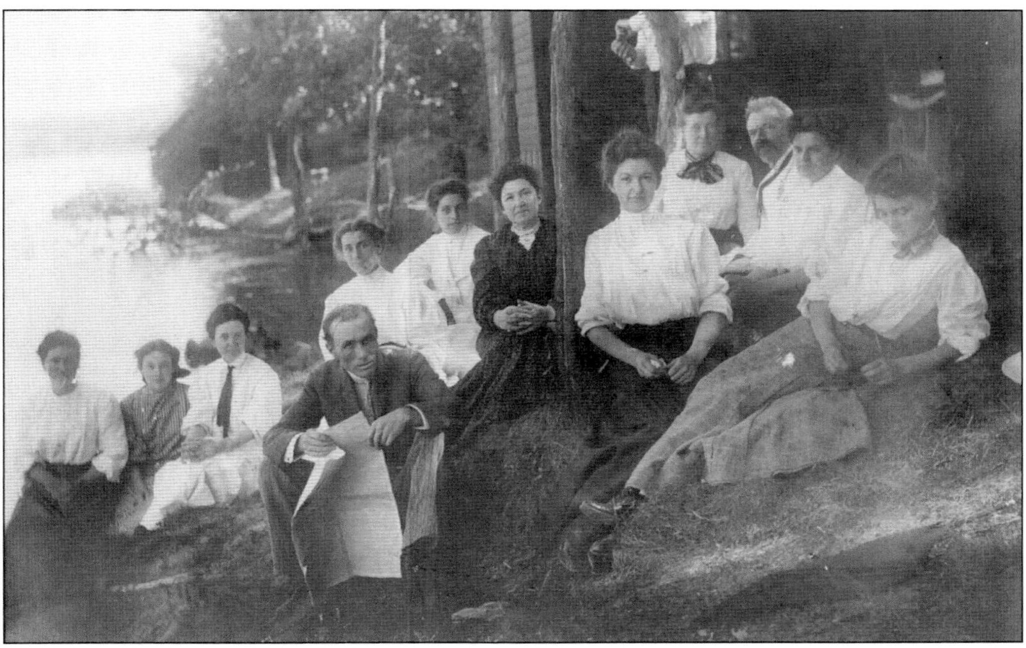

It would be hard to imagine this group of picnickers chasing "pinkies" down Oak Street; in their day, this type of relaxation was the norm.

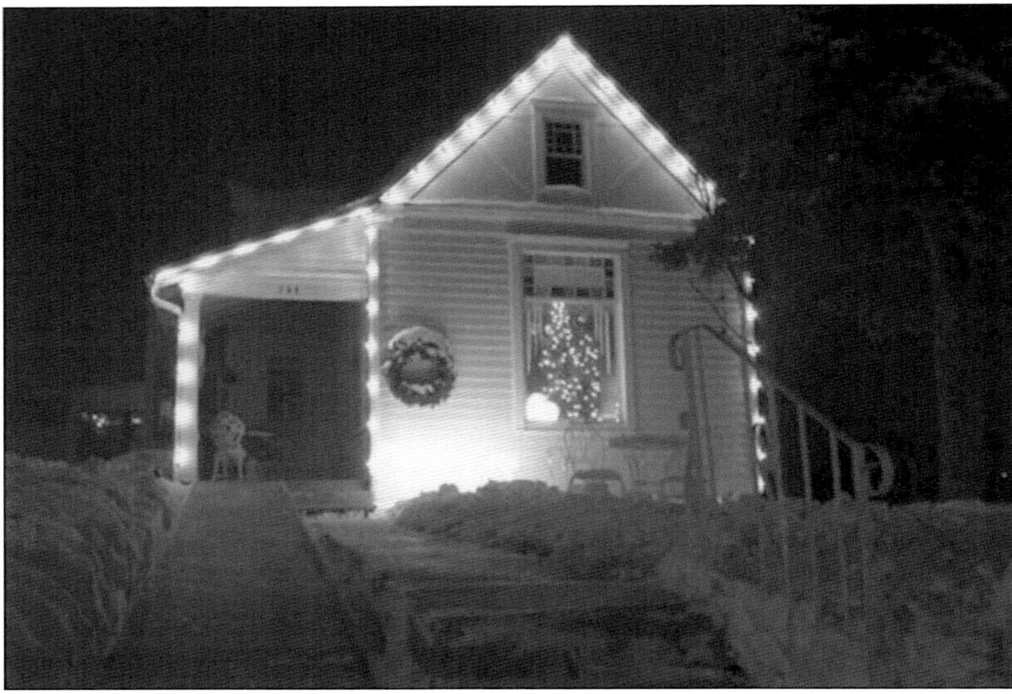

For years, the chamber of commerce has sponsored a Christmas lighting contest for both homes and businesses. While this home was probably not a winner, it is an early example of decorating for the season.

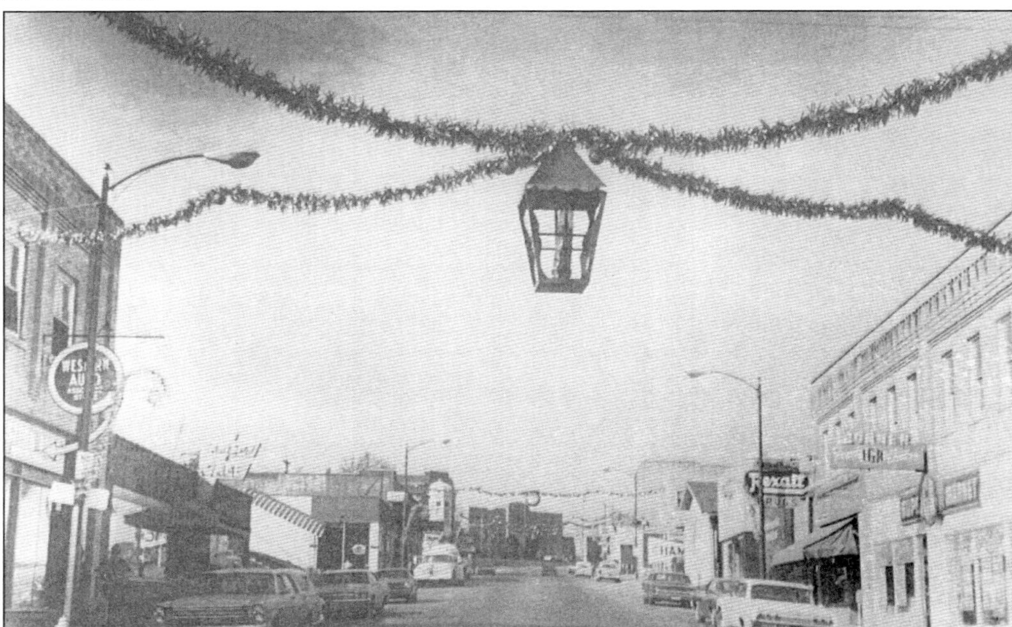

The Jaycees started lighting the downtown area in the late 1960s, and an early example of their work is seen here. The city has taken that responsibility now, and lights are hung along Oak and Front Streets during the Christmas season.

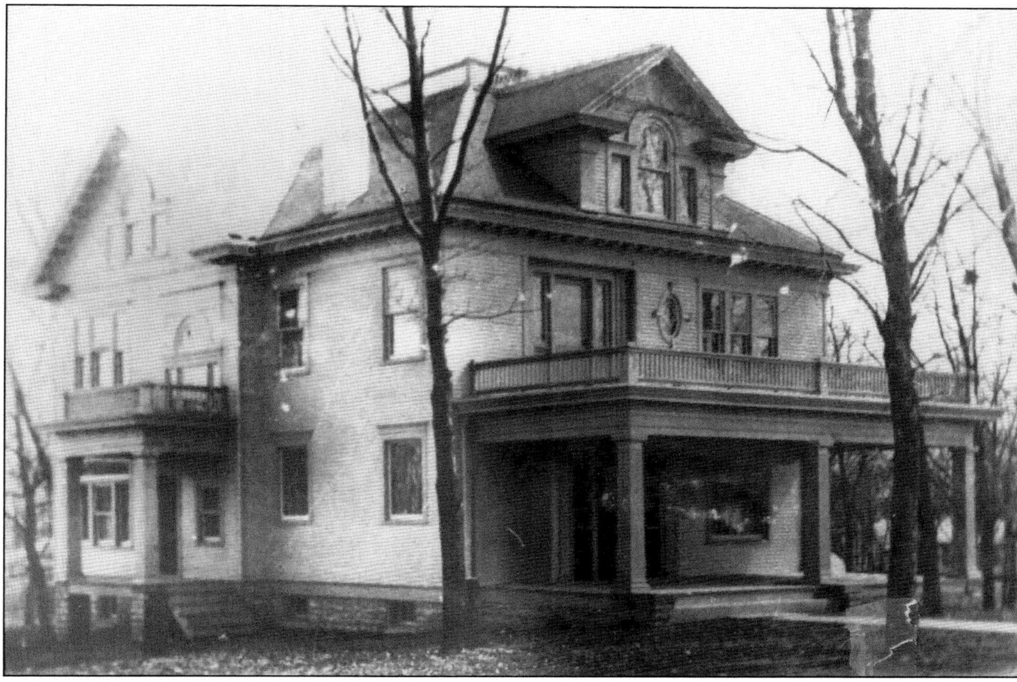

Many of the homes in Bonner Springs are over 100 years old, including this house, at 201 South Nettleton Avenue, seen here in 1908.

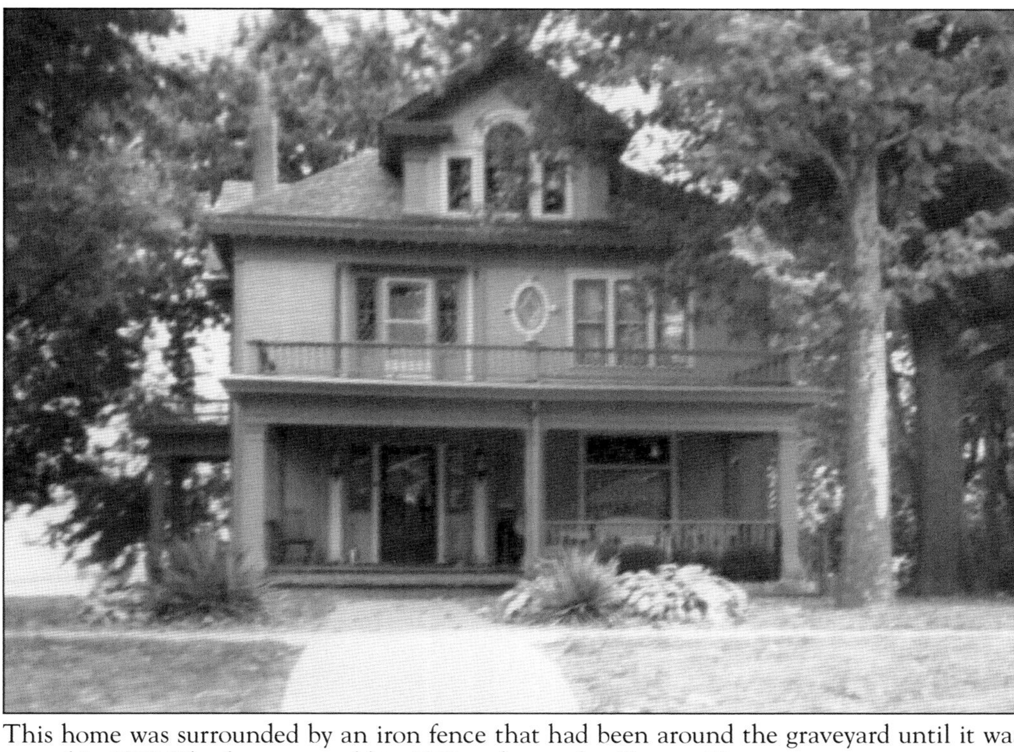

This home was surrounded by an iron fence that had been around the graveyard until it was moved in 1910. The fence was sold in 1967 and moved to Kansas City.

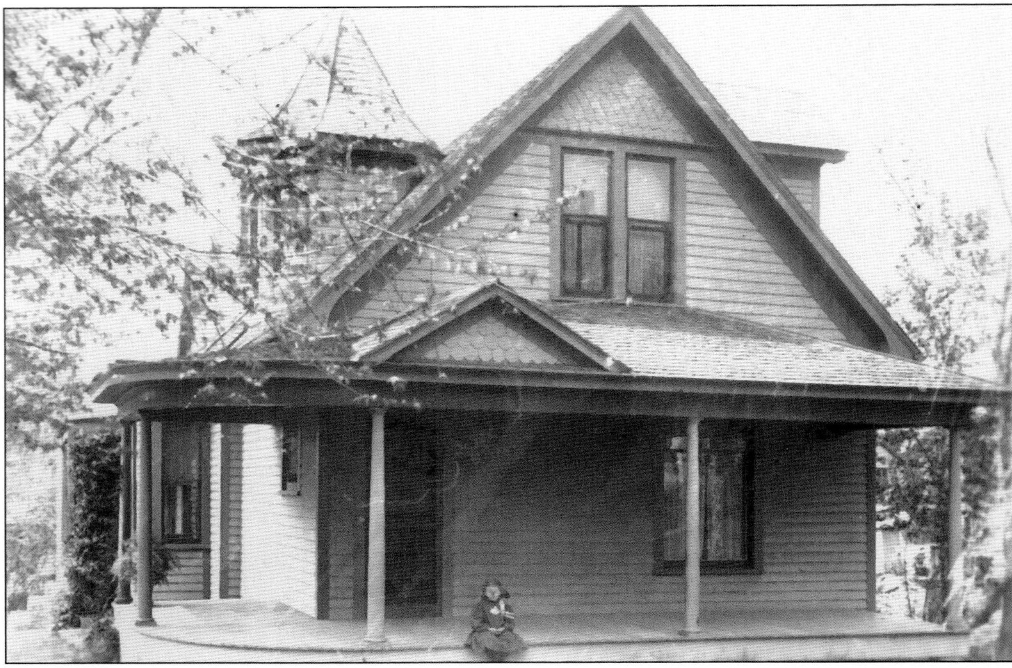

The John Kuhn home, at 126 Allcutt Street, is seen here in 1907. A youngster sits sedately on the front porch, waiting for the photograph to be taken.

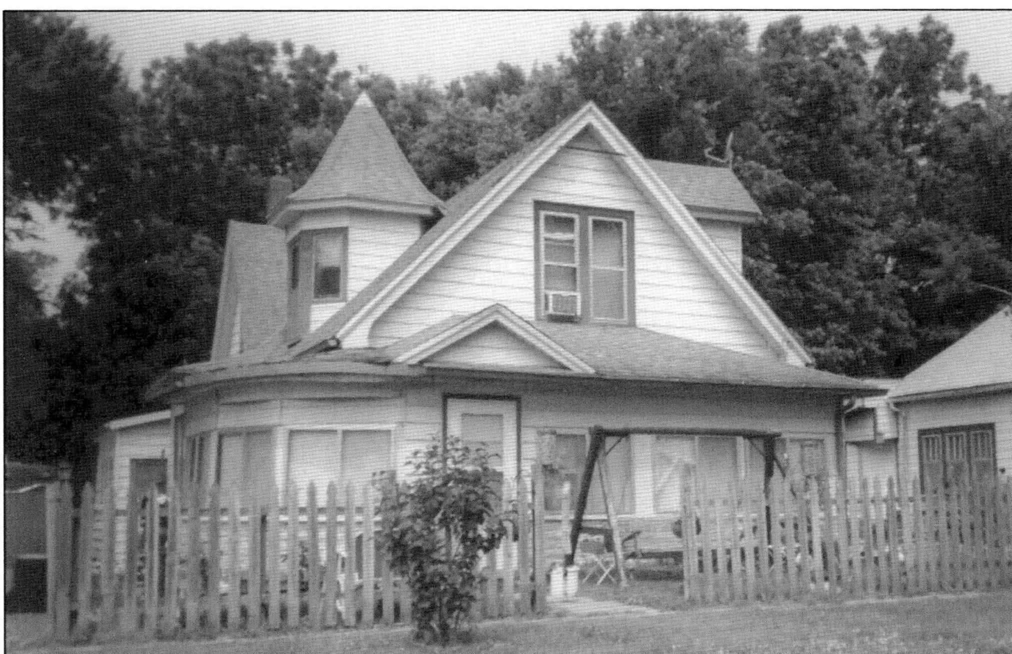

The John Kuhn home has had its porch enclosed, but otherwise it is still in its original state today. It is seen here more than 100 years after this photograph was taken.

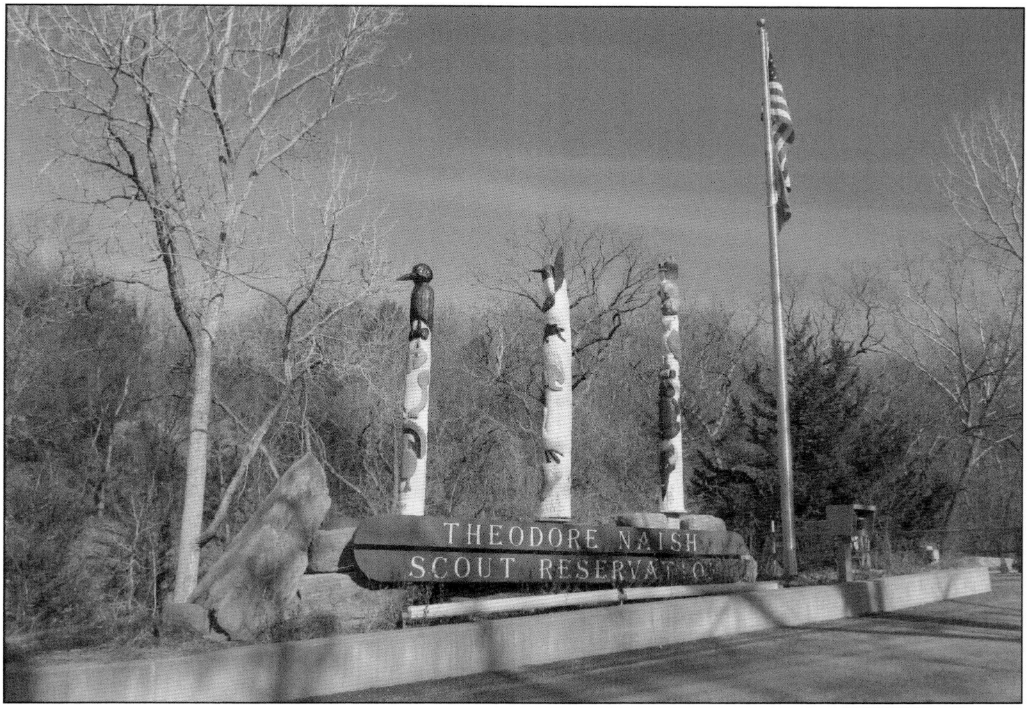

In 1920, Belle, the widow of Theodore Naish, who died on the *Lusitania*, donated over 100 acres of land to the Boy Scouts of America. The Scouts created Camp Naish, located east of the cement plant in Bonner Springs. Since then, more than a million Scouts have spent weekends or summers at the camp.

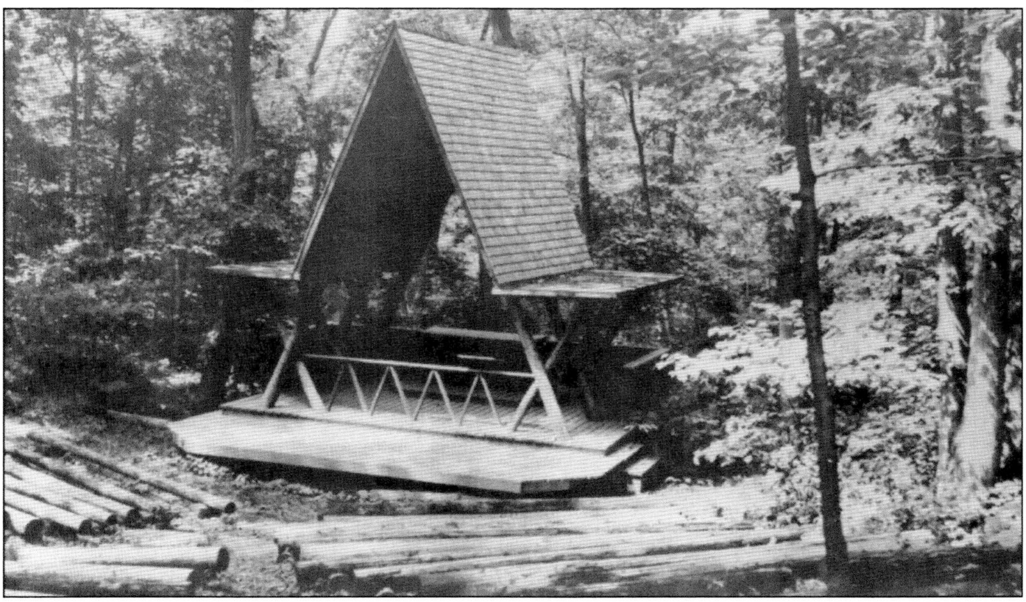

This chapel was one of the first buildings at Camp Naish. Until cabins were constructed, the Scouts camped out in tents, as many still do as they complete the requirements to get their camping merit badges.

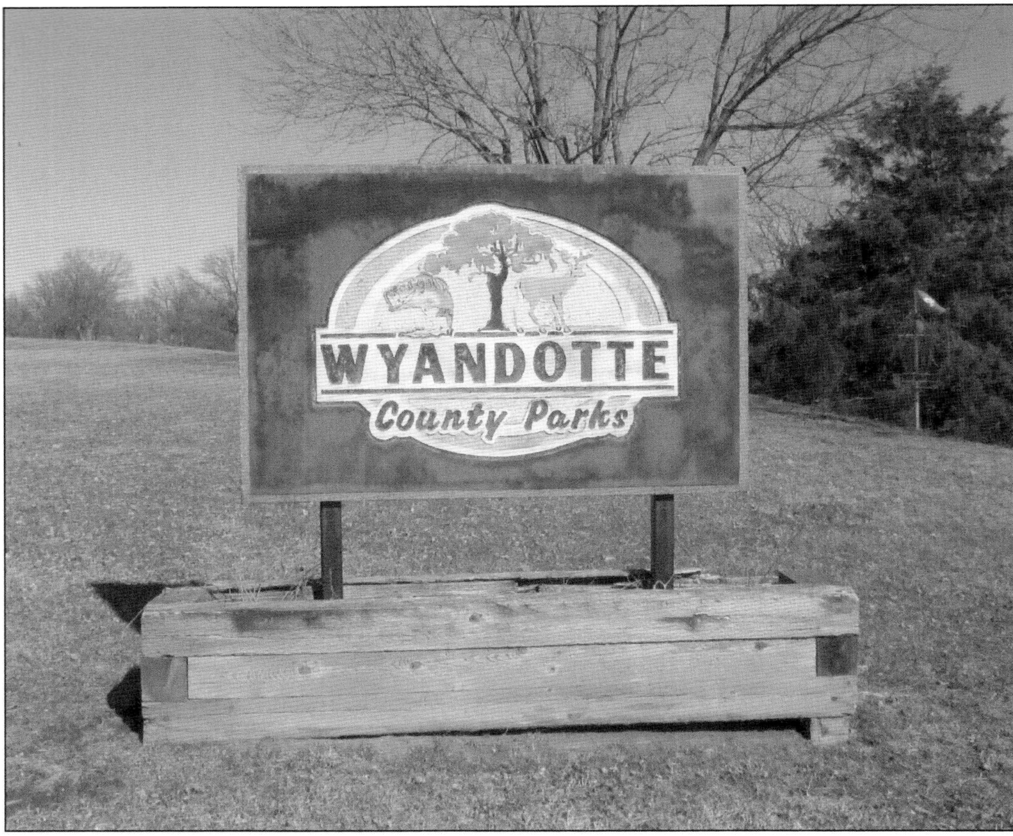

Wyandotte County Park is located in Bonner Springs but is managed by the Unified Government of Wyandotte County. Besides numerous picnic areas with A-frame structures, the park also includes tennis courts, soccer fields, a skateboarding area, a disc golf course, a model airplane flying area, and baseball diamonds. The George Meyn Community Center hosts many community events.

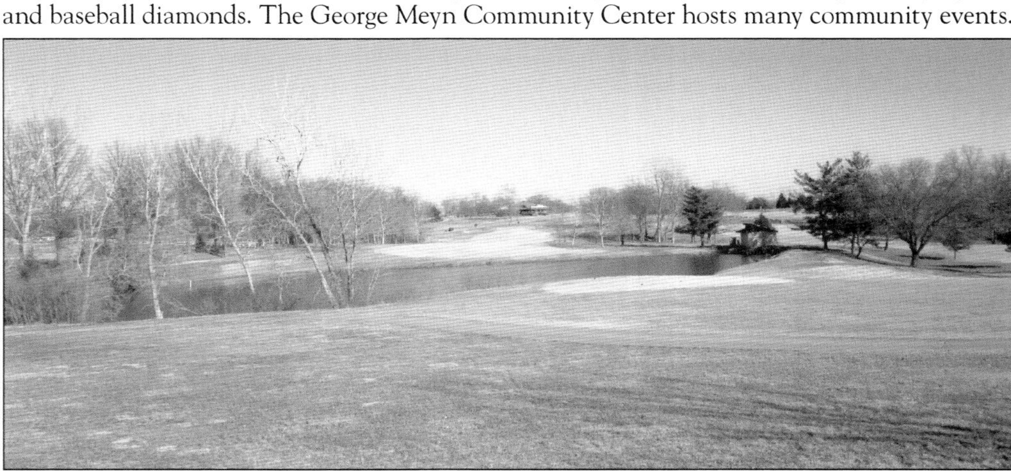

Sunflower Hills Golf Course is also a part of the Wyandotte County Park. It opened in May 1977 and has proven to be a challenge to golfers of all abilities. It hosts many tournaments and has a senior league and a ladies league. This view looks down the 18th fairway towards the clubhouse. Driving over water is one of the many obstacles encountered at Sunflower Hills.

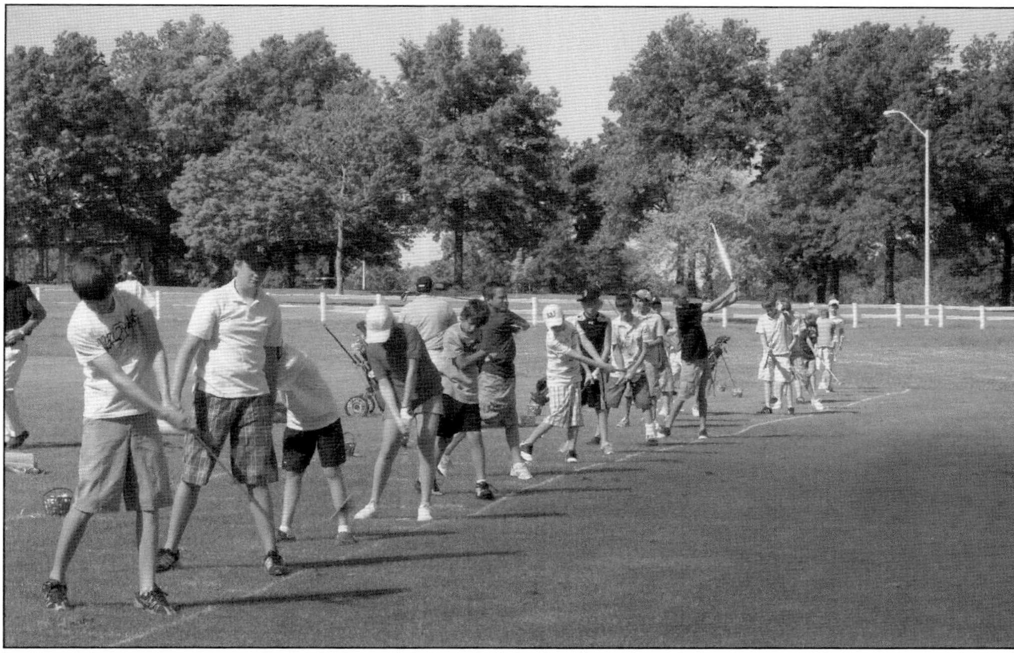

The First Tee is an organization that teaches golf to youngsters, including the kids practicing here. Golf equipment and instruction is offered free to those enrolled. They have their own golf course within the park, with six shorter holes that still have regulation greens. (Courtesy of Sunflower Hills Golf Course.)

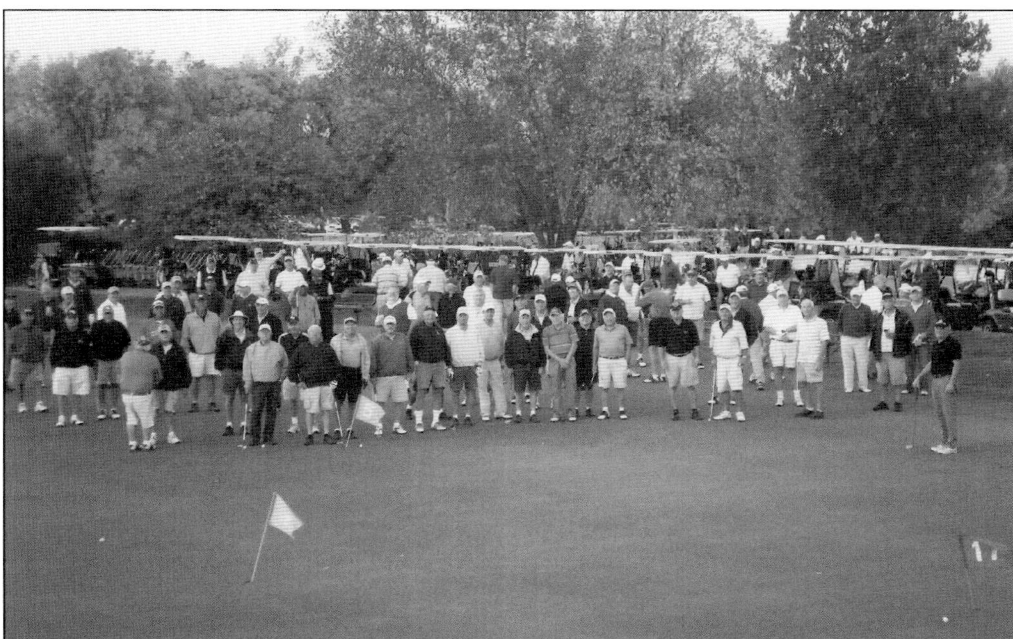

This group of golfers is ready for the tournament about to start. Over 32,000 rounds of golf are played yearly, which makes Sunflower Hills one of the busiest public courses in the area. (Courtesy of Sunflower Hills Golf Course.)

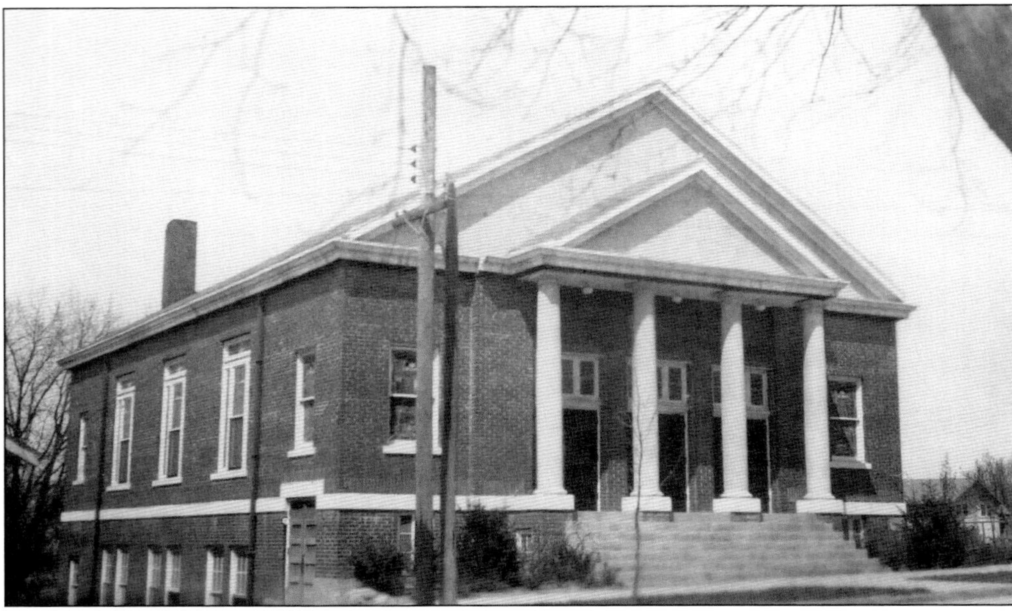

The Christian church erected its third building in 1927 to replace the 1902 structure across the street on Nettleton Avenue. It burned in December 1969, and, during the building of their fourth church, the congregation met in the Methodist church.

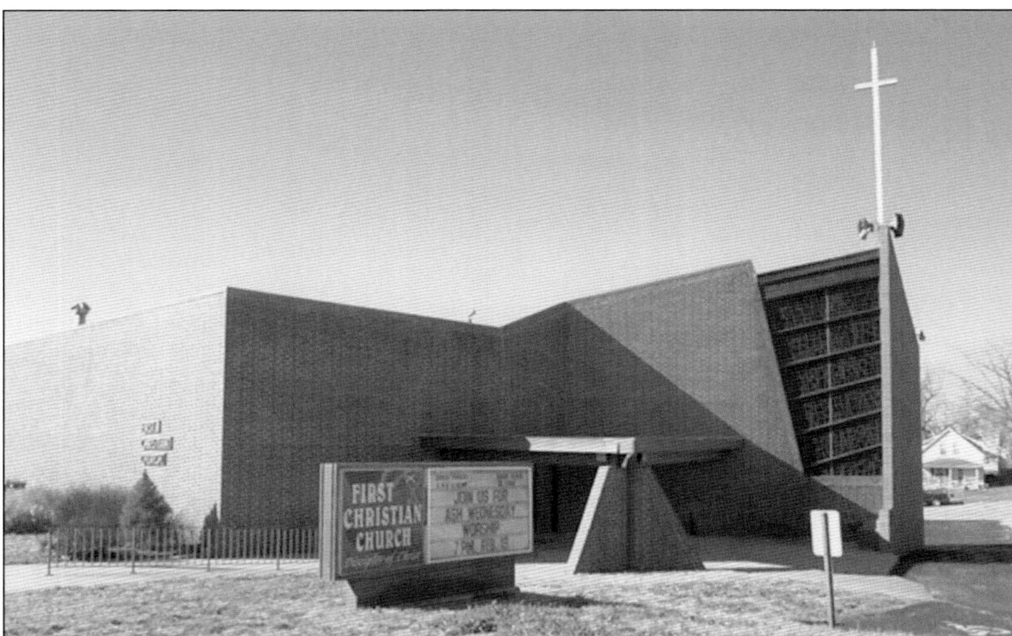

This more modern structure replaced the third church and still hosts the congregation today.

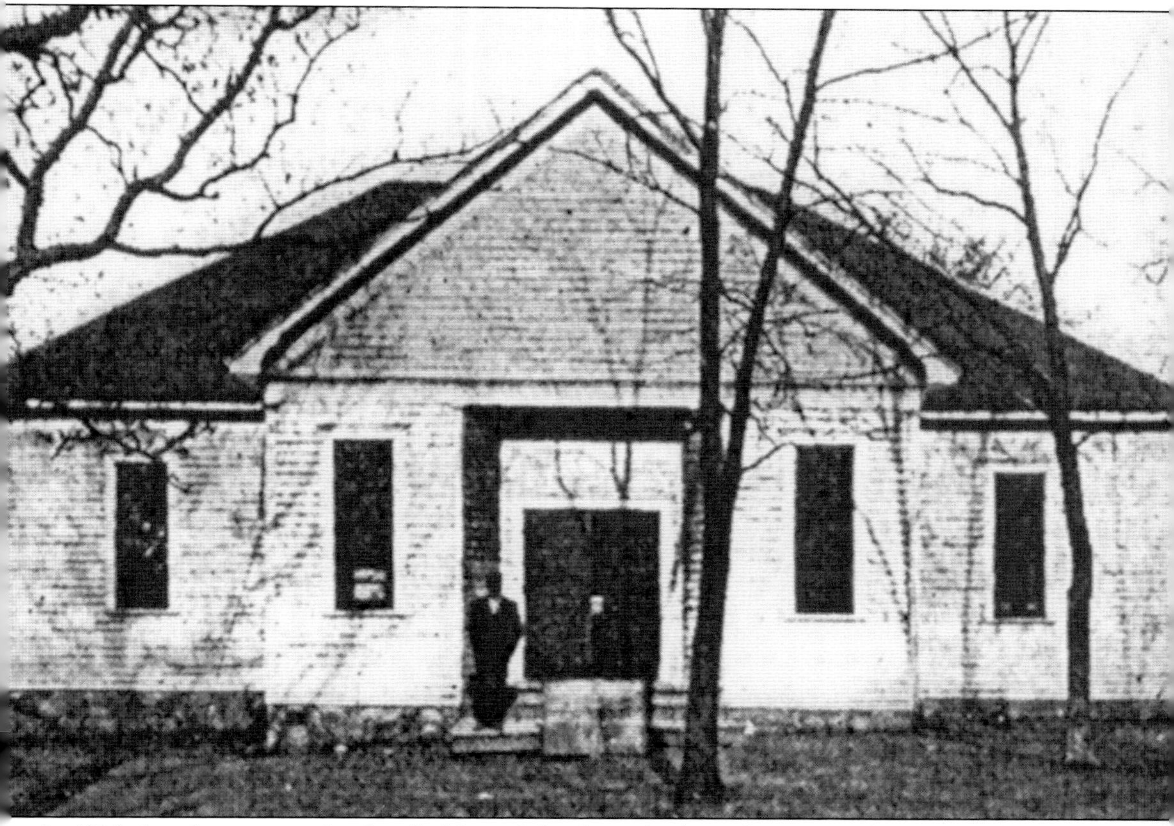

In 1905, this elementary school, called Pratt School, was built on the corner of Neconi and Pratt Avenues. African American parents did not send their children to the school, so the high school and eighth grades were assigned to the building. In October 1905, Afican American parents voted to use the building, so the eighth-grade and high school students were moved, and 33 African American students were enrolled. The school was renamed Lincoln School. Wilma Johnson was the principal from 1905 until 1949. In 1941, a total of 60 students were enrolled, with three teachers—Wilma Johnson, Lonetta Groves, and Gladys Lewis. There were 18 African American students enrolled in the high school. In 1946, Lincoln School was destroyed by fire and replaced by a new building, called Northwest School. In 1958, the elementary school system was desegregated, and the students attended Southwest School, McDanield School, and Northwest School.

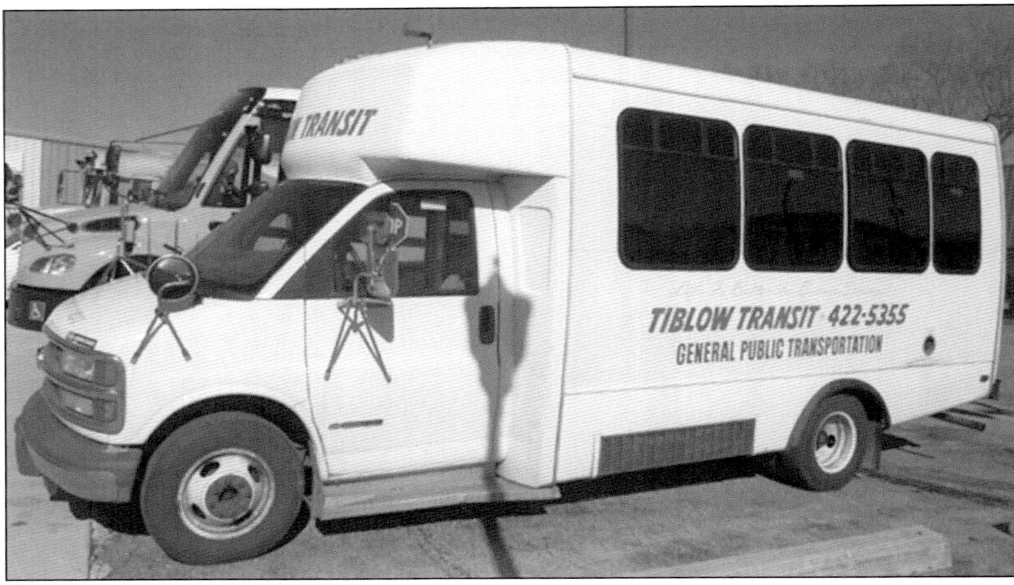

Public transportation is provided by the city, with a fleet of vehicles called Tiblow Transit. Seniors ride free, and others pay a minimal amount per ride. The vehicles are on an on-call basis, but there are scheduled trips to surrounding area attractions. The city slogan, "Life is Better in Bonner Springs," adorns each vehicle.

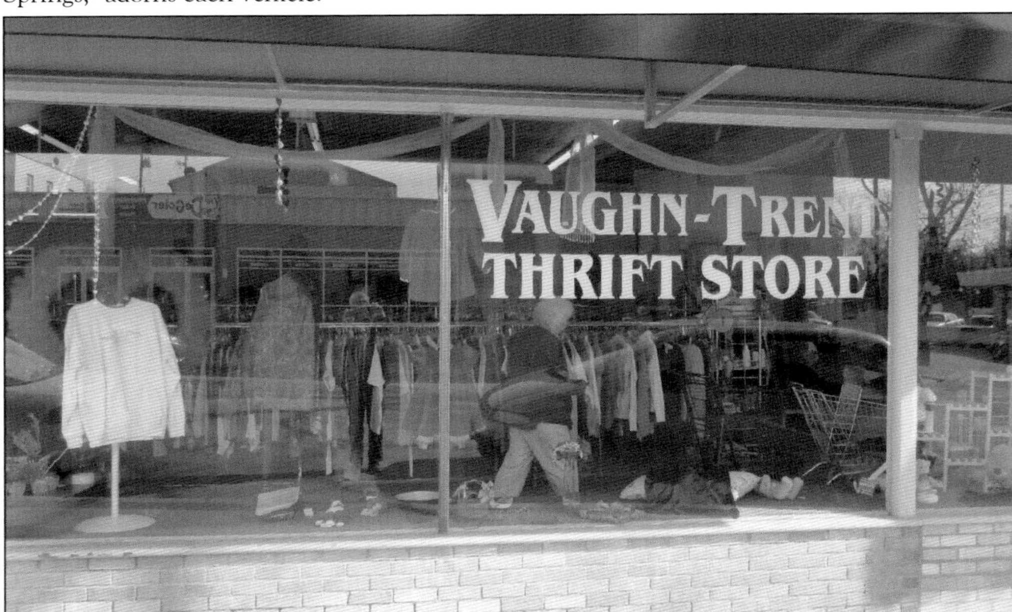

Vaughn-Trent Community Services was officially organized in 1989, but it has been active in the community since 1965, with the start of the traditional Christmas baskets, filled with food, that are still given to over 200 families in the Bonner Springs Unified School District. The center has a food pantry that provides staples for qualified residents, as well as help with utility payments and other emergencies. The 99-percent volunteer organization operates this thrift store at 205 Oak Street, which provides some help with funding.

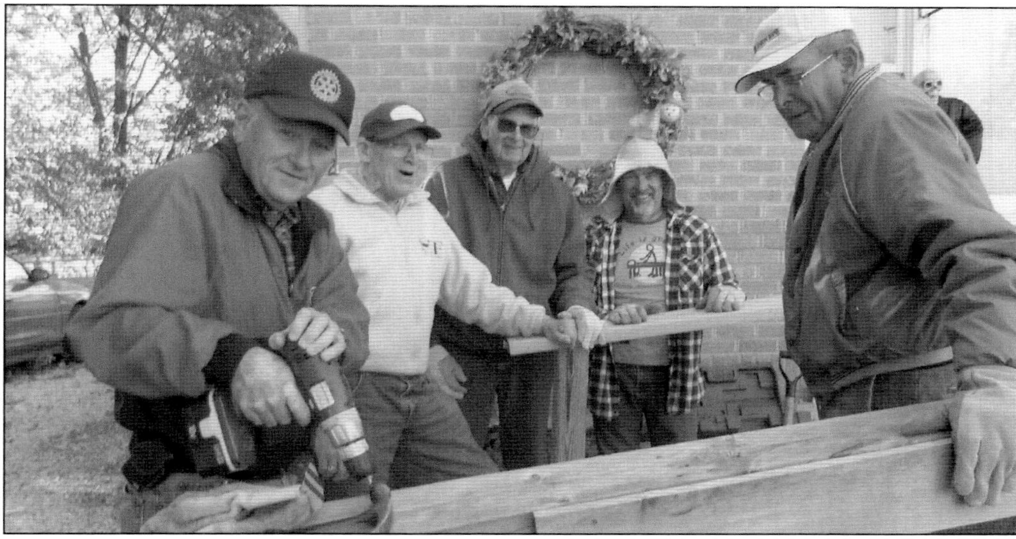

Bonner Springs has several active service organizations. The Rotary Club, founded in 1936 in Bonner Springs, conducts a variety of projects that benefit the community. Here, members help renovate a home during the Christmas in October project. Pictured, from left to right, are Del Coleman, Mike Miller, Darrel Donahue, Bill Miller, and Al Ramirez. The club also sponsored the Tiblow Trot, a 5K race that was held during Tiblow Days for 35 years. An annual Christmas auction raises money for Vaughn-Trent. Bonner Springs High School students are honored and awarded college scholarships each year at the scholarship banquet. The Kiwanis and Optimist Clubs are also active with community projects.

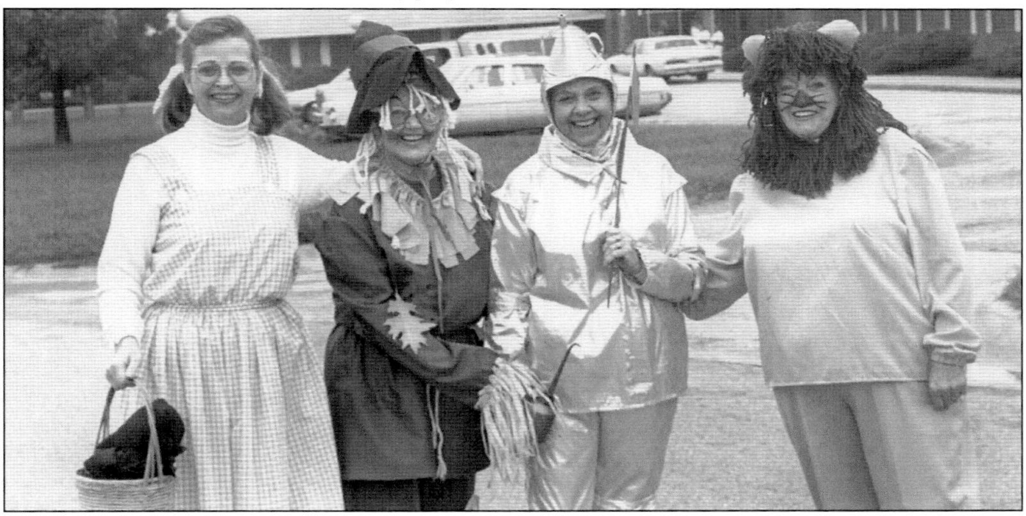

The Bonner Springs Business and Professional Women organization was founded in 1945. One of its earlier projects, named Fairesta, was a fundraising lawn party for the entire community. Besides offering educational programs for their members, the group also provides college scholarships to graduating seniors. These members are ready for a *Wizard of Oz* skit at a local nursing home. They are, from left to right, Donna Wallace, Kay Shevling, Caroline Summers, and Bernice Scheidt. The local organization has provided leadership on the state level, with Debe Birzer, Jane Hanks, Julie Smith, and Susan Roberts all serving as state presidents. (Courtesy of Bonner Springs Business and Professional Women.)

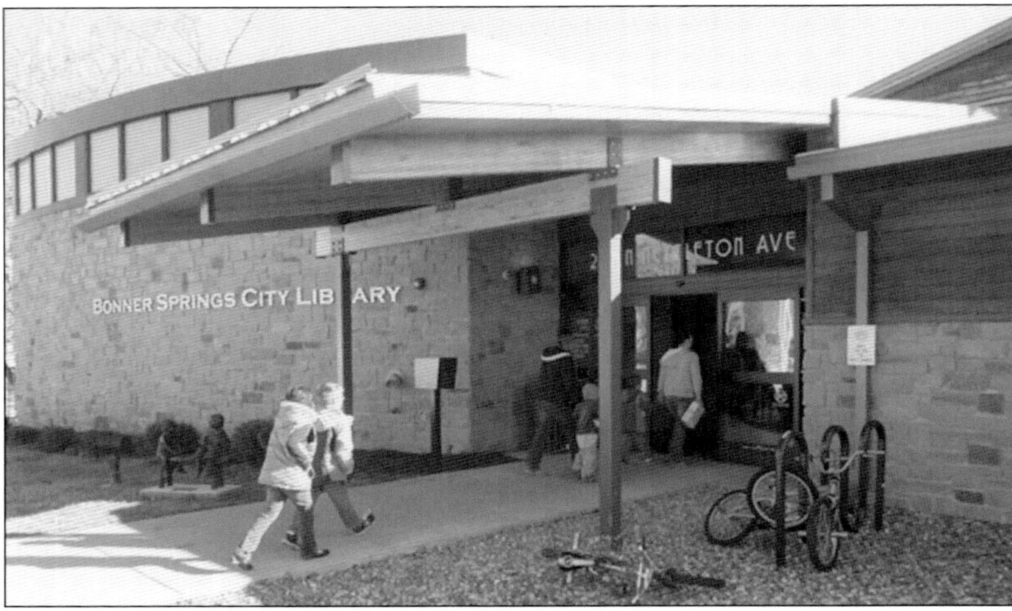

Seeing the need for a larger library, Bonner Springs citizens approved a $3 million bond issue to build a new facility. The city already owned the site of the former Sacred Heart Church, school, and rectory, in the 200 block of North Nettleton Avenue, which proved to be an ideal location. With community input, plans were approved, and construction was completed in July 2009. The library houses 40,000 items available for checkout. The Friends of the Library oversees the used bookstore and sponsors programs with visiting authors.

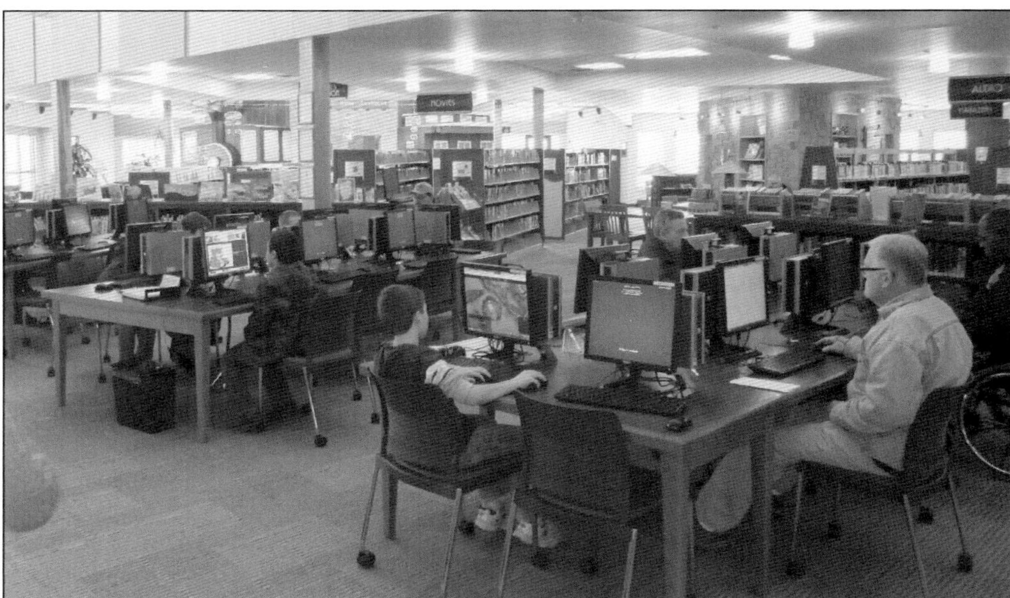

The library features 26 computers, which are in constant use. There are also quiet reading areas and a special children's nook. The Kansas Room houses books relating to Kansas and offers access to every issue of the *Chieftain* newspaper from its beginning in 1896.

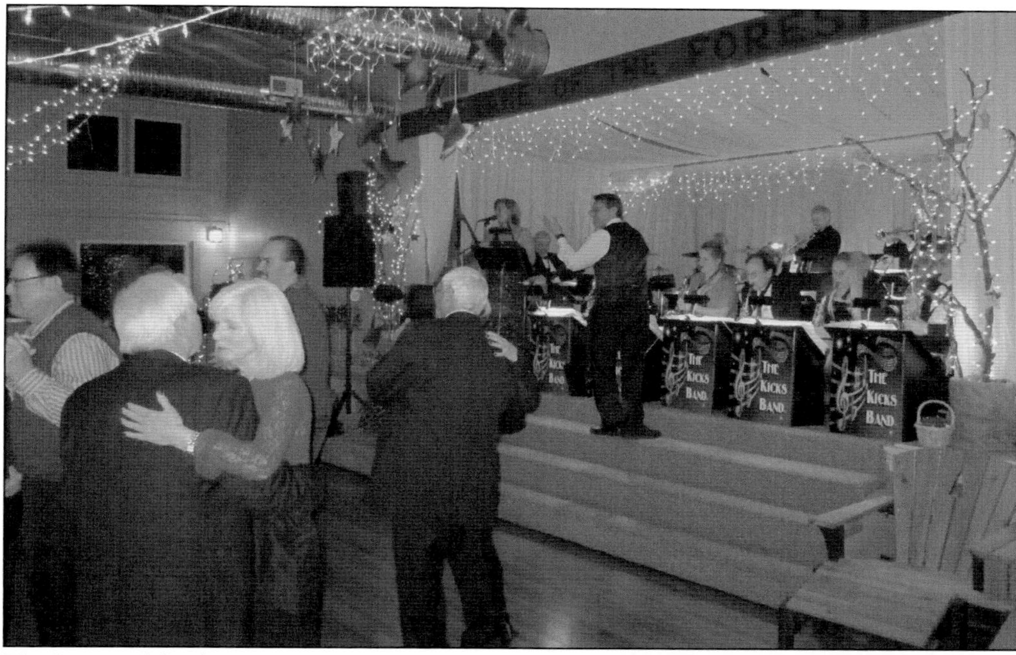

The biannual fundraiser for the library's children's educational programming is Jazz at the Lake, a dinner, dance, and auction held in the Lake of the Forest clubhouse. The Kicks Band, led by Ross Woolf, provides the music. The band had its start in Bonner Springs in 1988. Originally named the Bonner Springs Kicks Band, the group saw its popularity expand, forcing it to drop the first half of its name.

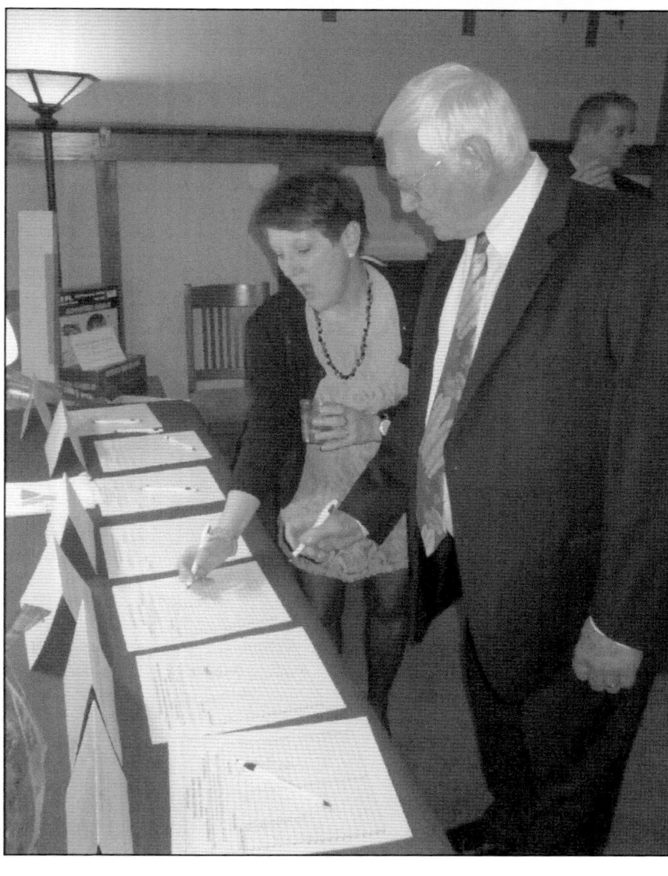

Besides the live auction of everything from dental care to lawn care to pool parties, the silent auction has also become popular. Here, these two library patrons figure out who wants the item the most.

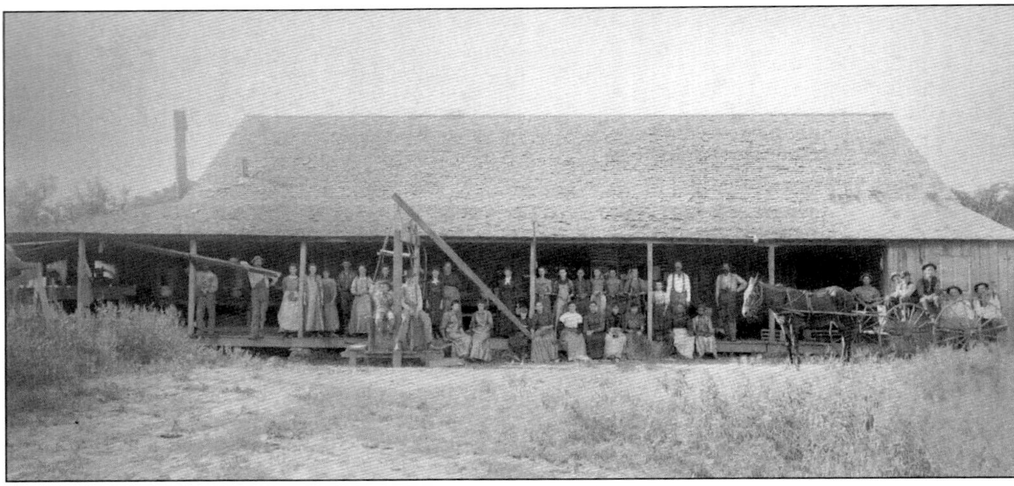

Potatoes grew well in the Kaw River bottomland, and the early thriving industry necessitated a cannery, seen here around 1903.

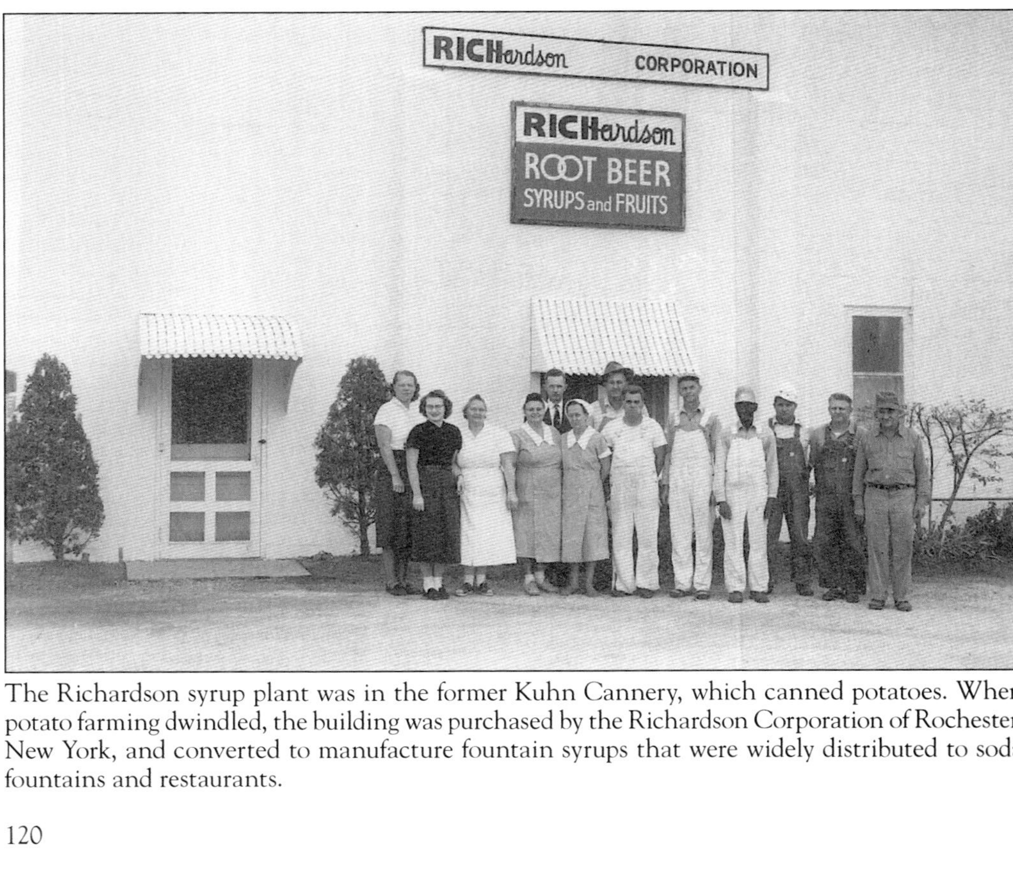

The Richardson syrup plant was in the former Kuhn Cannery, which canned potatoes. When potato farming dwindled, the building was purchased by the Richardson Corporation of Rochester, New York, and converted to manufacture fountain syrups that were widely distributed to soda fountains and restaurants.

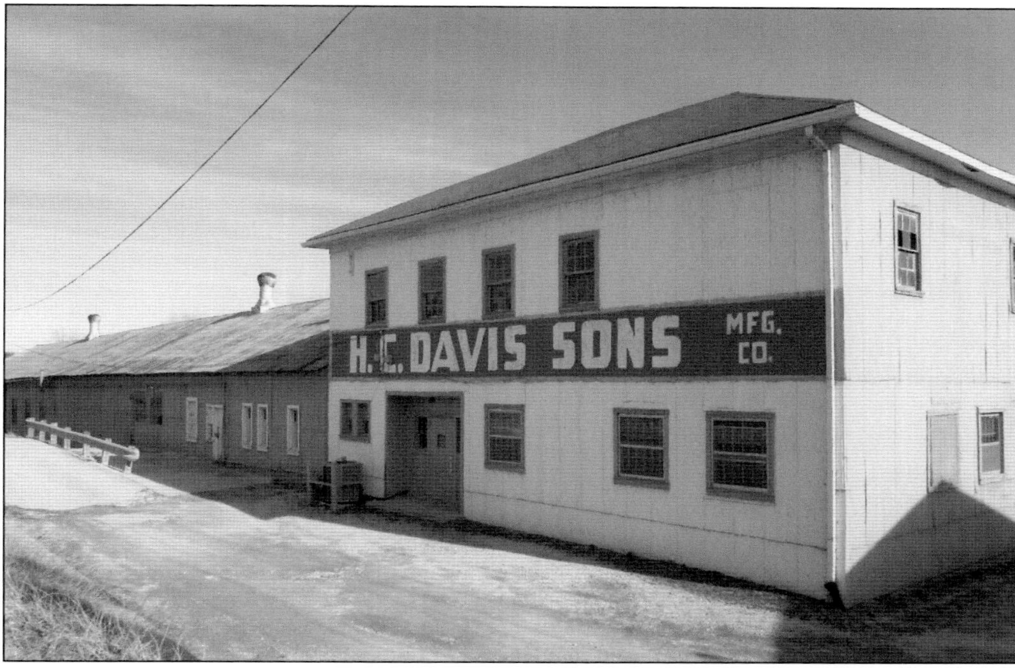

The H.C. Davis Sons Manufacturing Co. makes mixers of all kinds, which are shipped worldwide from the plant on Front Street. The company was started by Howard C. Davis, who was succeeded by his sons Barney and Jack and then by their sons Dick and Ramsey.

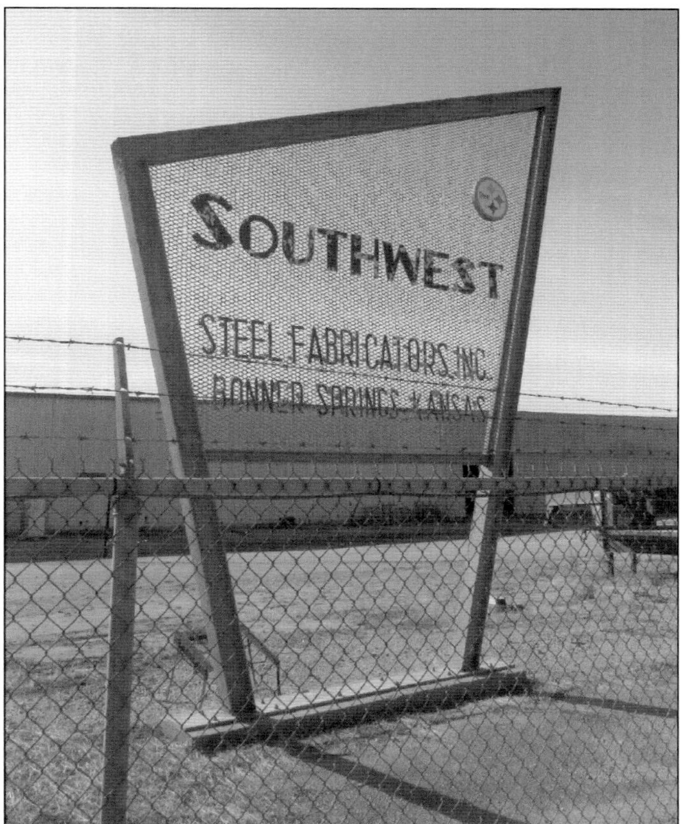

Southwest Steel Fabricators was known as Southwest Ornamental Iron when it moved to Bonner Springs in 1961. It had been in business since 1910 in Kansas City, Kansas. The company was started by Michael Nelsen, who was succeeded by his son Norman and then by Norman's son Craig. The company has sent fabricated steel all over the country, providing materials to build everything from the St. Louis Arch to the fence around the White House in Washington, DC.

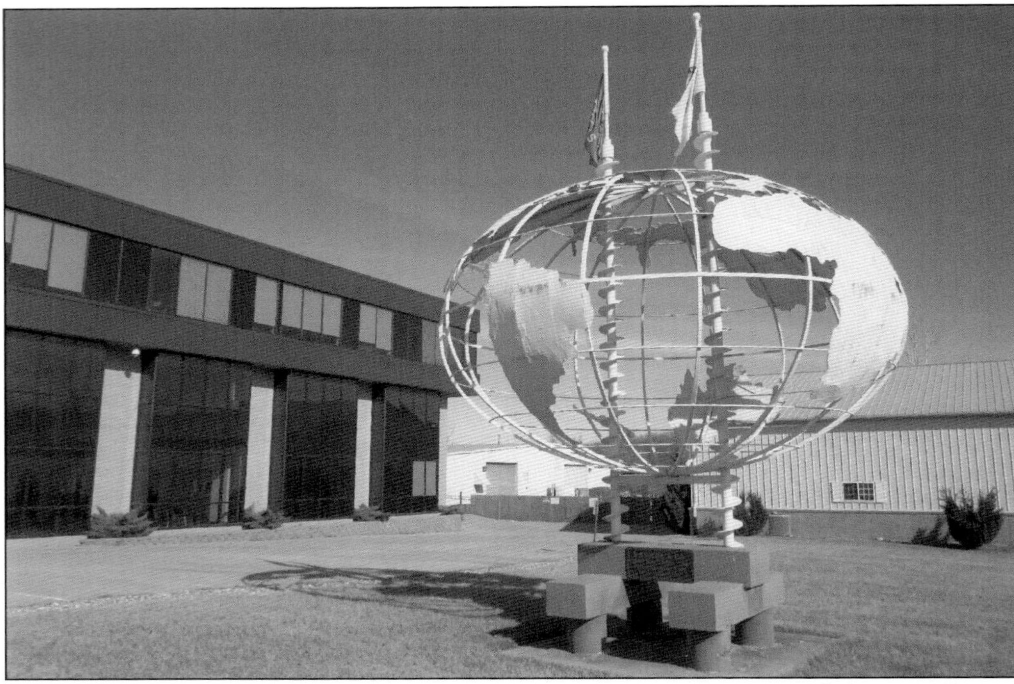

Berkel & Company Contractors has been a community supporter since C.J. Berkel came to Bonner Springs in the 1970s. It has grown into a worldwide company, as illustrated by this structure on its corporate grounds on 142nd Street. The drills are representative of the way they reinforce concrete structures, from dams to pilings, as concrete is forced into the drilled hole as the drill is extracted.

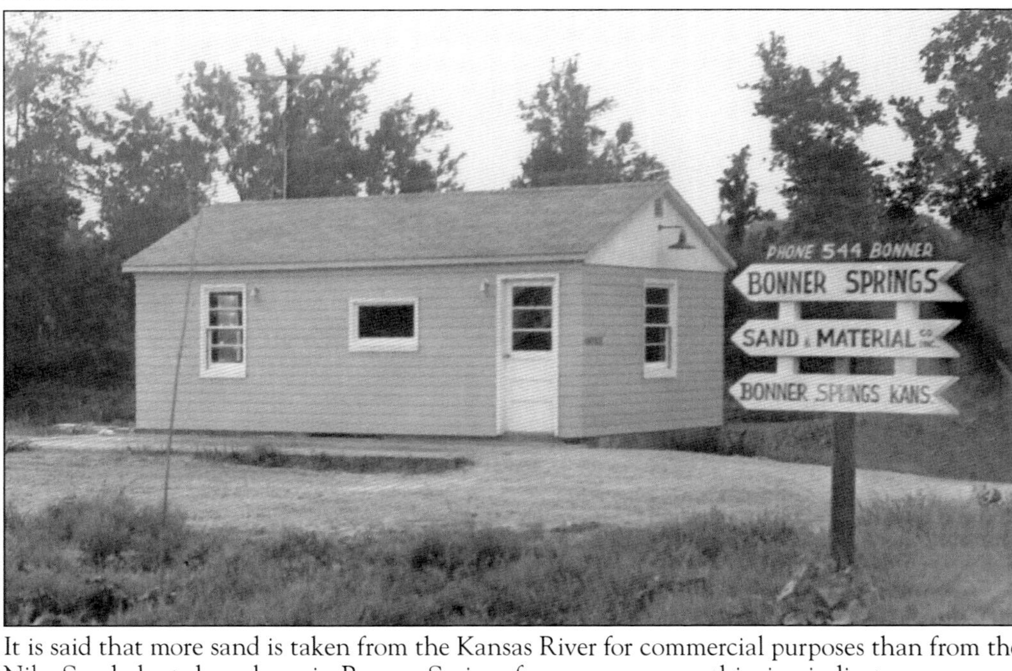

It is said that more sand is taken from the Kansas River for commercial purposes than from the Nile. Sand plants have been in Bonner Springs for many years, as this sign indicates.

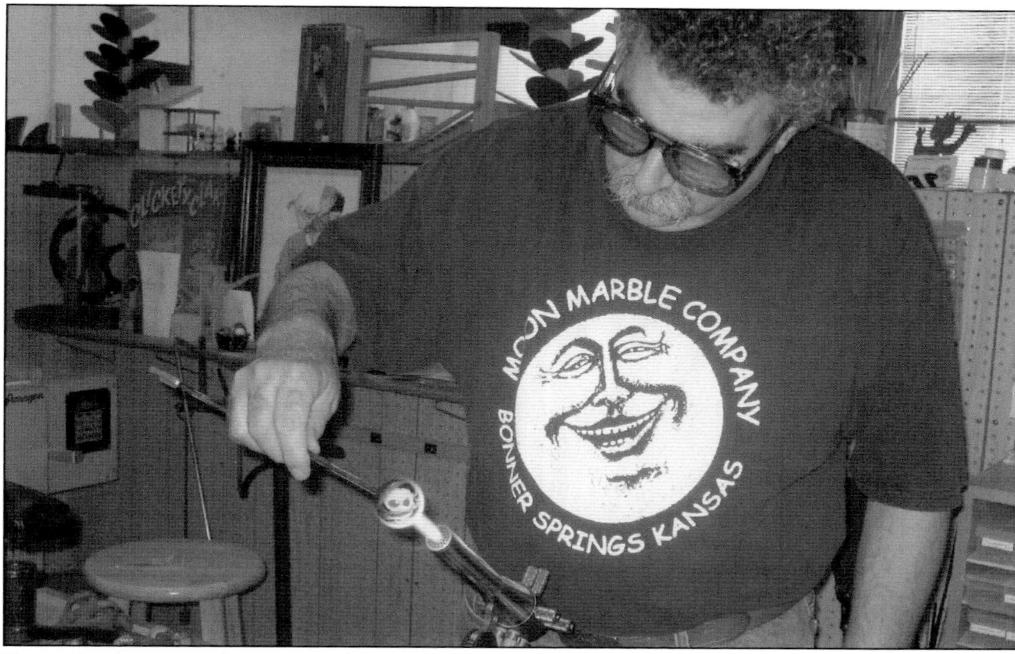

Bruce Breslow started Moon Marble Company in 1997. He had been in the woodworking business, making marble games, when he found himself in need of marbles for them. He has developed the art of marble-making to a high degree and gives demonstrations regularly. Moon Marble was voted one of the Eight Wonders of Kansas Commerce and is featured on Rand McNally maps as a destination for travelers to visit. (Courtesy of Moon Marble.)

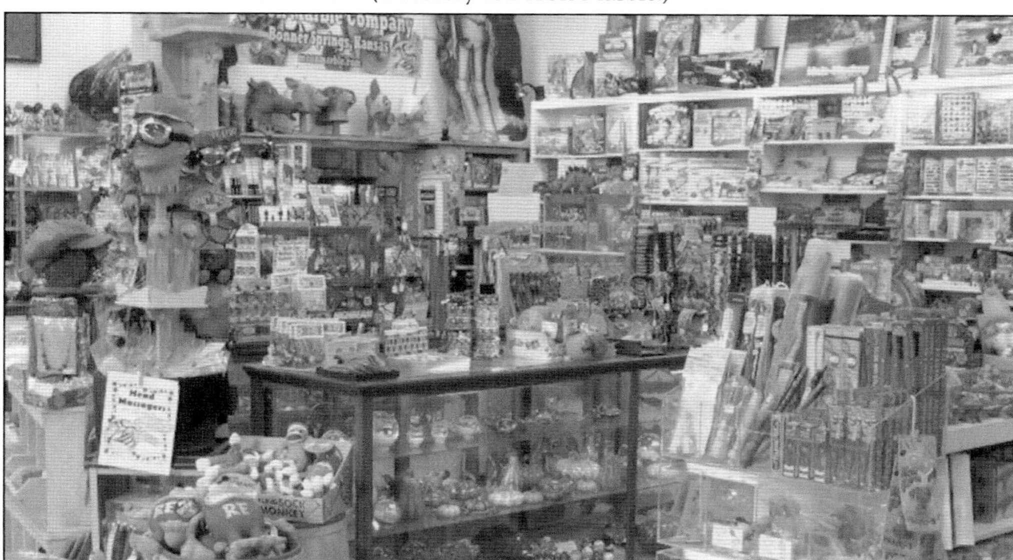

The interior of Moon Marble provides a visit back in time and is one of the most unique retail shops one could encounter. Displays of old marble games line the walls, while the shelves hold every game, gag, or puzzle imaginable. Marble Crazy is held one weekend a year, during which visiting artisans give demonstrations and offer their spectacular marbles for sale. (Courtesy of Moon Marble.)

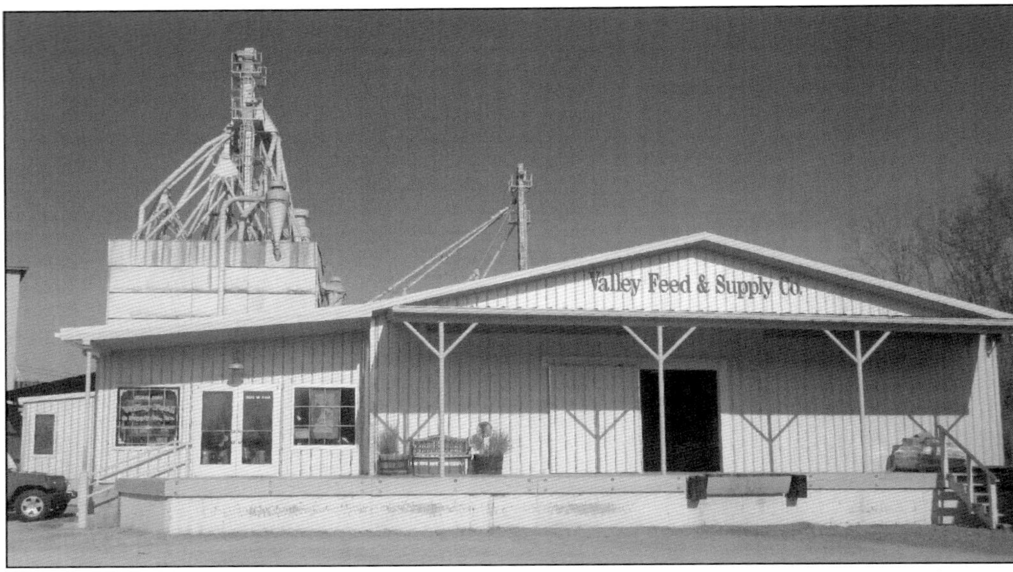

Valley Feed & Supply Co. was started in 1923 by Fred Stubbs Sr. as Stubbs Feed & Coal. The name was changed in 1956. Originally located along Front Street, the building burned in 1940 and again in 1970, at which time this new facility was erected at 600 West Second Street. Fred Stubbs Jr. and his brother John managed the business until 1982, when John's son Neal assumed control.

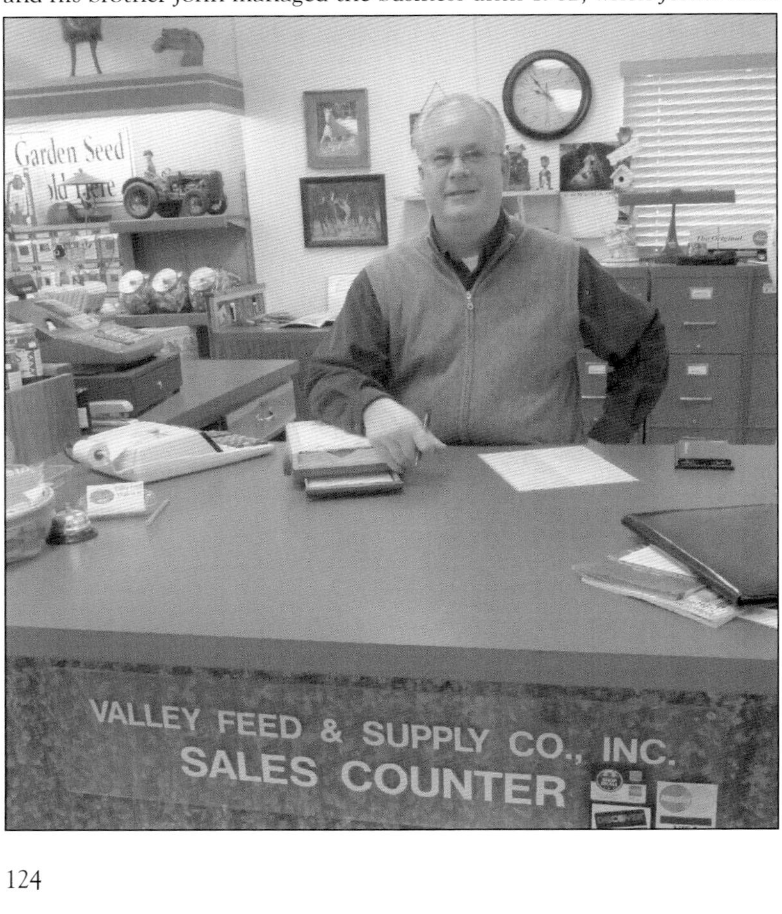

Neal Stubbs will take an order for any one of the numerous varieties of KawMix feed that Valley Feed & Supply Co. offers. Even though the company still supplies the large-animal trade with feed and hay, pet owners and bird lovers can also find what they need at the store.

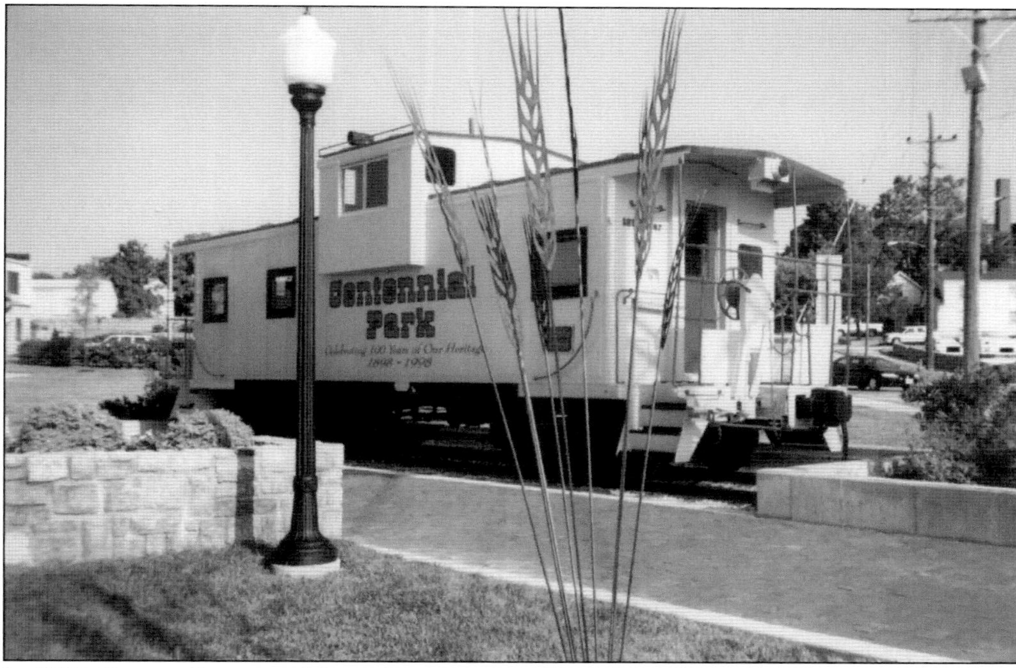

In 1998, Bonner Springs celebrated its centennial with a yearlong celebration. One idea that came out of the celebration was the creation of a park to replace an old electric substation and vacant lot. The Kansas Power & Light Company donated the land, and the Burlington & Santa Fe Railroad donated one of its last cabooses. The park was completed and dedicated in May 2004. A pond was created by the Bonner Beautiful Commission. The caboose is open to enjoy and includes information about Bonner Springs and the surrounding area attractions. (Courtesy of City of Bonner Springs.)

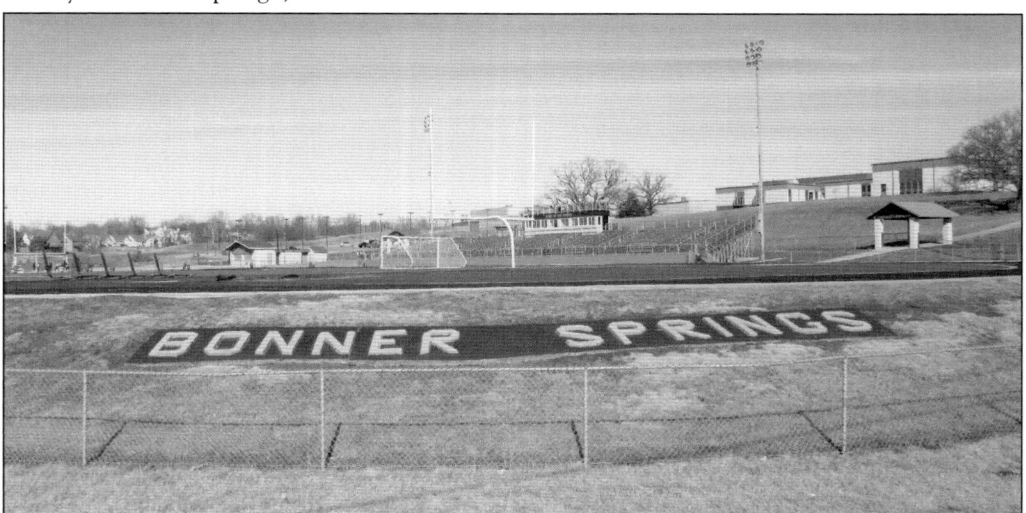

The concrete "Bonner Springs" letters that were near the railroad tracks were moved to the athletic field at Bonner Springs High School. The school colors are orange and black, so the letters were painted orange. They still welcome drivers approaching the city from the west on Kansas Highway 32.

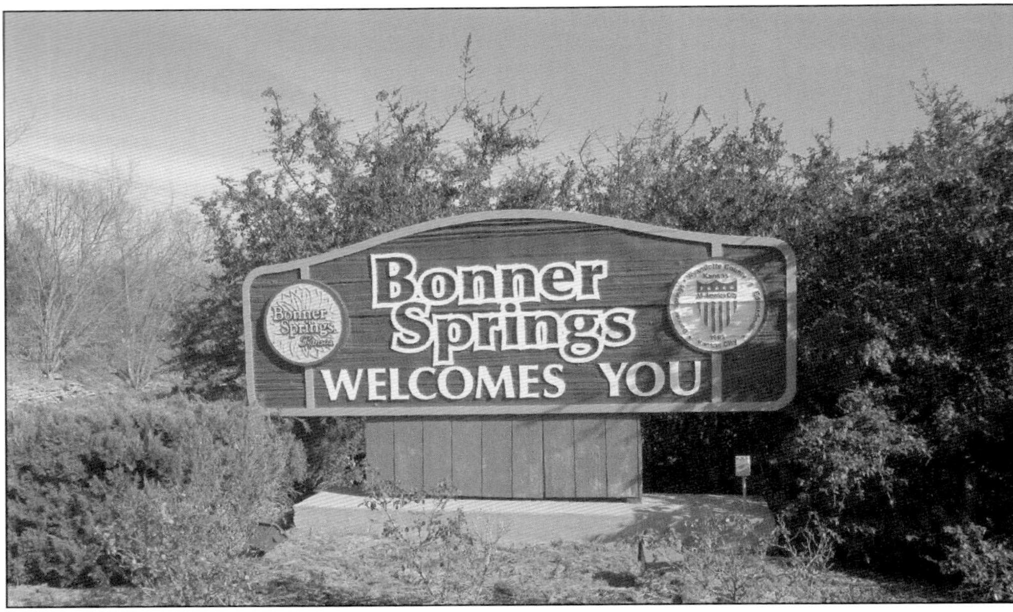

Welcome signs like this one are placed at every entrance to Bonner Springs, inviting all to come and visit.

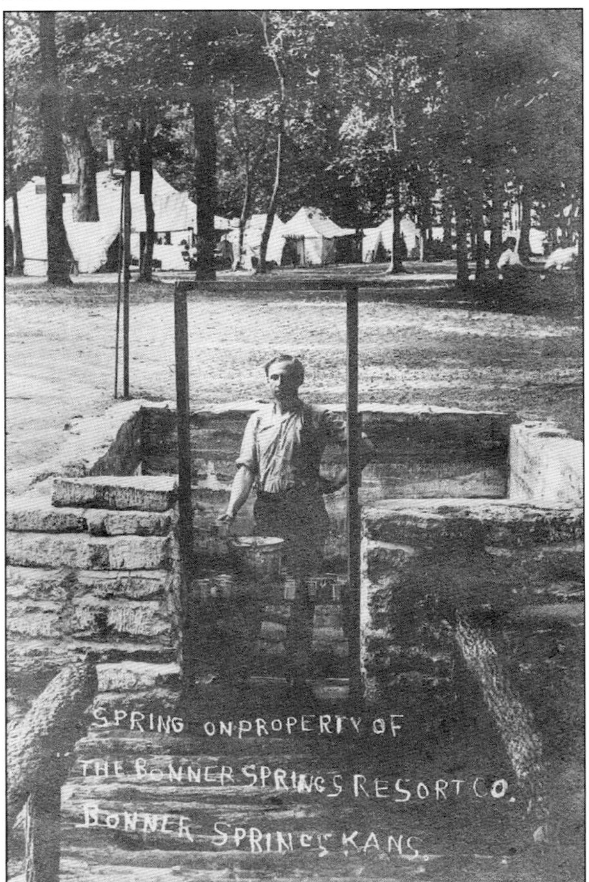

This early postcard from the Connie Harrington collection shows one of the area's mineral springs. Visitors to the resort were offered cups of the healing water. The resort and the springs are long gone, but the town continues to welcome visitors.

BIBLIOGRAPHY

Taylor, Loren. *The Historic Communities of Wyandotte County*. Sec. on Bonner Springs by Ella Mae Mitchell, Larry Berg, Connie Harrington, and Roger Miller. Bonner Springs, KS: Wyandotte County Historical Society and Museum, 2005.

Tewell, Kenneth. *Bonner Springs School System: Lincoln School*. Bonner Springs, KS: privately published, n.d.

Discover Thousands of Local History Books Featuring Millions of Vintage Images

Arcadia Publishing, the leading local history publisher in the United States, is committed to making history accessible and meaningful through publishing books that celebrate and preserve the heritage of America's people and places.

Find more books like this at
www.arcadiapublishing.com

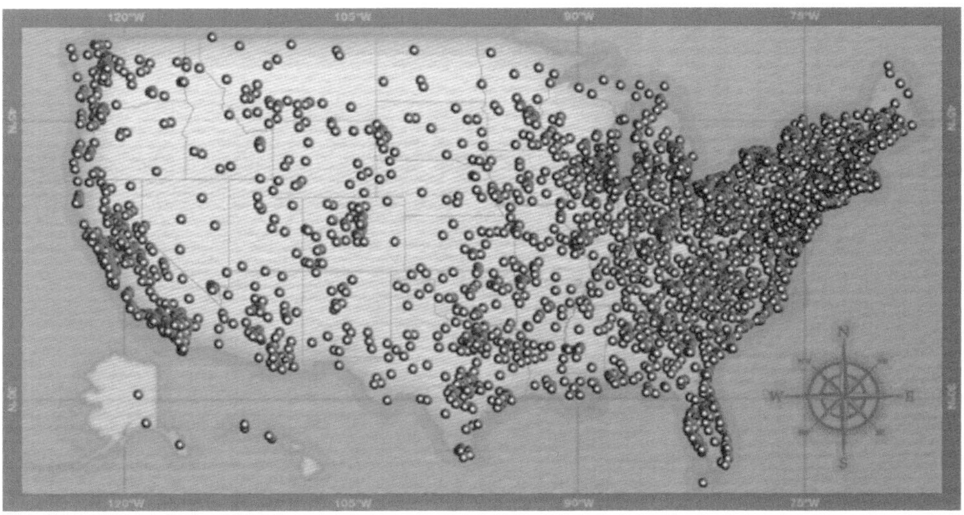

Search for your hometown history, your old stomping grounds, and even your favorite sports team.

Consistent with our mission to preserve history on a local level, this book was printed in South Carolina on American-made paper and manufactured entirely in the United States. Products carrying the accredited Forest Stewardship Council (FSC) label are printed on 100 percent FSC-certified paper.

MADE IN THE USA